Praise for

Reverse Mergers

Taking a Company Public Without an IPO

By David N. Feldman

With contributions by Steven Dresner

"This is the book our industry has been waiting for!"

TIMOTHY HALTER

Chairman and CEO, Halter Financial Group, Inc.

"A perfect primer on reverse mergers, equally appealing to the seasoned lawyer or the first-time executive. The practical advice and numerous easy-to-understand examples are but two reasons that David Feldman is the leading expert on reverse mergers. A must-read for anyone contemplating such a transaction."

MITCHELL C. LITTMAN, ESQ.

Founding Partner, Littman Krooks LLP

"With this book—the first of its kind—David Feldman has created an invaluable guide to the varied and increasingly complex world of going public. It is essential for any investment banker, lawyer, accountant, or private company that is seeking a rational alternative to an IPO."

TIMOTHY J. KEATING

President, Keating Investments, LLC

Reverse Mergers

Reverse Mergers

Taking a Company Public Without an IPO

David N. Feldman

With contributions by Steven Dresner

Bloomberg Press
New York

First edition published 2006

1 3 5 7 9 10 8 6 4 2

Library of Congress Cataloging-in-Publication Data

Feldman, David N.
    Reverse mergers : taking a company public without an IPO / David N. Feldman ; with contributions by Steven Dresner. -- 1st ed.
       p. cm.
    Includes index.
    ISBN 1-57660-231-1 (alk. paper)
  1. Going public (Securities) 2. Going public (Securities)--Law and legislation--United States.
3. Corporations--United States--Finance. I. Dresner, Steven II. Title.

HG4028.S7F45 2006
658.1'64--dc22   2006014703

Edited by Janet Coleman

To the loves of my life:

the inside-and-out beautiful Barbra,

the superbly talented Sammi,

and the always happy Andrew.

CONTENTS

PART THREE | A FEW OTHER SIMPLE WAYS TO GO PUBLIC

PART FOUR | MANUFACTURING SHELLS AND CURRENT TRENDS

ILLUSTRATIONS

Figures

Reverse Mergers

Introduction

Recently, Wall Street has discovered that there are more ways to go public than through the traditional initial public offering (IPO), making it easier for more companies to reap the benefits of public status. Public companies find it easier to attract investors than private ones do because investments in public companies are more liquid. Because of this liquidity, public companies can also use their stock more effectively to fund acquisitions and reward executives. Having various options to go public is good news to the vast majority of smaller companies, most of which do not fit the typical profile investment banks use when deciding which companies can successfully accomplish an IPO.

The two most popular alternatives to IPOs are reverse mergers (including mergers with specified purpose acquisition companies, or SPACs) and self-filings. The following well-known companies have gone public through reverse mergers:

- ❑ Texas Instruments Inc.
- ❑ Berkshire Hathaway Inc.
- ❑ Tandy Corporation (Radio Shack Corporation)
- ❑ Occidental Petroleum Corporation
- ❑ Muriel Siebert & Co., Inc.
- ❑ Blockbuster Entertainment
- ❑ The New York Stock Exchange

Less well-known deals are no less interesting:

- ❑ In February 2005, an investor group led by billionaire Robert

F. X. Sillerman, former owner of well-known concert promoter SFX Entertainment, raised $46.5 million contemporaneous with the acquisition of a public shell company called Sports Entertainment Enterprises, Inc. and the acquisition of an 85 percent interest in Elvis Presley's name, image and likeness, and the operations of his home at Graceland. Since then the company, now known as CKX, Inc., has completed several more acquisitions including the proprietary rights to the *American Idol* television show and, in April 2006, it paid $50 million for an 80 percent interest in boxer Muhammad Ali's name, likeness, and image.

❑ In 2002, RAE Systems went public in a reverse merger at $0.20 a share. As of this writing in early 2006, the stock was trading around $4.

❑ Global Sources reverse merged into Fairchild. As of this writing, it has a market capitalization of approximately $430 million.

Alternatives to IPOs have grown in popularity over the last six years. The number of closed reverse mergers has increased fourfold since 2000. (See **FIGURE I.1**, Closed Reverse Mergers by Year.) All signs indicate that this fast-paced growth will continue for the foreseeable future.

There are several reasons for this. First, the IPO market effectively closed in late 2000 following the dot-com bust. Those seeking to go public were forced to find other ways to accomplish their goals. Second, the alternatives to IPOs offer benefits that traditional IPOs do not, especially to companies interested in raising capital in the $3 million to $20 million

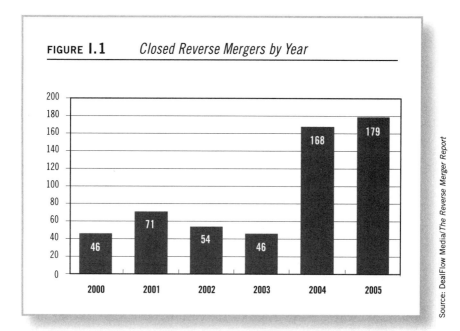

FIGURE I.1   *Closed Reverse Mergers by Year*

Source: DealFlow Media/The Reverse Merger Report

range. Third, new SEC regulations and enforcement policies have turned reverse mergers and self-filings into completely aboveboard, legitimate methods of accessing the capital markets. (There is a history here, which we will cover in Chapter 2. Some of the early practitioners of alternatives to IPOs in the 1970s and 1980s were shady characters.) Fourth, in the past several years the number of investors ready and willing to make private investments in public equity (PIPEs) in connection with alternatives to IPOs has increased dramatically. PIPEs are defined as follows: A private placement of equity or equity-linked securities effected for a public company, typically with immediate required registration of the equity sold to the investor. These days PIPE investors are constantly on the lookout for soon-to-be public companies to invest in.

The idea behind the reverse merger is simple, yet powerful. To achieve the goal of publicly traded shares, a private company merges into a public one. (The public company has minimal, if any, day-to-day business operations. For this reason, it is called a "shell.") The public company may be the remnant of a bankrupt or sold organization or specially formed for the purpose of investing in a private company. Either way, the basic maneuver is the same: the private company purchases control of a public one, merges into it, and when the merger is complete becomes a publicly traded company in its own right.

Self-filings take advantage of the SEC regulation that allows private companies to become public by voluntarily following the same rules (and filing the same documents) that public companies follow. After agreeing to mandatory compliance with the SEC reporting regime, a company earns public status and can then offer securities to the public market or complete a PIPE.

This book is written for seasoned pros and beginners alike. It is—as of this writing—the first and only book to explain the business and legal issues specific to reverse mergers and self-filings. My goal was to create a text that would be useful to both company CEOs and CFOs and the professionals who advise them—lawyers, accountants, consultants, and investment bankers. Please note: I wrote this not just for lawyers; it covers legal issues in plain English.

This book is my best effort to codify what I have learned about alternatives to IPOs over the thirteen years since Feldman Weinstein & Smith, the twenty-three-attorney law firm I lead, and a predecessor firm, began this part of our practice. During that time we have worked with hundreds of clients contemplating reverse mergers and self-filings. Steven Dresner, my friend and contributor to this book, has enriched the text with the wisdom he has gleaned in his capacities as editor of *PIPEs: A Guide to Private Investments in Public Equity* (Bloomberg Press, 2005), and as the organizer of numerous business conferences on PIPEs and reverse mergers.

The Structure of This Book

The book is divided into four parts. Part One covers the business of reverse mergers. Chapter 1 discusses the pros and cons of going public. Chapter 2 compares the benefits of a reverse merger to the benefits of an IPO. Chapter 3 presents an overview of the market for shells, how they are formed, and basic reverse merger deal structures. The shell market is changing rapidly, in no small part due to recent rule changes by the SEC. Chapter 4 reviews the history behind the famous SEC Rule 419 which in the early 1990s all but stopped the market for creating shells from scratch and taking them public for awhile. Chapter 5 covers the financings that typically accompany a reverse merger, especially those done as PIPE investments. It includes examples of a few specific transactions which are analyzed in depth from the fields of biotechnology, entertainment, technology, and sports. Issues of disclosure and valuation are discussed. An acknowledged challenge following a reverse merger is building and obtaining support for the company's newly trading stock. Chapter 6 covers this issue in depth with the goal of changing attitudes toward the issue. Rather than seeking an immediate "pop" in a stock as sometimes happens after an IPO, reverse merged companies require patience for support to build over time. Chapter 7, the last chapter of Part One, provides a road map for those (hopefully all) seeking to steer clear of unsavory and illegitimate activity in this field. Covered here are bad shell owner tactics and bad investment banker tactics. A list of signs that are consistent with behavior of a credible, legitimate player is included. As in all things Wall Street, it is difficult to go anywhere without finding some bad guys. Indeed, the venerable IPO suffered a black eye when state and federal regulators fined IPO underwriters over $2 billion for illegal excesses in the IPOs of the late 1990s. But reverse mergers also have a checkered past, something many of us are working hard to reverse both in terms of perception and reality.

Part Two covers legal issues and traps. Chapter 8 describes deal structures and issues in completing merger agreements. The famous "reverse triangular merger" is examined. Issues in a shell's capital structure and availability of shares are also discussed. How parties back up their statements and promises is another issue, as is changing the name of the shell after a deal. Chapter 9 covers a critically important issue in reverse mergers: due diligence. This involves "scrubbing" a shell which may have a history of prior operations, as well as working to avoid or minimize risks from dirty or messy shells (these are two different things). So-called Footnote 32 shells, which have been targeted by the SEC in its recent rulemaking as being of questionable validity, are discussed. These are particularly thorny shells to examine, because they *appear* to be real businesses that went public, when in fact they are either fake start-ups or very small real businesses that will be stripped out or shut down upon a merger. Chapter 10 discusses the regulatory regime in greater depth. In particular, the chapter explores the sweeping and dramatic legislation, known as the Sarbanes-Oxley Act, that was passed in 2002 following the Enron and WorldCom debacles. This law requires many changes—most of them for the good—in how public companies act. But, among other things, it has led to increases in the cost of being public. This chapter also reviews the new SEC rulemaking of June 2005 which imposed significant new disclosure requirements immediately following a reverse merger. By means of these rules, the SEC sought to eliminate more bad players at the same time as it affirmed that these techniques are perfectly legitimate means of structuring companies.

Part Three covers self-filings in depth and a few other methods of going public without an IPO or reverse merger in overview. There are two ways to go about a self-filing: either by means of a resale registration to allow existing shares to start trading, or through filing a Form 10-SB, which simply puts the company on the mandatory SEC reporting list. Once it is fully reporting, if shareholders have the ability to sell without having their shares individually registered with the SEC, trading can commence. Part Four covers the most contemporary techniques of going public without an IPO. Chapter 14, which looks at SPACs, may be the first primer on a technique that has taken off recently. A SPAC, or specified purpose acquisition company, is a public shell, created specifically to enable a company to go public. It raises large amounts of money that can then be given to the private company it merges with. A SPAC's shares are permitted to trade (most other manufactured shells do not trade), and investors in the SPAC get to review and approve the proposed merger. Each SPAC generally has an industry or geographic focus, and has a management team experienced in that sector to review potential merger candidates. As of this writing in early 2006, over eighty SPACs have been formed just since 2004 and thirty-eight of them have successfully completed IPOs. These shell vehicles are generally raising anywhere from $20 million to over $100 million each. The next intense area of current activity, covered in Chapter 15, is manufacturing Form 10-SB shells. The SEC appears to favor these over some other types of shells (such as those created under Rule 419). Nearly one hundred of these shells are being formed by clients of my law firm alone! The last chapter of the book, Chapter 16, reviews a variety of other current issues: The intense desire of PIPE investors and investment banks to benefit from the "public venture

capital" returns that are possible when one invests in reverse mergers. The "yuan rush" to complete deals involving Chinese companies.
And future prospects for SPACs, Form 10-SB shells, and the like. This
chapter includes extensive quotes and thoughts from over a half dozen
leading industry players, from accountants to investment bankers to
venture investors and others.

CHAPTER 1

Why Go Public?

Before deciding how to go public, a company must decide *whether* to go public. Or, as Tim Halter of Halter Financial Group asks his clients: *"If everything else in your company was the same, but you had a publicly trading stock, would that be better?"*

Advantages of Being Public

In general, there are five major advantages to being public: easier access to capital, greater liquidity, ability to grow through acquisitions or strategic partnerships, ability to use stock options to attract and retain senior executives, and increased shareholder confidence in management.

Access to Capital

It is easier for public companies to raise money than private companies. This has little to do with a reasoned assessment of the merits of any specific private company. Public companies have five characteristics that make them more attractive than private companies to investors.

First, public companies are required to disclose their financial results, good or bad, and other material developments to the U.S. Securities and Exchange Commission and the public regularly and in great detail. Disclosure requirements build investor confidence because it is harder for a public company to hide problems than it is for a private one.

The second major benefit to an investor, which increases a public company's access to capital, is an easier opportunity to create liquidity for the investment. Those who invest in private companies always worry about the "exit strategy" and look for companies wishing eventually to be sold or go public. If a company is already public, the ability to exit is significantly enhanced. And, typically, public company investors are able to obtain the ability to sell their shares publicly within three to five months after the investment. This is significantly faster than the three to five *years* a venture capitalist generally expects to wait for an investment to pay off. The fact that a public company's stock can be traded creates liquidity through the sale of an investor's stock in the public markets.

The third major benefit to a company completing a financing as a public company rather than a private one concerns the restrictions and covenants customarily required by private equity or venture capital investors. Venture capitalists view themselves as management's partners, and require veto power on many different aspects of decision making in a company. In general, once a company is public, investors stop demanding these powers. Thus, even if a private company is able to attract private equity investors, it still may want to consider being public since PIPE investors or others financing public companies generally put fewer restrictions on the company's activities, decision making, and so on.

The fourth advantage of seeking financing after going public is valuation. The markets judge shares in a public company to be worth roughly twice as much as shares of similarly situated private companies. When a financing takes place as part of the going-public event itself, the value of the company before the investment (known as the "pre-money value") is almost always materially higher than the value a private equity investor would place on the same company. This makes perfect sense when one considers that a premium is placed on liquidity.

Even though it is easier for public companies to raise money than private ones, this is not a sufficient reason for going public, as many companies who go public solely to obtain one round of financing learn to their dismay. Companies that follow this path frequently regret the decision; many, in fact, end up going private. Companies that make the most out of being public also make use of the following benefits.

Liquidity

Liquidity gives all investors the opportunity to enhance their exit strategy by being able to turn their investments into cash. New investors are not the only ones who want to be able to exit. Sometimes one of the main reasons for bringing a private company public is so the company founders, former investors, and senior executives holding stock positions can take money out of the business without selling it outright or losing practical control. There are as many reasons owners might want cash as there are owners.

The challenge in this situation is to avoid a great wave of share sales by company insiders. There are two reasons for this. First, if too many insiders sell out, those who built the company in the past will lose the incentives that would encourage them to continue building the company in the future. Second, Wall Street notices when insiders are selling out. Generally, a wave of insider sales discourages outsiders from investing in a company. Therefore, a company should consult its advisers and design an appropriate, rewarding, but measured selling plan.

For example, a former client took his company public through a reverse merger. Shortly thereafter, the company founder actively began to sell his stock. He sold nearly $5 million worth of stock before the price began to drop precipitously. This caused prospective investors to lose interest in the company. Today the company is out of business and in bankruptcy. According to the rumor mill, an SEC investigation into whether or not the founder's selling activities constituted insider trading will get under way shortly.

Another client took a more circumspect approach, with great success. He restricted when, how much, and how often insiders could sell their shares. He meticulously consulted with legal counsel before each insider sale to determine whether there was a risk of insider trading. Today, the company is growing, its stock price is rising steadily, and the founders have been able to sell enough stock, slowly and deliberately, to begin to realize their exit strategies.

PRACTICE TIP

To senior executives of newly public companies: don't get greedy.

Growth Through Acquisitions or Strategic Partnerships

The most popular reason for going public after the need to raise capital is to pursue a strategy of growth through acquisition, joint venture, or strategic partnership. As noted above, investors are more willing to provide financing to a public company, even when the purpose of the financing is to fund acquisitions. In addition, a public company often can use stock as currency or "scrip" in the package of consideration to be provided to a company being acquired or partnered with. Sometimes the only consideration given is stock.

In general, the value of the stock provided exceeds the agreed-upon value of the transaction because there is some risk the stock will drop in value down the road. In other words, if a company is to be acquired for $20 million, including $10 million in cash, a seller may demand the balance to be equal to $12 million or $13 million in stock to offset the risk of volatility in stock price. Public buyers generally are willing to be flexible in this regard as purchasing with stock avoids the need to raise cash for the purchase. It also allows a company to retain its cash for other purposes, reserves, and so on.

Stock Options for Executives

Many companies have difficulty attracting talented senior management. Public companies have an advantage over private ones in the competition for top people because they can offer stock options and other equity incentives—the "brass ring" of affiliation with a public company—as part of the compensation package. Frequently, compensation for top executives at public companies seems exorbitantly high. But the fine print often reveals that the vast bulk of a multimillion-dollar compensation package comes not in the form of wages, but in the form of stock or stock options. (Stock options aren't just for high-ranking executives. Many stories have been written about the millionaire secretaries at Microsoft, eBay, and other companies.)

Private companies do, of course, have the option of setting up stock option plans; however, the problem, as with all investments involving private companies, is liquidity. Private company executives know that they cannot make money from owning stock unless there is some form of liquidity event. The company must go public, be sold, or initiate a major dividend distribution in order to turn shares into cash. Stock options in a public company are much more versatile.

Options are attractive to those who lead public companies because they align management's incentives with company performance as judged by the market. Option holders are highly motivated to build the company's success so that its stock price will go up. The vesting process, by which options become available based on an executive's time with the company, encourages a long-term commitment. I know many senior executives who stay with a company longer than planned simply to ensure that their options vest.

Confidence in Management

Because of SEC disclosure requirements, shareholders of public companies feel more confident that the actions of management and the operation of the company will be transparent. The SEC requires reporting companies to regularly reveal financial results (including explanations of period-to-period changes), executive compensation, related party transactions, material contracts, liquidity, capital resources and the like. Public companies create this stream of information as required by SEC rules, and the result is to help a shareholder feel knowledgeable about the company's operations and challenges.

On the other hand, state laws generally *limit* the type and quantity of information that a shareholder of a private company may obtain. Rarely can a shareholder legally obtain a financial statement and a list of shareholders more than once a year. Some states even require a showing of cause or even a court proceeding to obtain this or other information. Investors in private companies typically negotiate broader and more frequent information delivery, but still find extracting pertinent information to be a constant challenge.

That being said, it must be remembered that even public company filings can be misleading or fraudulent. The lessons of Enron, WorldCom and others are recent and will linger. Nonetheless, private companies still have greater incentives to play games than do public ones. After all, the public company that plays fast and loose with disclosure requirements runs the significant risk of SEC investigations, criminal prosecutions, and class action lawsuits.

It is not unusual for a senior executive of a public company to ask my firm to figure out how *not* to disclose something, almost always something bad. Even when disclosure is not absolutely mandatory, we usually take the view that disclosure is recommended. (Not in absolutely every case of course. The departure, for example, of a CEO's longtime personal assistant generally would not need to be disclosed. But the departure of a CFO or other senior executive probably would.)

Disadvantages of Being Public

There are five well-recognized disadvantages of being public: pressure to please Wall Street by emphasizing short-term results; mandatory public disclosure of company information, which makes "warts" hard to hide; vulnerability to fraud (even after Sarbanes-Oxley); higher annual expenses necessary to fulfill SEC reporting and auditing requirements and vulnerability to lawsuits.

Emphasis on Short-Term Results

If a public company is lucky enough to be covered by Wall Street analysts, the pressure to please "the Street" is intense and constant. Every quarter, the question on analysts' minds is whether the company will meet or beat expectations in the market.

There is a healthy aspect to this because management must keep its eye on stated goals. But the negative, of course, is that short-term results become more important than the long-term goals every company must pursue in order to build shareholder value.

A public company must concentrate both on making wise decisions and on how those decisions will be perceived by analysts. This can cause problems. Say a company with a strong cash position decides to spend a portion on longer-term capital expenditures. Some Wall Streeters will see the long-term benefit and some will simply see the erosion of cash. Another example: If the underwriters in an initial public offering (IPO) did not insist that the company shed an early stage or R&D opportunity and it continues to drain cash, Wall Street may not respond kindly. Investments in systems, real estate, or overhead in anticipation of future business may be negatively received.

Conflicts also arise when companies "do the right thing." I make financial decisions in the course of running my law firm based on my business philosophy of doing right by my vendors, my clients, and my staff. This may mean, for example, keeping problem employees on if I feel they are working diligently and with great effort to correct their deficiencies. Or it may mean a larger raise for an employee who is going through tough times, getting married, or experiencing unusual personal circumstances. Or cutting a client's fee, even when he does not request it, if I feel that we may have spent too much time on something. If my firm were public, I would feel more pressure to limit my decisions to the smartest financial ones regardless of whether or not I was doing the right thing.

Public Disclosure

Earlier I described some of the advantages of the public disclosure of financial results, executive compensation, and the like; however, public disclosure is not always beneficial. All of a company's problems have to be revealed, without delay. If financial statements are being restated, or a major customer was lost, or an executive has strong personal or family ties to a major vendor, the public will find out immediately.

Disclosure requirements also make it more difficult to keep important information away from competitors. I had a public client, since sold, whose business primarily involved obtaining military contracts. SEC rules require that major new contracts must be filed and disclosed. Unfortunately, one contract included a copy of the company's original bid, which was very specific and detailed regarding pricing, etc.

The company challenged the filing requirements on the grounds that the original bid was confidential. Unfortunately, the SEC ruled that the contract must be disclosed, confidential bid and all. Thereafter, the company's competitors were able to obtain this information on the SEC's website with the ease of a mouse click. Granted, the information was also obtainable with a Freedom of Information Act (FOIA) request (which was the reason the SEC deemed it not confidential). But the process of obtaining information through FOIA is more cumbersome, and our client's competitors generally would not seek information in that manner.

The flip side of public disclosure is that good news travels fast. When positive things are happening at a company, press releases and SEC filings help promote the company's success.

PRACTICE TIP

In deciding what to disclose, be consistent, and as quick and determined to disclose the bad as well as the good, or risk shareholder and regulator ire.

Fraud and Greed (Even After Sarbanes-Oxley)

Congress passed the sweeping Sarbanes-Oxley Act of 2002 (SOX) in reaction to the scandals at Enron, WorldCom, and other corporations. SOX instituted the most wide-ranging changes in securities laws since 1934. (See Chapter 10 for more about SOX and its impact.)

Yet fraud and greed are still alive and well in corporate America. In some respects public companies have more incentives to engage in deceptive practices than private companies. This is because, as described earlier, they are under so much pressure to meet or exceed Wall Street's expectations for their performance. Here are some of the tricks companies still use.

Unscrupulous management may engage in "Enronomics," defined by wordspy.com as "a fiscal policy or business strategy that relies on dubious accounting practices, overly optimistic economic forecasts, and unsustainably high levels of spending."

Then there is the euphemistic term "earnings management," which works like this: A product has been ordered and produced and is sitting on the shipping dock of the company-owned warehouse. On March 31, a customer informs the company that a truck is on the way to pick up the product within a couple of days. Is this a sale under accounting rules on March 31? Absolutely not. A sale does not occur until the product is picked up by the customer's truck; however, some companies will record this as a sale anyway. That's earnings management: improving sales in the current quarter. Earnings management is a risky business. I had at least one public client whose earnings management, in the form of questionable inventory auditing techniques, caused it ultimately to lose its key lender, and therefore its nearly $100 million business, leading to bankruptcy.

Companies also "manage" expenses. In this scenario, a bill arrives on March 31 for work done by a consultant. The CEO places the bill in his bottom drawer until the next day. Is this an expense on an accrual basis?

Absolutely. Do some companies pretend this expense is not incurred until the next day? Absolutely. Earnings management, again: reducing expenses in the current quarter.

Other tricks include complex off-balance sheet transactions and multitiered corporate structures designed to hide underperforming assets or the involvement of a questionable player. In the reverse merger world, unsavory types have their own repertoire of shady tricks, which will be discussed later.

It's Expensive!

A company that is considering going public needs to prepare for significant additional costs—both hard and soft—in connection with this change in status. Even the smallest private company could see annual expenses rise anywhere from $300,000 to $700,000 when it goes public. For some companies, these additional expenses are the difference between positive and negative net income.

Additional costs include:

❑ retaining attorneys to deal with the SEC (which can cost anywhere from $50,000 to $150,000 per year just for basic service)

❑ instituting internal financial controls that comply with SOX section 404 (implementation of some of the SOX provisions for small businesses has been delayed and may ultimately be eliminated)

❑ hiring auditors to perform the annual audit and review each quarterly financial statement

❑ paying SEC filing costs

❑ adding additional company staff, in particular finance and shareholder relations staff, to deal with additional requirements

❑ engaging a public relations and investor relations firm (can easily be $150,000 per year)

❑ paying travel and entertainment costs in connection with Wall Street activities

Many expected that the increase in these costs due to the passage of SOX would discourage companies from going public. This has not been the case. Instead, more companies that aspire to be public either have the ability to raise enough financing, or are larger than in the past so that their existing business covers the additional costs. Thus, the deals taking companies public are bigger and stronger.

Public Companies Attract Lawsuits

In 2004, more dollars were paid to settle class action lawsuits than in any previous year. A recent issue of *Forbes* magazine had Mel Weiss, one of the leading class action plaintiff lawyers, on its cover, dubbing him "one of the most feared men in corporate America."

It is well known that in some of these plaintiffs' law firms, attorneys take turns sitting in front of a Bloomberg stock quote machine, watching to see if any particular stock takes a precipitous drop. When that occurs, a lawsuit is filed, even if there are no facts whatsoever to suggest any wrongdoing. In many of these cases, companies settle quickly to avoid the negative publicity and the costs of defending even a frivolous suit.

In the United States, the threat of such a case is enough to send a stock price reeling. Most of the time cases eventually get dropped. Occasionally one is successful, and the purported "rights of shareholders" are defended. I have received several notices of my being part of various classes in these cases. When, for example, a major alleged case of overbilling involving my cell phone provider was settled, each of us received a $10 phone card as our settlement. The lawyers received a $2.5 million fee.

Unfortunately, most cases are no more than legalized extortion. It is no surprise that Mel Weiss and his partners were criminally investigated for alleged illegal payments to so-called lead plaintiffs in dozens of cases.

A new class action bill signed into law by President George W. Bush in early 2005 may help reduce some of the more egregious cases.

A few American companies, in a minor but discernible current trend, actually have chosen to go public in other countries, in particular the United Kingdom, rather than face the burdens of SOX and the litigious environment here in the United States. This trend may well continue unless greater relief is forthcoming—especially since domestic U.S. hedge fund investors seem more than willing to invest in companies whose stock is traded on foreign markets and exchanges.

In the meantime, however, there is no question that private companies considering going public sometimes choose not to do so primarily because of the concern over potential litigation.

Weighing the Pros and Cons

Each company must evaluate the pros and cons in light of its specific circumstances. This is how one potential client did the math. The company, in the industrial equipment business, had generated about $25 million in revenues annually for each of the past five years. It expected to stay at this revenue level for the foreseeable future. From this revenue, the company derived earnings of about $2 million, all of which went to the founder, who was enjoying his success and working hard. The company wished to purchase a large warehouse as well as a significant piece of equipment. But the founder, a post–Depression era gentleman, abhorred debt and did not want to make the purchases with a mortgage or equipment financing.

His CFO suggested he meet with a hedge fund investor, who seemed willing to provide $15 million in equity financing for the purchases, if the company was willing to go public. The investor would provide everything necessary to get the job done—what amounted to a turnkey solution. The result would be a much stronger balance sheet, the elimination of certain warehousing and other outsourcing costs, no debt, and a fair equity position for the investor. It sounded logical.

I advised the potential client that he should think very seriously before going forward with the transaction, and ultimately the client decided not to. On the one hand, going public would neatly provide the capital he wanted to pursue his business goals. But on the other, raising this single round of capital was his only reason for going public. He did not want to make acquisitions, did not need stock options, and had no plans for future financings. And he had no plans to pursue a growth strategy—something investors practically demand from public companies.

If he went ahead, he would incur the extra costs of being public, possibly eliminating a meaningful portion of the company's earnings (offset only in part by cost savings with the new warehouse and equipment). In addition, he would expose his company to the risks of lawsuits, scrutiny of quarterly results, and burden of hiring additional financial staff. In sum, after this one round of financing, the company would see no other benefit from being public and bear all of the costs and burdens.

Ultimately, the company found a private investor to put up money to buy the building and equipment. The structure of the transaction allowed the company to buy out the investor at a future date. This occurred five years later with a healthy return to the investor and the continued benefit of using the newly acquired assets.

PART ONE

THE BUSINESS OF REVERSE MERGERS

CHAPTER 2

IPOs Versus Reverse Mergers

Once a company has decided that the advantages of going public outweigh the disadvantages, it must begin to evaluate the different methods for achieving this objective.

The IPO is the most well-known means of going public. (An initial public offering is the first time a company sells stock to the public and has its stock listed on an official market or exchange.) Investment banks underwrite the offering (in other words, they raise the money from among their customers in exchange for a commission) and handle the transaction. Most investment banks will only do IPOs for companies they expect to be able to grow fairly rapidly after the transaction.

Many companies could benefit from being public but are not good candidates for IPOs. The investment bankers who are responsible for finding people to invest in the new stock look for very specific characteristics in the companies they represent. Companies that are in a stage of development considered premature for an IPO or who wish to go public at a time when the IPO market is inhospitable or who are in an unfashionable industry will find it impossible to find an underwriter for their IPO. Nevertheless, they can often achieve their goal by other means. In addition, even some companies who qualify for an IPO may find some of the negatives leading them to consider other choices.

Some companies work around this by doing an IPO without using an underwriter to raise the money. This is called a "self-underwriting." The company may engage agents to work on raising money, but none stands as lead underwriter in the traditional sense.

The problem with a self-underwriting is that it is not clearly beneficial although, theoretically, a trading market can develop earlier than in some reverse merger situations and the stock might initially be a bit more broadly distributed. However, a self-underwriting involves both the National Association of Securities Dealers (NASD) review (assuming brokers are involved or might be engaged to assist) and state securities regulation or "blue sky" review (if the company is not listed directly on Nasdaq or a higher exchange). These reviews take time. In addition, companies trying the do-it-yourself approach for a public offering may find—as one client did several years ago—that substantially less capital than hoped for is raised, and ultimately a traditional PIPE (private investment in public equity) financing becomes necessary once the company is public.

However, if a company believes the only way it will be able to sell stock is if investors can immediately resell into the public market, and the company has the contacts to obtain these investors, then a self-underwriting may be worth the extra hassle. The concern, of course, is that investors who care predominantly about liquidity may seek it early. An early wave of selling right after the self-underwriting could hurt the stock price if many more sellers than buyers come to market and pressure prices downward.

There are several alternatives to IPOs whether self- or investment bank underwritten. This book covers the two most popular types—reverse mergers (Chapters 3 to 10) and self-filings (Chapters 11 to 13)—in depth and briefly reviews several of the other, mostly disfavored, approaches. Each has advantages and disadvantages when compared to an IPO.

A reverse merger is a transaction in which a privately held company merges with a publicly held company that has no business purpose other than to find a private company to acquire, has no assets (other than possibly cash), and no or nominal existing business operations. For this reason, such a public company is called a "shell." At the end of the reverse merger, the private company is publicly held, instantly. Often financing arranged at the time of the merger provides needed capital, just as with an IPO. In a self-filing, a private company becomes public by voluntarily following all the U.S. Securities and Exchange Commission rules that govern the behavior of public companies. By doing so, a private company can become public and then offer securities to raise money.

Some private companies merge into, and take over, smaller operating businesses that are public. The New York Stock Exchange's widely publicized merger with the much smaller public company Archipelago Holdings in 2006 is such a transaction (the seat holders of the Exchange owned approximately 70 percent of the combined company after the transaction). Although technically a reverse merger, the focus of this book is on mergers with public shell companies, or "shell mergers."

For reasons which will become clear as this book goes along, most companies that go public through reverse mergers initially are penny stock companies that end up listing their shares on the OTC Bulletin Board or the Pink Sheets. (Penny stock refers to stocks that usually sell for under $5.00 per share. These stocks are not traded on the larger exchanges.) Some graduate to larger exchanges as their businesses grow, and that is typically the goal. By contrast, most companies going public with an IPO are immediately listed on Nasdaq, the American Stock Exchange, or the New York Stock Exchange. This is generally because most companies do reverse mergers at an earlier stage of development than most companies completing an IPO (although there are legal reasons as well which will be discussed later in the book).

As the introduction to this book states, the number of successfully completed reverse mergers has increased exponentially in recent years. During the same time, the average value of newly post-reverse merged companies has also increased. In the third quarter of 2005, closed reverse mergers with SEC reporting shells had an average market capitalization of approximately $48 million. In the fourth quarter, the average market capitalization continued to creep up to approximately $53 million. Anecdotal evidence suggests the value of post-reverse merged companies was much lower in prior years (although data is sparse due to the recent changes in SEC reporting requirements). An examination of the data reveals two possible explanations for these trends. First, the IPO market has been virtually inaccessible since 2000. When IPOs are hard to complete successfully, people find other ways. Second, a new group of investors has recently discovered reverse mergers. PIPE investors have become enthusiastic financiers of reverse mergers, which they have begun to refer to as "public venture capital." Third, the SEC and the financial community have accepted reverse mergers as a legitimate technique for going public.

It was not always thus. Reverse mergers have a checkered past. In the early days of the practice—the 1970s and 1980s—a number of unsavory players used the technique fraudulently. Because, relatively speaking, small amounts of money were involved, shareholders seeking retribution generally could not convince lawyers to take their cases so the bad guys often got away with their schemes.

Some shady dealers would form new public shells, raise money from investors, and then take that money in the form of "fees," salaries, and perks in exchange for "running" the shell. In many cases, these shells were simply milked for the cash they had until it was gone.

Others sought to manipulate stock prices. A promoter would leak false information into the marketplace, such as about a pending merger, which was either very speculative or simply made up, and then watch the stock rise, after which he would sell some shares.

A general lack of regulation created an ideal environment for unscrupulous participants. At the time there were no restrictions on completing a public offering of a shell company. Practices varied widely. Sometimes shares in these companies were widely distributed for pennies or even without consideration. Sometimes fewer than ten shareholders existed in a shell prior to a merger. Sometimes a shell raised quite a lot of money through an IPO, but other times only a small amount was raised—just enough to pay lawyers and auditors. In time, many complaints were lodged with the SEC and other regulators.

In 1989, the National Association of Securities Administrators of America's Report on Fraud and Abuse in the Penny Stock Industry declared, "Penny stocks are now the No. 1 threat of fraud and abuse facing small investors in the United States." It almost didn't matter that there were many other fraudulent activities being undertaken against small investors at that time. (These included scandals in the savings and loan market, insider trading, and others.) The perception was that this was the place to attack, not dissimilar to what I consider to be Congress's overreaction to the Enron and WorldCom scandals which took the form of passing onerous corporate governance regulation in 2002—the Sarbanes-Oxley Act of 2002 (SOX). That said, penny stock swindles were responsible for at least $2 billion in losses for investors each year at that time.

This was a serious problem, so serious Congress passed the Penny Stock Reform Act of 1990 (PSRA) to address the situation.

The PSRA's key provisions included greater corporate disclosure and increased availability of information for investors wishing to purchase lower-priced stocks, or stocks not trading on major exchanges. In addition, brokers selling penny stocks were required to obtain much more information about their customers before allowing them to purchase these securities.

As required by the PSRA, a few years later the SEC adopted a new rule, Rule 419 under the Securities Act of 1933 (see Chapter 4 for details), designed to chase the unscrupulous out of the reverse merger business.

Reverse mergers have—finally—shed most of the taint of past association with shady dealers and become respectable vehicles for taking small- and mid-cap-sized companies public. In its reverse merger rulemaking in June 2005, the SEC corroborated this when it announced: *"We recognize that companies and their professional advisors often use shell companies for many legitimate corporate structuring purposes."* This is a dramatic change. As recently as 2004 the SEC took a different view as manifested by then SEC Chairman William Donaldson's question to his staff at a public hearing, "Well, are there any legitimate reverse mergers?" (The staff advised him that, indeed, there are.)

Advantages of a Reverse Merger Versus IPO

Reverse mergers provide seven major benefits when compared to traditional IPOs:

- ❑ lower cost
- ❑ speedier process
- ❑ not dependent on IPO market for success
- ❑ not susceptible to changes from underwriters regarding initial stock price
- ❑ less time-consuming for company executives
- ❑ less dilution
- ❑ underwriters unnecessary

Lower Cost

A reverse merger usually costs significantly less than an IPO. Most reverse mergers can be completed for under $1 million. (This includes the cost of acquiring the public shell.) Total costs can be much less than $1 million, depending on the cost of the shell and whether or not the private company has already completed proper audits of its financial statements. I have seen transactions costing less than $200,000, and this is not unusual.

Another advantage of reverse mergers is that most of the costs can be predetermined. Some law firms (including my own) use flat fee structures to ensure no surprises. The costs of the shell and the fee for the investment bank's services are determined up front. Auditors' costs usually fall within the range of their estimates.

An IPO is much more expensive, costing at least several million dollars. And that does not include underwriting commissions to be paid to those raising the IPO money, which can add several million dollars more. Law firms rarely complete an IPO for a flat fee, and costs almost always exceed everyone's expectations. The company going public also generally bears the legal and other costs of its underwriter, which can be significant.

One of the biggest variables in the total cost of a reverse merger is the cost of the public shell into which the private company will merge. The cost of shells that are trading and have significant shareholder bases has gone up dramatically in the past several years as demand outstripped supply and the quality of available trading shells has markedly diminished. As of the writing of this book, some shells have sold for as much as $900,000—not including the equity that the original shell owners will retain after the merger. In fact, I recently heard about a shell board that turned down an offer of $1.2 million. That said, some savvy shell buyers, even today, are sometimes still able to find shells for $400,000 to $500,000.

The shell market will be discussed in much more detail in Chapter 3, but one trend is worth reporting here. In order to cash in on the demand for shells, people are creating them from scratch. Because these new shells do not trade, they cost less than shells that do, at least in terms of cash. The people forming new shells are generally more interested in equity and are willing to take less cash because of the lower up-front costs of creating the shell.

Speedier Process

In general, a reverse merger can be completed much more quickly than an IPO. Prior to the SEC's reverse merger rulemaking in June 2005, most transactions involving legitimate players completing proper due diligence and negotiation of documents were taking two to three months from start to finish, even if a contemporaneous financing was taking place. If no financing was involved, the transaction could be completed in a matter of weeks.

The SEC's new rules, which require significant disclosure about the merged company within four business days after closing, should not cause extensive delays. It is estimated that complying with the new rules will add approximately one month to most transactions, meaning a three- to four-month process if there is a contemporaneous financing. Some companies thinking about a reverse merger can reduce this time by preparing some or most of the information to be filed upon closing even before identifying a shell with which to merge.

This is much faster than a typical IPO, which usually takes nine to twelve months from start to finish, and can easily take longer. Reverse mergers are quicker because they are accomplished in fewer steps and with virtually no regulatory interference. The first step is due diligence in both directions. Then the merger agreement is negotiated and financing documents are completed. Next, a disclosure document is filed with, but not reviewed by, the SEC.

There are also fewer parties involved in reverse mergers than in IPOs. In a typical reverse merger, only two or three parties must come to terms: the controlling shareholders of the shell, the owners and managers of the private company, and the source(s) of financing. Of course, attorneys represent each party. Most important, in many cases reverse mergers can be completed entirely without review or approval by regulators.

An IPO involves more players, any one of whom can delay the transaction, and a much more extensive review process. Parties include: the private company's owners and managers and the underwriter (or frequently a group of managing underwriters). The IPO disclosure document must be prepared and reviewed by each player after very complete due diligence. Then the document, called a registration statement, is filed, reviewed, and approved by the SEC. This can take many months. The prospectus for the IPO is printed, and often delays at the printer can be frustrating. Next, the NASD must approve the underwriter's compensation in the IPO. The NASD is notoriously difficult, slow, and unpredictable in its handling of underwriter's compensation issues. Small IPOs involving listings on the OTC Bulletin Board rather than a major exchange require a particularly cumbersome review process in which the IPO must be approved in every state where the company seeks to offer securities under each state's securities laws, referred to as the blue sky laws. Some states have the reputation of being particularly difficult when they handle IPOs.

In one IPO my law firm went through *seven* comment letters from the NASD on underwriter's compensation. Responding to each took a week and they took anywhere from two to four weeks to respond back each time. In almost every letter, comments previously responded to were repeated. New comments came with each response that should have or could have been addressed in the first letter. The NASD gives the impression that it is entirely unconcerned with a company's desire to complete the process as quickly and efficiently as possible.

Reverse mergers do not involve any approvals or filings with the NASD, even if there is a contemporaneous PIPE or other private financing, because the NASD does not rule on agents' compensation in private placements such as a PIPE that don't involve a public offering such as an IPO.

Most IPOs require management to travel extensively to promote the deal. This takes weeks or sometimes months and causes further delay, not to mention it's a major distraction for the private company's management team, which has to take time off from running its business. PIPE investors in reverse mergers typically do not require extensive road shows.

No IPO "Window" Necessary

Sometimes there is absolutely no market for IPOs. During these times, the IPO "window" is said to be "closed." In 2000, after the stock market crash, the IPO window slammed shut. The market has opened slightly since then, but only for larger companies. (In the first half of 2005, fewer than twelve IPOs raising under $25 million occurred.) The window opens and shuts without warning and at extremely inopportune moments. Numerous dot-com companies were left with uncompleted IPOs after the market crash of April 2000. (Some of these completed reverse mergers in order to obtain the benefits of public status.)

One of the reasons IPOs have not come back—and may never come back as in their previous incarnation—is that the market is still reeling from the scandal-plagued Internet era when billions of dollars in fines and settlements were levied in connection with allegations of fraud and favoritism in IPOs of the 1990s. This does not bode well for the return of a strong IPO market for smaller companies anytime soon and leads one to wonder what is indeed the most "legitimate" way to go public.

Unlike IPOs, reverse mergers continue in all markets. In a down market with limited opportunity for IPOs, companies can use reverse mergers as an alternative route to going public. In an up market with many opportunities for IPOs, many companies still choose reverse mergers as the vehicle of choice because of their other benefits: lower cost, speed, and less dilution.

One type of reverse merger, involving a specified purpose acquisition company (SPAC™*), is the exception that proves the rule. These are market-sensitive vehicles; they flourish only when the IPO market is weak. As mentioned earlier, SPACs (discussed in detail in Chapter 14) are public shells, formed from scratch to raise money in an IPO and then use that money to back a high-level management team. A SPAC's IPO can take place even in a weak IPO market because of many protections offered to investors purchasing equity in the SPAC. The stock of the SPAC trades publicly in anticipation of a merger with a private company, generally in a particular industry or geographic sector. As SPACs are a more direct alternative to IPOs than reverse mergers, they tend to be less successful when the IPO market is strong.

No Risk of Underwriter's Withdrawal

One of the riskier aspects of an IPO is that an underwriter can decide to terminate the deal or significantly change the share price of the offering at the last minute. Unfortunately, much of the success of an IPO depends upon the state of the market during the week that the stock begins to trade. What this means is that after months of preparation, the receptivity of the market to shares trading in a given price range can change dramatically and at the last minute. It is not unusual for an underwriter to request a big reduction in the offering price just before finalizing the deal. This significantly increases the dilution, or amount of stock given to new investors, thereby reducing the ownership stake of founders and entrepreneurs.

---

*David Nussbaum of boutique investment banking firm EarlyBirdCapital is essentially the founder of the SPAC movement. Nussbaum advises that "SPAC" and "specified purpose acquisition company" are trademarks of his company, and I hereby provide such disclosure.

More dramatically, sometimes IPOs are simply canceled for lack of interest in a tough market.

As mentioned above, reverse mergers are not market-sensitive. Certainly, cataclysmic events such as the September 11 attacks or wartime events have an impact on everything, including reverse mergers. But for the most part, reverse mergers continue regardless of the direction or timing of the stock market. An IPO's market sensitivity relates to the fact that the underwriter is intensely focused on its original investors in the IPO and getting them, in many cases, in and then right out of the stock within a matter of hours or days. Financiers in reverse mergers understand that immediate liquidity is not generally realistic, and thus are less worried about the state of the markets on the particular day that trading commences.

Much Less Management Attention Required

Most senior executives do not realize what they are getting into when they pursue a traditional IPO. Endless road shows, due diligence meetings, late nights at the printer, and international travel are the norm. A year away from building the business while pursuing an IPO can damage a company's ability to execute its business plan.

In general, reverse mergers demand significantly less management attention than IPOs, for a number of reasons. The transaction is quicker and less complex. Most of the work can be handled by a capable CFO working with counsel and auditors. There are no delays at the printer. Road shows to drum up interest in the offering are minimal.

No matter what route a company takes to go public, management must still learn the rules, requirements, and operational mandates that apply to public companies but not to private ones. These additional burdens were discussed in Chapter 1.

Less Dilution

A rule often quoted in finance is, "If money is being offered, take it." Another one is, "However much money you think you need, multiply by two." An often forgotten rule, however, which should also always apply, is, "Don't take more money than you know you comfortably need if you plan on growing, since you are taking money at a lower price per share than will be applicable in only a few months' time." Well, that one doesn't exactly roll off the tongue, but the idea is clear.

Too often in IPOs, underwriters essentially force the company to take more money than it could possibly need. A significant "working capital" line item in the use of proceeds section gives that away. Why do they do this? Because underwriters get paid based on what is raised. So raising more makes sense to them, regardless of whether the company needs it.

In general, a company's valuation at the time it goes public will be lower than six months or a year later, assuming the company grows and successfully executes its business plan. Therefore, the best time to raise money is after that appreciation in company value.

In a reverse merger context, financings tend to be smaller than in IPOs. In most cases, the PIPE or other financing provides money needed initially, and a follow-on financing can be pursued later. At a recent reverse merger conference, a PIPE investor speaking on a panel was asked why he decided to get into reverse mergers. He answered, "I got annoyed too many times being the investor *after* the financing that took the company public, since the first got a much better valuation."

As a result of raising less money in a reverse merger, there is less dilution. This allows a private company's management, founders, and prior investors to retain a greater percentage ownership of their company following a reverse merger than following an IPO.

No Underwriter

IPO underwriters provide a valuable service by helping larger companies obtain public status and raise significant sums. But underwriters, in the end, typically have one goal—to make a company look just right for an IPO, regardless of the long-term implications. Often management barely recognizes their company after the underwriters and counsel are finished writing the IPO prospectus.

The private company may be managed heavily through debt, which an underwriter may seek to convert or shed. It may be developing new areas of business which have exciting long-term potential but currently are draining cash and losing money. Management may be asked to terminate this area of business so as to separate it from the financials and make the company appear more profitable.

Early in my career I worked on an IPO for one of the first intended chains of adult day care facilities. It was a pure start-up, and had experienced management and a strong plan. But the underwriter felt that some operating business needed to be included, so it acquired a senior-focused book publisher doing a few million dollars in sales. Management really had no interest in book publishing, and sold the operation a few years after the IPO, once some day care facilities were actually established. Nothing illegal or improper, but clearly this move had no part in management's actual long-term plan.

Disadvantages of a Reverse Merger Versus IPO

IPOs have two advantages over reverse mergers. One, IPOs generally raise more money. Two, the IPO process makes it easier to create market support for a stock. Fortunately, with careful planning and artful execution, those engaged in reverse mergers can overcome these disadvantages.

Less Funding

Typically, a company receives more money in an IPO than in a financing tied to a reverse merger. As mentioned above, in some cases this amount is more than a company reasonably needs. But even where the reverse merger financing does not solve long-term needs, an additional public or private financing months after the reverse merger is usually possible, and at a higher valuation. Thus, at least in the current capital markets environment, there is generally no need to complete an IPO as the sole method to obtain all necessary financing.

Market Support Is Harder to Obtain

One of the most common criticisms of reverse mergers is that "market support" for the newly public company does not exist in the same manner as it does following an IPO. This is because in an IPO, the underwriter's job is to arrange that support. No Wall Street firm really follows stocks trading below $5 per share. Without analysts and major market makers, these stocks often trade "by appointment" since no buzz is created.

In a typical IPO, the underwriter seeks to create buzz and place the company's stock on a major exchange. Frequently, this market building causes a post-IPO pop in the stock price, something companies that complete reverse mergers cannot expect.

In fact, if a post–reverse merger pop occurs, it may be a sign that unscrupulous players are trying to manipulate the situation. Unfortunately, there are some players in the reverse merger field who do these transactions solely for the purpose of creating an opportunity to manipulate the stock price, either up or down. (They generally achieve this by distributing false or misleading information about the company or by betting the stock will go down through a method called "selling the stock short.") There are ways to mitigate this risk, discussed in detail in Chapter 7.

After a reverse merger, support for the stock develops over months, sometimes even a few years, after the company has logged a number of publicly disclosed quarters of operating activity. Ultimately, this earned support will be greater than the manufactured support following an IPO.

Post–reverse merger companies can take steps to increase the support for their stock. They engage capable and reputable public relations and investor relations firms to expose reverse merger companies to potential investors. They use an investment banker experienced in developing market support to handle the transaction, thereby increasing their chances of attracting more attention from Wall Street. But in the end, it is the company's performance that earns attention. If a company can grow to the point that it is able to move its stock listing to Nasdaq or the American Stock Exchange, at which point it is more likely that the analyst community will begin to notice, the company's success, not hype from underwriters, will be the key to the stock's performance. Chapter 6 covers the market support issue in depth. A good mantra: Wall Street's attention should be earned, not manufactured!

CHAPTER 3

Shells and Deal Structures

For those heading into their one-hundredth deal, and for individuals learning about these techniques for the first time, this chapter offers Reverse Mergers 101. Some experienced practitioners may choose to skip ahead to the next chapter; others will find a refresher of the fundamentals valuable.

Public Shells

In June 2005, the U.S. Securities and Exchange Commission defined a shell company as a company with "no or nominal operations, and with no or nominal assets or assets consisting solely of cash and cash equivalents." This definition caused much debate, in particular as to what constitutes "nominal" operations or assets. (This will be examined in more detail later in the chapter and again in Chapter 10.) But for now it is sufficient to understand that a real, seasoned operating business generally would not be considered a shell. The intent of the definition is to describe a public entity which is essentially dormant and waiting for a transaction.

Until the SEC sharpened its definitions in 2005, these companies were often called "blank check" or "blind pool" companies. Many in the industry use these terms interchangeably; however, there are fine distinctions in meaning, which sometimes become problematic. (See Chapter 10 for details.)

Another type of public shell, the SPAC, is created to raise large sums through an initial public offering with the intention of giving this money to a private company in a specified industry or sector with which they later merge. The shell is promoted as a one-stop shop to obtain both public status and needed capital without a third party going out to raise money.

It has recently become popular for PIPE investment banks and investors to manufacture nontrading public shells from scratch to use in their reverse merger transactions. These shells are as yet unnamed but are sometimes referred to as Form 10-SB shells because of the SEC form used to take them public.

Value of Shells

Economics 101 explains supply and demand, forces that influence all markets, including the market for shells. This market in recent years has seen rapidly growing demand outstripping a dwindling supply of shells. Thus, the value of the average shell has more than tripled in the last five years.

To identify and value an appropriate shell for a specific company's purpose, it is necessary to understand six important characteristics of the shell:

- ❑ How it was created
- ❑ Whether it has assets and/or liabilities
- ❑ Whether it is a trading or a nontrading shell
- ❑ Whether it is a reporting or a nonreporting shell
- ❑ The size of its shareholder base
- ❑ Whether it is clean or unclean

Together, these six characteristics give the prospective buyer a way to gauge the shell's value and utility for the purpose at hand. Some publicly trading, clean, OTC Bulletin Board shells have been sold for close to $1 million, plus an ongoing equity interest for the former owners of the shell. Prices generally go down from there based on whether or not the shell is trading, where it is trading, the size of its shareholder base, and the other factors described above.

Creation of Shells

Public shells are created in one of two ways. Some are created from scratch: a founder or group takes public an empty company whose business plan is to acquire a private company. Either a public offering is undertaken under SEC Rule 419 (or in the case of a SPAC through an exemption under Rule 419), or a company voluntarily subjects itself to the reporting requirements of the SEC by filing Form 10-SB. (See Chapter 13 for details.)

Other shells are created after the termination of operations of a "real" company. In other words, if a company went public through an IPO or reverse merger, operated a business, then was either sold, went out of business, or otherwise became dormant, the resulting entity is a public shell. If SEC filings are kept up to date, the stock can continue to trade though often exchange listed companies are moved down to the OTC Bulletin Board and the shell can be marketed to private companies for a potential merger. Recently, some have taken over struggling or dormant *private* companies for the purpose of creating a public shell by putting them through bankruptcy and using a little known provision of the bankruptcy code to allow free-trading shares to be issued to creditors and others in the reorganization.

Assets and Liabilities

Some shells have significant amounts of cash, such as SPACs. Other shells have little or no cash, and if capital is needed, funds will have to be raised through other methods.

Some shells have other valuable assets, such as an old claim the company is asserting against a third party from its operations. For example, one shell that a client looked at was in litigation against a customer to collect a large, old receivable. The lawyer had taken the case on contingency, so no additional legal fees would be payable after the merger. This asset was included as part of the value of the shell. Other shells have potentially valuable intellectual property.

In some cases shells carry old liabilities on the books. These are presumed to be assumed upon the merger, and have to be included in the value of the shell. For example, if a shell shows $100,000 in old payables, the value of the shell to a buyer is reduced by that amount. More commonly, the promoter of a shell seeks to eliminate these liabilities or convert them to equity prior to or upon closing a merger.

Occasionally a shell promoter will suggest that creditors owning old payables will never seek to collect. In that case, an indemnification arrangement with control persons of the shell may be in order. Our experience has been that, even if creditors have not sought payment, once they learn of the impending merger they are much more likely to seek payment. In many cases, as long as the creditor has not reasserted the claim, the statute of limitations runs out in about six years.

Trading Versus Nontrading Shells

Shells are also distinguished by whether or not their stock is trading. Shells formed from scratch, except SPACs, generally do not and cannot have their stock trade prior to a merger. Public shells resulting from a former public operating business typically do continue trading.

The marketplace for shells deems trading to be a positive, and generally values a trading shell higher than one that is not trading. This is not completely rational.

Assume a trading shell, which was formerly a real operating business, has 1 million shares trading in its public float. Upon a merger, a formerly private company negotiates to take over 90 percent of the shell, obtaining 9 million new shares out of 10 million then outstanding. These newly issued shares cannot trade until they are registered with the SEC, which can take months.

In the meantime, only 1 million out of 10 million shares (those originally held by the owners of the shell) are tradable. Further, in most shells, one or two people control a significant majority of the stock. Assuming that two-thirds of the stock is so controlled, and that those controlling shareholders will not be selling, that leaves 333,000 shares in the "real" public float. Thus, 333,000 out of 10 million shares may be actively trading after a merger, or barely 3 percent of the stock.

Further, those holding the 333,000 shares typically have been holding them for a long time. They probably purchased the shares at a higher price when the business was operating. At the time of the merger, there is really only one thing they want. They want out. So immediately following a merger, there is typically a strong sell-off of what little float there is, providing downward pressure on the stock price post-merger. Thus, until a large portion of the remaining 9 million shares are registered and increase the public float, the company never gets to real trading.

Trading shells have another risk factor. In some cases insider trading takes place in the shell's stock prior to announcements relating to the potential deal. In this case, those doing the trading are not the only ones liable. As will be discussed later, if the person trading illegally also controls the shell, the shell itself can be liable on an "alter ego" theory. The private company that merges into the shell inherits this potential liability, if it exists.

PRACTICE TIP

Watch the trading of the shell's stock throughout the transaction and consider backing out if insider trading is suspected.

A nontrading shell has none of these problems—no unexplainable downward pressure, no insider trading, and so on. Trading can be achieved fairly quickly following a merger with a nontrading shell if the company immediately registers its shares. Real trading can begin in the same three-to four-month time frame as with a trading shell.

Our clients have learned this, and as a result, currently more than twenty PIPE investment banks and investors have engaged us to manufacture nontrading shells for them. They see no concern with the lack of trading in the shell for the reasons stated above and prefer a totally clean entity with no history to "scrub."

Reporting Versus Nonreporting Shells

Some public shells "report" under SEC rules; others do not. A reporting company is obligated to file quarterly, annual, and other regular reports with the SEC and is subject to other rules regarding insider trading, soliciting proxies and the like.

Companies that trade on the Pink Sheets may do so without reporting. The mechanics vary, but if a company does an IPO, it is subject to reporting requirements only for one year. After that year, the company may cease reporting and the stock may continue trading. The only requirement is that certain basic information be provided to brokerage firms who are making a market in the company's stock. None of the other stock exchanges permit this. Cromwell Coulson, chairman of Pink Sheets LLC, the company that operates the Pink Sheets market, is implementing some higher level trading opportunities for companies that disclose more information than is currently required.

A third category of companies is known as "voluntarily reporting." These public companies are not subject to the reporting requirements (i.e., they have passed the one-year required period) but they have chosen to continue to file quarterly and annual reports with the SEC, have their financials audited and so on.

What does this mean for the valuation of public shells? The marketplace generally assigns a higher value to a shell that is required to report and is current in those reports; however, some take the opposite position and assign a higher value to a voluntarily reporting shell or even a nonreporting shell because it is obligated to disclose less information. The reason for this is that certain filing requirements leading into and after a reverse merger might be avoided if the shell is not obligated to report. Only reporting companies have to file the new disclosure document required by the 2005 SEC reverse merger rulemaking. Only reporting companies have to mail a document to shareholders prior to closing a reverse merger if a change in the control of the board is contemplated. (It almost always is.) Only reporting companies' officers, directors, and five percent or greater shareholders have to report their ownership. Only reporting companies are required to use an SEC-approved proxy statement when shareholder approval of a matter is required.

Making the transition from nonreporting to reporting became easier after a little-known SEC telephone interpretation given in 1997. (A telephone interpretation is where the SEC staff answers in writing a specific question asked by an individual.) This particular "telephone interp" established that a voluntarily reporting company could become a mandatory reporting company by completing a Form 8-A—a relatively simple filing compared to the alternative, Form 10-SB. To choose this option, the company must have voluntarily completed all periodic filings, and all information that would be in a Form 10-SB must be contained in those periodic filings. Thus, a voluntarily reporting shell that is current in its filings may be able to become a mandatory reporting company through a relatively simple filing immediately prior to completing a reverse merger.

There is a concern, however, that nonreporting or voluntarily reporting shells do not provide sufficiently reliable information for due diligence purposes. In general, I find that my clients prefer a reporting shell.

Shareholder Base

In addition to public status, the other major asset a shell has to offer is a shareholder base. The only way meaningful trading in a stock can build is through the addition of a good number of shareholders. A public company with twenty or thirty shareholders is simply less valuable than one with 2,000 or 3,000 shareholders. Thus, one of the factors influencing how shells are valued is the number of shareholders. The OTC Bulletin Board unofficially requires at least thirty-five to forty shareholders with at least one hundred tradable shares each (known as "round lot shareholders") to allow a stock to trade there. Thus, some of those who are manufacturing nontrading shells generally are planning to include at least forty to fifty shareholders in each shell at some point. This permits them to market the shells as "Bulletin Board-ready."

Clean Versus Unclean Shells

Another item that meaningfully influences a shell's value is whether it is considered to be "clean." (See Chapter 9 for details.) At this time, suffice it to say that problems in a shell's past history or management can adversely affect its current value.

Reverse Merger Deal Structures

Now that much of the industry's jargon has been explained, it's time to describe in more detail how reverse mergers work. As explained earlier, the private company takes over the public shell and becomes instantly public. The "reverse" happens because the public shell survives the transaction, although control of the new organization usually passes to the private company's owners. The public shell must survive in order to maintain the trading status of the new enterprise and to avoid complex issues of being a "successor" to a public company through a process known as a "backdoor" registration.

The private company's shareholders generally receive between 65 percent and 95 percent of the stock of the public shell, and often pay cash as well. The allocation typically gives the owners of the operating business control of the public shell. In addition to the factors affecting shell valuation described above, the percentage of shares allocated to the private company's owners will depend on the value of the private business. A typical start-up will end up with a smaller share of the public shell than a company with $50 million in revenues and $2 million in profit.

The Reverse Triangular Merger

When public shells and private companies merge, they fall under the jurisdiction of the states in which they are incorporated. (Two corporations from different states also may merge, and then they are subject to the laws of both states in completing a "foreign," as opposed to "domestic," merger.) In most states, companies that want to merge cannot do so without the approval of the shareholders of both companies. If the shell is reporting and is a party to the merger, this requires that a complex and cumbersome proxy statement be approved by the SEC and mailed to shareholders before a shareholders' meeting is held. This process can be very expensive and time-consuming.

Shell companies that trade on the OTC Bulletin Board or Pink Sheets can circumvent this process by using a "reverse triangular merger."

In a merger, reverse or otherwise, two corporations join together. One becomes the "surviving corporation"; the other becomes the "nonsurviving corporation." The surviving corporation swallows up the assets and liabilities of the nonsurviving corporation and the latter simply ceases to exist.

In a reverse triangular merger, the public shell creates an empty, wholly owned subsidiary. The subsidiary then merges into the private company. This merger must be approved by the shareholders of the private company (who typically give their consent in writing) and the shareholder of the shell's new subsidiary, which of course is the shell itself, acting through its board, must approve the merger. The shareholders of the public shell need not be consulted.

Shares of the private company are exchanged for shares of the public shell. As a result, the newly formed subsidiary of the shell, as the nonsurviving corporation, disappears and the private company, as the surviving corporation, becomes a wholly owned subsidiary of the shell, with the owners of the formerly private company owning the majority of the shares of the shell following the deal's closing.

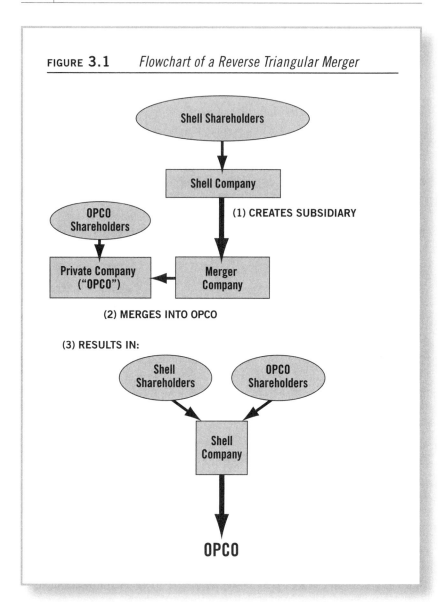

FIGURE **3.1**   *Flowchart of a Reverse Triangular Merger*

One major advantage of this structure is that the operating business remains intact. If it has valuable vendor numbers with customers, they do not need to change. Bank accounts, employer identification numbers, virtually all contracts (even leases) remain the same since all that has changed is the ownership of the private company. And even so-called change of control default or consent provisions in contracts generally would not be triggered, since the same people control the enterprise both before and after the transaction.

This option is not available to shells that trade on a major market or exchange such as the Nasdaq because their trading rules insist that any reverse merger, including a triangular one, be subject to shareholder approval. They also require that companies present a "new listing" application when control changes hands. To complete this application, a company must meet all initial listing standards, not just maintenance standards, following the merger. Generally, the initial listing standards (relating to number of shareholders, share price, public float, size of business, etc.) are much higher and more difficult to meet than the maintenance standards.

Thus, to avoid having to seek shareholder approval, it is sometimes recommended that a Nasdaq shell delist from Nasdaq and move to the OTC Bulletin Board prior to the merger. A merger with a Nasdaq shell is possible, and I have participated in several. The parties simply have to be sure they have the patience to prepare and have approved by the SEC a proxy statement relating to the transaction.

Other Deal Structures

Some reverse mergers are structured as an exchange of shares or a simple asset acquisition. This is sometimes necessary when the private company is a non-U.S. entity, because most state laws on mergers only contemplate transactions between U.S. companies. Sometimes the accountants advising the parties prefer these structures as well. At the end of the day, the transaction generally ends up as a tax-free reorganization under Internal Revenue Service regulations, and whether a merger, share exchange, or asset acquisition, the net result taxwise is typically the same (except that in the case of an asset acquisition, the private company's existence generally ends). In general, the tax treatment of reverse mergers is very straightforward and in almost all cases avoids the payment of tax as a result of the transaction.

Reverse Stock Splits

It may be possible to complete a reverse merger with minimal involvement from the shareholders. But other desirable actions—including a reverse stock split or name change—may require shareholder approval.

A company generally must have shareholder approval if it wants to change the number of shares it issues or the number of shares owned by the public. Every corporation, including every public shell, has a maximum number of shares of stock it is authorized to issue under its corporate charter, the document under which it was incorporated. This number cannot change without a shareholder meeting or written consent and, in the case of a reporting shell, an SEC-approved proxy (or "information statement" if proxies are not being solicited). Each corporation also has a number of shares that people own, known as the issued and outstanding shares. A corporation cannot have more issued or outstanding shares than those that are authorized.

In the process of completing a reverse merger, however, a public shell often finds itself with too many issued and outstanding shares and not enough authorized shares.

For example, assume a shell is authorized to issue 20 million shares. It has issued 10 million shares and it has negotiated a reverse merger which gives the owners of a private company a 90 percent interest in the merged entity. This means that the company has only 10 million shares available to give to the owners of the private company. Unfortunately, this is not enough to give the private company a 90 percent ownership stake in the company. (Providing ten million shares gives them a 50 percent stake.)

This problem has two solutions, both of which typically require shareholder approval. One option is that the 10 million outstanding shares can be the subject of a reverse stock split where each share is turned into, say one-tenth of one share, so that the 10 million outstanding shares turn into 1 million. At the time of the split, each shareholder still owns the same overall percentage interest in the company. Most states' laws require a reverse stock split to be approved by shareholders, through a proxy or information statement under SEC rules.

The other solution is to amend the company's charter to increase the number of authorized shares. This also requires shareholder approval.

Either solution frees up the proper number of new shares for the former owners of the private company. Depending on the circumstances, it may be possible to postpone shareholder approval until after the merger so as not to delay the transaction.

Reverse stock splits are more common than increases in authorized shares. This is because promoters of these transactions generally seek to limit the number of outstanding shares so as to increase the average per share trading price after the merger. We discuss this further in Chapter 6.

Doing a Deal

A reverse merger with a reporting shell (other than a SPAC or a shell formed under Rule 419, to be discussed in Chapter 4) generally follows a typical path.

Both the private company and the shell engage in a due diligence review of each other's finances, legal documents, and so on. A merger agreement is then prepared and negotiated. In this document, which generally runs from twenty-five to seventy-five pages, each side makes certain representations, or statements of fact, to the other about its business and history.

If shareholder approval is required for any action, the appropriate proxy statement is prepared and filed. If a financing is to take place at the same time as the merger, documents relating to that are also prepared. This might include a securities purchase agreement, registration rights agreement, and other documents such as the form of a warrant issued in a transaction. In many cases this also includes a full disclosure document, known as a private placement memorandum or PPM. Any problems from the shell's past, such as converting or paying off old liabilities, are cleaned up while the merger agreement is being negotiated.

If a change in the shell's board is anticipated upon completion of the reverse merger (it typically is), an additional SEC filing known as a Schedule 14F must be prepared, filed with the SEC, and mailed to shareholders of the shell at least ten days prior to closing the deal. This document looks like a typical public company proxy statement for a board election and includes information about the nominees for the board to take over after the merger.

This filing is often forgotten or ignored, but it is technically required. The legal section of this book covers a simple, legal way around this filing for those who wish to avoid it. Proponents of nonreporting shells often focus on their low filing and mailing costs, and ability to avoid delays related to Schedule 14F, since the nonreporting shell is not subject to the rules which require that filing.

Under the SEC rules passed in June 2005, one more document must be prepared before closing and filed with the SEC within four business days after closing. This document, to be filed as a "current report" on Form 8-K, must include all the information that would be included in a Form 10-SB with respect to the merged company. This includes, among other things, several years of audited financial statements; executive compensation; related party transactions; period-to-period comparative analysis; full business description; and a list of stockholders, officers, and directors.

In other words, the filing must include essentially all the information that would be contained in a prospectus if the company were pursuing a traditional IPO. The very important difference, however, is that the IPO filing is reviewed and scrutinized in great detail by the SEC before becoming effective.

The Form 8-K to be filed after a reverse merger is not required to be reviewed, and is effective immediately upon filing. But the amount of effort needed to prepare it is the same. Although review is not required, the SEC always may choose to review any filing. Many practitioners in the reverse merger field anticipate that the SEC will, at least for a while at some point, choose to review and provide comments to 8-K filings. However, the 8-K is still effective upon filing and the review should not interfere with the completion or effectiveness of the reverse merger.

PRACTICE TIP

Assume that the SEC will look at the Form 8-K filing.

CHAPTER 4

Introduction to Rule 419

Over the last twenty years, and in particular the last five to ten, reverse mergers have been transformed from sometimes-shady deals into legitimate transactions. One of the most influential events guiding this transition was the passage in 1992 of SEC Rule 419. This rule was designed to protect shareholders from fraud in reverse merger transactions.

Then, during the Internet boom (1995–2000), major investment banks began raising money for companies that had gone public through reverse mergers, something they previously had been unwilling to do. This completed the transformation of reverse mergers from dubious to legitimate transactions. This chapter first describes how Rule 419 protects shareholders, then explains how reverse mergers entered the mainstream during the Internet boom, and finally describes how PIPEs (private investments in public equity) are now transforming the reverse merger market once again.

Rule 419

In 1992, the U.S. Securities and Exchange Commission began treating registration statements from shells (including those pertaining to initial public offerings) differently than those from operating companies. Rule 419, passed in 1992 under the Securities Act of 1933, spells out requirements for shells that were designed to protect shareholders and investors from fraud. It is important to note that the SEC decided not to end the practice of reverse mergers. Instead, it used Rule 419 to make shell IPOs and reverse mergers safe and legitimate. There was, however, a price to be paid for this protection. The price was more onerous filing requirements for shell promoters. (Eventually, practitioners of reverse mergers learned that there was a legitimate way around Rule 419 by taking a shell public through the filing of Form 10-SB. See Chapter 15 for details.)

Rule 419 uses the term "blank check company" to include companies for which the following statements are true:

1 The company is in the development stage.

2 The company is issuing penny stock. (Penny stock is any equity security that is not traded on Nasdaq or a U.S. securities exchange or is issued by a company that fails to meet certain net tangible asset/revenue criteria.)

3 The company either has no specific business plan or purpose or its business plan is to merge with an unidentified company or companies.

To clarify: a legitimate start-up business, say, with a goal of developing software, would not be a blank check company subject to the restrictions of Rule 419. Equally, any company that can meet the standards for listing on a major market or exchange is exempt from Rule 419. Finally, having certain assets and revenue also means exemption from the rule. If a company has more than $5 million in assets (or $2 million if it has been in existence for more than three years), or is raising $5 million in a so-called firm commitment underwritten IPO, it is exempt from Rule 419 and its restrictions.

Rule 419 has been an important influence on the practice of reverse mergers. For example, specified purpose acquisition companies (SPACs) which generally raise at least $20 million, are exempt from Rule 419 because they raise more than $5 million. However, as will be discussed in Chapter 14, many SPACs adopt many of the restrictions of Rule 419 voluntarily because doing so attracts investors and may prevent unwanted attention from the SEC.

Basics of Rule 419

Rule 419 is intended to address a situation where a founder of a blank check company wants to use it to first raise money in a public offering, and then look for a company with which to complete a reverse merger. In the case of a registered offering (in other words, typically an IPO) of a penny stock by a blank check company, the rule requires that the gross proceeds, less certain authorized deductions, be deposited in escrow. This is the provision that drove away most of the scam artists, since the money raised could no longer be used simply to line the pockets of promoters. Rule 419 caps expenses related to the offering at 10 percent, in addition to customary underwriting commissions.

Second, the stock issued in the blank check's IPO also must be placed in escrow, and cannot be transferred until a reverse merger is completed. Therefore, while the company is waiting to do a reverse merger, those who purchase the IPO shares in the blank check cannot sell the shares. This was not intended to punish the purchasers, but rather to eliminate another wrongful practice, namely, the substantial amount of abusive trading that took place in the secondary market following the IPOs of blank check companies prior to a reverse merger. This served to eliminate short sellers and rumormongers.

In order for the stock and funds to be released from escrow, three conditions must be met under Rule 419:

1 The blank check must agree to *acquire a business the fair value of which is at least 80 percent of the maximum offering.* Therefore, one cannot raise $1 million in the shell, and then merge with a company that has a legitimate value of $100,000. Although one could argue that a company with a $100,000 value could benefit from a $1 million investment, it appears that was overshadowed by the SEC's concern that bogus companies not commensurate in size with the amount of money raised would come in and use up the proceeds improperly.

2 The *investors in the IPO must reconfirm their investment* after receiving a prospectus-like document regarding the company to be acquired. In other words, enormous detail about the business to be merged with must be put together in a prospectus for the operating company. This document must be filed with and approved by the SEC, which can take a number of months. The merger cannot be completed until this document is approved and mailed to investors, who must then reconfirm their investment in order for the merger to close.

3 *The merger must be completed within eighteen months of the public offering* or all funds invested, less expenses incurred, are returned to investors. If the funds are returned, however, the shell remains as a public company, but its only remaining shareholders are those who owned shares prior to the shell's IPO—in other words, the founders. This creates a "second life" for the shell, but those who invested in the IPO do not have the ability to participate.

Life After Passage of Rule 419

What happened after Rule 419 was passed in 1992? There was an immediate and dramatic positive effect on abuses. Most of the bad guys moved on (they were next seen in municipal securities and so-called Regulation S transactions), but the quality players also were hurt. Those who stayed in the game looked at several alternatives.

Grandfathered Shells

As the rule was being considered, smart players pushed through as many new blank checks as they could knowing these would be grand-fathered under the new rule. It took several years for those shells to be merged. I still represent one shell that was created prior to the passage of Rule 419.

Public Shells from Operating Companies

It became more common to look for public shells formed from the end of a public operating business rather than to create shells from scratch. Very few people were interested in using the burdens of complying with Rule 419 as a method to actually form shells. The technique of using a recently bankrupt or virtually dormant former operating company as a shell in a reverse merger candidate became more in demand.

SPACs

The market for SPACs also developed during this time, particularly in the mid-1990s, just before the IPO market really took off as part of the Internet boom. Investment bankers were willing to endure many of the burdens of Rule 419 in exchange for substantial underwriting fees, as well as commissions earned from trading in the stock of the SPAC while it awaited a merger. As indicated above, while SPACs were exempt from Rule 419, their promoters adopted many of its restrictions for marketing purposes.

Form 10-SB Shells

Though it took a little time, it was discovered that Form 10-SB shells could be formed from scratch as a legal end-around Rule 419. There was a reason this took time, which I will now explain. The legal analysis is simple. Rule 419 was passed under the Securities Act of 1933 (Securities Act), which governs primarily the public offering market and was the first congressional reaction to the great stock market crash of 1929. This meant that Rule 419 applied only to those seeking to register for public sale individual shares to be sold by a company, or resold by existing shareholders.

Form 10-SB is filed under the Securities Exchange Act of 1934 (Exchange Act), passed a year after the original Securities Act. The Exchange Act followed up the Securities Act with the creation of the U.S. Securities and Exchange Commission; regulation of brokers and dealers and the trading markets; and regulation of proxies, tender offers, and other activities undertaken by public companies. The integrated disclosure system of regular reports by public companies also was established in the Exchange Act.

Form 10-SB allows a company to voluntarily subject itself to the SEC reporting requirements under the Exchange Act without registering individual shares for sale or resale. In order for a trading market to develop in these companies, shares have to be registered for sale at some point under the Securities Act. Alternatively, under Securities Act Rule 144, shares held for a certain period of time, generally one to two years, can be publicly sold whether or not they are registered.

Therefore, a company can file a Form 10-SB, become subject to reporting requirements, and then have a trading market develop through the use of Rule 144. Unfortunately, the SEC has ruled that shares acquired in a public shell or blank check can never be sold under Rule 144. Therefore, shares owned in a shell formed through filing a Form 10-SB have to be registered at some point after the reverse merger.

In any event, a blank check can go public by filing a Form 10-SB and avoid the proscriptions of Rule 419. The SEC rebuffed early efforts to create Form 10-SB shells after the passage of Rule 419, including one on behalf of one of my clients. In a filing we attempted in 1993—just one year after the rule was passed—the SEC commented on our Form 10-SB filing saying, "You cannot do this because of Rule 419." We knew the SEC's analysis was incorrect, and that Rule 419 by its terms did not apply to a Form 10-SB filing. However, my client indicated his desire not to make an enemy of the SEC, so we decided to withdraw the filing.

By 1998, we saw a flood of Form 10-SB shells. I surmised that someone must have fought the fight and been successful, as was appropriate. Until only very recently, however, many practitioners (including myself) took the position that Form 10-SB shells were to be avoided, since at best they appeared to be disfavored by the SEC, even if legally permissible. As a result, many (but by no means all) of the Form 10-SB shells formed during this period were promoted by questionable players.

As a result of numerous conversations with SEC and Nasdaq officials in recent years, I have concluded that the SEC and the major exchanges do not appear to have any problem with Form 10-SB shells. Indeed, recent attempts at filings for these shells have received extremely favorable treatment in the review process. Yet recent attempts to form Rule 419 shells have met with significant resistance from SEC staffers in the form of major comments in each successive filing seeking to take blank check companies public.

In the end, the timetable is basically the same to get a private company public and get to "real" trading post-merger, whether going through a Rule 419 shell or a Form 10-SB shell. In the case of Rule 419, it takes several months for the "reconfirmation" prospectus to be approved and then the merger closes and trading can commence. In the case of a merger with a Form 10-SB shell, the merger happens quickly but trading only develops after a "resale" registration covering the sale of securities, which generally takes several months. However, because a merger with a Form 10-SB shell is faster, a PIPE financing also can be accelerated and closed upon the merger. Thus, merging with a Form 10-SB shell seems preferable to a Rule 419 shell for this reason.

As previously mentioned, a current trend involves major PIPE investors and investment banks forming Form 10-SB shells to complete reverse mergers and PIPEs for the currently private companies in which they are interested.

The Internet Boom (and Bust)

During the Internet boom of the late 1990s, reverse mergers blossomed. This would seem illogical, since traditional IPOs also flourished during this time; however, as mentioned earlier, reverse merger activity generally remains healthy in both weak and strong stock markets. This is because in a down market, especially when the IPO market is weak, there are still plenty of companies that can benefit from being publicly held.

In an up market, a reverse merger is faster and less dilutive than a traditional IPO. In addition, in every IPO boom some companies seeking public status lack some element required for a traditional IPO. A company may be seen as too early stage, or operating outside of an industry in vogue with the investing community. Still, these companies could grow if afforded the opportunity to have a publicly traded stock.

During the Internet era, some companies were able to go public even though they had barely passed the initial formation stage and had little more than a business plan on a paper napkin. What seemed most important was to have the words "dot-com" somewhere in the company name. A milder version of this frenzy had occurred in the biotechnology area. Another minifrenzy is occurring as of this writing in the nanotechnology, oil and gas, and security industries, as well as for Chinese companies, and to a lesser extent, in health care.

During the late 1990s boom, companies wanted to go public faster than even the most aggressive investment banks could get them there with a traditional IPO. Enter the reverse merger, which became a very popular method for going public at the time.

This trend had a positive and unexpected consequence. As mentioned above, previously all the largest "bulge bracket" investment banks of the Goldman Sachs and Lehman Brothers league had shunned reverse mergers and the companies that had gone public this way.

During the Internet period, these old biases were virtually eliminated as bulge bracket firms fell over each other trying to grab as much reverse merger business as they could get. Thus, these major firms learned they could sometimes invest, with the same confidence (or lack thereof) as with other financings, in reverse merged companies. They learned the importance of focusing on the company itself, rather than on how it went public. And they began, slowly, to learn how to distinguish the good guys from the bad in the reverse merger business.

The market crash of 2000 created a different dynamic. Companies that were doing fairly well but missed the late-1990s IPO window used reverse mergers in panicked attempts to go public any way they could. A number of companies in registration to complete an IPO saw their dreams dashed, then sought salvation through a reverse merger. In some cases, these attempts paid off; in others, they simply created the next wave of shells as they hit bankruptcy or liquidation one after the other.

Today's Reverse Merger Market

In the last several years, PIPE investors and investment bankers have discovered the reverse merger—with the "pile on" mentality common to any Wall Street trend. In this case, however, there are good reasons for reverse mergers and PIPEs to come together. Why have reverse mergers suddenly become so popular? The short answer is, it has not been sudden, but rather an evolution that has taken about a dozen years. Most recently, however, a confluence of factors has caused this market to really take off.

First, since 2001, the IPO market has been essentially shut down for all but the largest private companies, making reverse mergers more attractive to middle market businesses. In addition, the private equity markets for growing private companies have been soft at best, making it tougher to stay private if large amounts of capital are needed to grow.

The PIPE market has been experiencing tremendous growth, creating more potential benefit to being a public company if access to the capital markets is important. Also, until recently, the merger and acquisitions market was very weak, and remains so for many companies. This limits the exit options that entrepreneurs and investors have.

An additional recent trend is a change in the PIPE market. In the past, PIPE investors were primarily interested in short-term liquidity and arbitrage opportunities in their investments. Typically, they did not look at companies in detail beyond their trading volume. Because of SEC scrutiny, along with issuer concerns about how PIPE securities are traded and a generally less liquid trading environment caused in part by recently enacted short selling rules, many PIPE investments now more closely resemble fundamental, longer-term investments.

PIPE investors are doing due diligence, meeting with management, taking more warrants to benefit from a stock's upside, and generally are more willing to wait for a larger return. As a result, PIPE investors are more active in pursuing investments in reverse mergers, where liquidity will probably take a little longer, but a greater upside potential exists. This, combined with the increased competitiveness for deals, has led PIPE investors and investment banks to see the benefits of what is now regularly called "public venture capital."

The most recent positive development in this area has come in the form of the SEC's new regulations, which will be discussed in detail in Chapter 10, The Regulatory Regime. In sum, the new regulation, which took effect in the fall of 2005, requires a significant increase in the amount of disclosure immediately following most reverse mergers. This is expected to help further improve the reliability and acceptability of these transactions. In its adopting release, in part resulting from strong encouragement from the private sector, the SEC declared that it acknowledges the legitimate use of the reverse merger technique. This is a major development. Given the history of abuse accompanying reverse mergers, it is very helpful that the SEC is prepared to encourage its proper utilization while continuing to come down hard on miscreants.

CHAPTER 5

Financing

Most reverse mergers are undertaken in order to obtain financing for a growing company. Companies effecting reverse mergers usually can raise somewhere in the range of $10 million to $25 million, significantly less than initial public offerings, which may raise anywhere from $20 million to $300 million. In some cases, only a few million dollars are raised as part of a reverse merger.

With an IPO, a company goes public and raises money in one transaction. Most reverse mergers take two separate but typically simultaneous steps (although frequently less time) to get to the same place: one, the private company buys the public shell and becomes public; two, the new company arranges for investors to purchase its stock. It would be difficult to overstate the importance of financing in reverse merger transactions.

That said, quite a number of deals involve no financing at all, but in most cases there is an intention to require financing at some point in the future, and being public is seen as a prerequisite to obtaining easier access to that capital.

In general, financing is easier in connection with a reverse merger than staying private because investors see liquidity as an opportunity, often within only a few months following the merger. Some are simply debt financings or factoring arrangements, others are more traditional private placements, PIPEs, or venture capital structures and the like.

The type of financing determines when purchasers may begin trading their stock. In private placements (sales of securities directly to individuals or institutional investors), purchasers generally must hold their stock for at least a year unless a registration process is completed with the U.S. Securities and Exchange Commission. If the deal is structured as a PIPE, a form of private placement providing for immediate registration, shares purchased can become tradable in as few as three months.

This chapter describes how financings both drive and slow a reverse merger transaction, valuation and structuring issues, documentation and other unique aspects of financings that are contemporaneous with a reverse merger.

How Not to Do It

As explained earlier, a very common mistake is for a company to pursue a reverse merger when its only goal is obtaining one round of financing immediately—or the hope of a round to come later—without the concomitant analysis of whether the company can otherwise benefit from being public (see Chapter 1). This shortsightedness can have unfortunate consequences. Here are two quick examples (some names and details are changed for obvious reasons):

A private company had a very exciting patent relating to certain entertainment technology. It had completed a small private placement to pay for additional research and development. A larger round was needed, and a group of investors agreed to provide $10 million as long as the company went public through a reverse merger.

The merger was completed, and the intention was to use the $10 million to help the company reach the point at which it could sell the product under development. As it turned out, more research was needed, the company was unable to raise additional financing, and consequently it went out of business. Since then, the resulting public shell has been merged with a different company, and the shares I received as part of my compensation have been reverse split from the 50,000 I held at a value of $2 per share to about 450 shares I now hold of a company trading at about $0.05 per share. As my accountant would say, "a good write-off."

In this case, the mistake was going public too early. The company was many months away from a commercial product. (This would have been unremarkable had the company been in the biotechnology industry, an industry that expects new companies to languish for years in prerevenue stages.) But, by its own industry standards, it took too long to get going. Investors got spooked and were unwilling to provide additional financing. This company went public because it wanted the $10 million and going public was a condition set by the investors.

Going public solely to raise one round of financing when a company sees no other benefits to being public almost always turns out to be a flawed strategy.

In addition, this company never made the effort to run itself like a public company. During my nine-month tenure as counsel (after which I resigned), the company went through three different chief financial officers. The CFOs never had second-level assistants, who are almost essential for a public company in the post-SOX environment. The well-intentioned chief executive officer was constantly traveling, trying to cut deals. Obtaining due diligence when we got started was like pulling teeth.

The second example involves a company that completed a reverse merger several years ago with the expectation of obtaining financing soon after the deal was done. The company, which was breaking even on about $15 million in sales, had a plan to benefit from being public by making acquisitions in its business, which relates indirectly to the sports industry. But it needed financing to pay for going public, as well as for searching for targets to acquire.

The investment bank it worked with provided the shell with which the company merged. The investment bank expected to raise funds after the merger, but for various reasons the financing was never completed. The banker would probably say that certain things in the company changed or were different than expected. The company would probably say that nothing was so different as to impair the ability to raise money.

In any event, the company did obtain some additional funds through traditional PIPE investors, but only enough to stay in business, which, by the way, is growing. As with so many businesses, however, while purchase orders and receivables grow, cash flow remains very tight. The management team is extremely dedicated and has worked hard to cut costs. Unfortunately, the difference between making and losing money in this company is represented by the combination of the costs of being public and the increasing cost of servicing the company's debt.

The company made several mistakes. First, because financing was essential, it should have arranged for it concurrently with the reverse merger. Second, when needed financing was not available, management probably should have considered returning to private status (which would not have been difficult in this case) at least for a short time so they could regroup and earn some money. Here's how they might have accomplished this.

Under current SEC rules, any reporting company with fewer than three hundred shareholders *of record* can voluntarily "deregister" itself as a public company, stop filing periodic reports, and have no further obligation to do so through a simple filing known as Form 15. A holder of record is one that actually holds a physical stock certificate. Many shareholders hold their shares in "street name," which means they own shares through an electronic entry at their broker, and therefore, all such street name shareholders count together as one shareholder. Thus, many public companies, some fairly large, have fewer than three hundred shareholders of record.

A company with more than three hundred shareholders of record must go through one of several complex filings in order to go private. It can effect a massive reverse stock split, cashing out investors who end up with less than one full share to reduce its number of shareholders to below three hundred. It can sell off its business to a related party, leaving behind the public shell to be used again. Or it can simply ask the share-holders to vote to "go private." In any of these cases, either state law or the SEC or both require shareholder approval, a full proxy, and often a related filing known as Schedule 13E-3, which describes in excruciating detail the plan for going private.

The ins and outs of going and staying private are of interest to growing numbers of companies. First, there are those who in the past several years have chosen to go private rather than comply with the onerous require-ments of Sarbanes-Oxley. Then there are those like the company described above. Under current rules, keeping the number of shareholders of record below three hundred provides important flexibility and usually is not that difficult to do.

There is one additional challenge to going private, one that the client mentioned above faces. That is, PIPE investors generally require that, for as long as they own shares, the company will retain its status as a reporting company and use its best efforts to maintain its exchange listing. Thus, any going private event results in a default in most PIPEs.

Several years ago, a client helped raise money in a private placement for a public company. There was no specific covenant to stay public; however, the company had a contractual obligation to register our client's inves-tors' shares so they could become tradable, which never happened. The company filed to go private the "simple way," by filing Form 15, a declara-tion that a company has fewer than three hundred shareholders of record. My client and his investors sued, and won a settlement that returned the money invested in a combination of cash and tradable stock of another company.

One last note on going private. In 2005, the SEC formed the Advisory Committee on Smaller Public Companies, which I testified before in June 2005. In April 2006, the committee submitted its final recommendations, which included amending SEC rule 12g5-1 to interpret the words *held of record* to mean what is known as "actual beneficial owners," but also increasing the number of shareholders one must have to avoid being able to use the simple Form 15 filing to go private. This inclusion of beneficial owners would encompass "street name" holders and not just those holding physical stock certificates. It is not clear whether the full SEC will adopt this or any other of the committee's recommendations.

In analyzing this issue, on the one hand, most everyone agrees that tying the availability of the simple filing to only those with physical stock certificates makes no sense: the rule is anachronistic and stems from a time when every shareholder held a stock certificate. In an era of electronic trading, it makes more sense to make the filing available based on the number of "beneficial owners"—including all those with shares held in street name. However, many—myself included—have urged the SEC to increase the maximum number of shareholders a company can have and still go private relatively easily.

In some few cases, such as in a reverse merger of a Chinese company I was recently involved with, there is no current need for financing. There may be a plan to raise money at some point in the future, but it is not required at the time of the reverse merger.

How Financing Drives the Deal

A leading venture capital firm approached an investment bank about providing a $15 million round of financing for a biotechnology company. The venture capitalist had already provided over $40 million in financing, and its partnership documents did not permit it to provide any additional financing (often funds are limited in the percentage of their overall pool of money that can be invested in a single company).

The company had successfully completed Phase II clinical trials and the preliminary results were positive. It was too early for a traditional IPO or even the sale of the company, and the venture capitalist knew this. Neither the company nor the venture capitalist was able to convince other private equity investors to put money into the company. Sometimes this happens when the original investor is unwilling to share his powers and rights with new investors.

The venture capitalist knew that an investment bank would raise money from a variety of sources and that it was likely the new investors would not demand substantial covenants, veto powers, and rights. (As mentioned earlier, investors in private companies such as venture funds generally seek to have more control over a company's decision making than investors in public companies. Also, public company shareholders do not want a small group of investors to have the right to veto important decisions.) In addition, the venture capitalist knew that the investment bank could raise multiple rounds of financing going forward, which would be essential to the company's achieving its business plan. The venture capitalist also knew that the valuation the company received from an investment bank was likely to be higher than a valuation from a private equity firm. All of this would be good for the venture capitalist and his interest in the company.

The investment bank was excited to get involved. They realized the most attractive way to raise money was for the company to become public. They consulted with advisers, including my law firm. The venture capitalist was clearly nervous about taking the reverse merger route. Indeed, while most of Wall Street has learned the value of this technique, the private equity and venture capital communities still remain somewhat skeptical and steeped in attitudes of the past (this was in 2003).

Thus, I found myself in the large conference room of a major law firm explaining the basics of reverse mergers to one of the firm's partners and the venture capitalist. My client was there as well, and of course helped fill in some of the details of the financing.

Recognizing that forming a new shell for the deal would take a few months and require substantial disclosure if a specific transaction was planned, the first step was for the investment bank to acquire an already existing public shell. They saw the benefits of acquiring the shell first rather than negotiating the reverse merger directly with the then-owners of the shell.

At that time, in early 2004, shells were readily available. The particular public shell they looked at, which was trading on the OTC Bulletin Board, cost about $450,000 (cheap by today's standards), plus a percentage of the deal going forward. Our client proceeded to purchase nearly a 90 percent interest in the shell, then immediately commenced negotiations with the venture capitalist and the company to complete both the reverse merger and the financing.

At this point, it is important to note a little known aspect of reverse merger financings. That is, if an investment bank or source of money also provides the public shell for the deal, it obtains an additional interest in the merged company simply for having provided the shell. In this case, at the end of the deal, our client's $450,000 investment in the shell turned into almost $1.5 million in value upon the closing of the reverse merger and financing only a few short months later.

It is considered both customary and appropriate in the reverse merger business to pay a fee to a shell's broker and, therefore, most private companies allow the investment bank or provider of the shell this extra interest. Some companies believe, however, it is a form of double-dipping when an investment bank earns fees on raising money as well as receiving an interest in the company for having provided the shell. I believe it is more than appropriate to receive these two forms of compensation because they are provided for separate sets of services, one for raising money and the other for providing a shell.

When a company balks at the additional compensation, however, there is still an advantage to the bank. Since it purchased the shell for cash as an investment, there is a tax benefit even to taking some of the fees for raising money by retaining its equity interest in the shell. In other words, if the bank were to receive warrants to purchase a 3 percent interest in the company as part of its compensation for raising money, it might be satisfied retaining an extra 3 percent through ownership in the shell. Thus, when it sells the interest later, it is taxed at more favorable capital gains rates rather than as ordinary income, which typically involves higher rates.

In general, though, banks supplying shells retain less of the overall post-merger entity if they also receive fees for raising money. Where a concern exists as to whether a bank has a conflict of interest raising money and also retaining an interest in the post-merger entity, it is not uncommon to obtain a fairness opinion from a valuation firm or investment bank. This third-party, theoretically objective opinion about the fairness of the transaction from a financial point of view helps assure the bank, the boards, and the shareholders that all parties were treated appropriately.

The two main purposes of obtaining such an opinion are (1) to confirm that the transaction is fair, and (2) to provide something of an insurance policy to the board of the shell. If the board has a fairness opinion in hand, it is much harder for shareholders to bring an action to challenge the valuation.

One must be very cautious when engaging a provider of a fairness opinion. In one case, a client owned a shell that was to merge. He sought a fairness opinion from a Midwest investment bank. The bank was hired, asked no questions, did no due diligence, got a check, and about two weeks later issued its opinion. Since the shell was traded on Nasdaq, a proxy was required to approve the deal. Only when the SEC insisted on much greater disclosure about the fairness opinion and how the investment bank did its analysis did the client feel forced to fire the original provider and engage another valuation expert who took six weeks, examined everything including comparable deals, and issued a well-researched, thorough, and insightful opinion.

When done right, the fairness opinion can provide some useful guidance. In fact, on at least one occasion a valuation expert was able to convince a client to change aspects of a deal to bring it more solidly into the realm of fairness.

Now, to get back to the biotechnology example: My investment bank client could not have completed its negotiations with the biotech company *before* acquiring the shell, as the $450,000 value of the shell at purchase would then come into question, given the value it achieved upon closing. In other words, the difference between the $450,000 purchase cost and the $1.5 million value on closing would be more suspect if the deal were prearranged prior to our client's acquisition of the shell. By purchasing the shell without any certainty as to whether the deal would proceed, our client had a strong argument that the $450,000 value was appropriate at the time of purchase. It felt the acquisition of the shell was worthwhile in any event, because if the biotech deal had not happened, it could have used the shell for another deal.

The next step was for the investment bank to work with the private company and the shell (i.e., itself as the owner of the shell) to craft both merger agreements and offering materials for the financing, while simultaneously working on due diligence reviews. Luckily, the client had completed a thorough due diligence review of the shell before its purchase, so it could focus on the private biotech company, the value of its patents, status of clinical trials, its financial results, and so on.

The most important step was yet to come, namely, valuing the company for purposes of the PIPE investment.

Many investors and investment banks have little experience with investments to be made at the same time a company becomes public through a reverse merger. They are accustomed to evaluating investments in private companies and investments in public companies, not investments that are hybrids of the two.

Several factors must be taken into consideration. First, different methods are used to value private and public companies. A private company often is valued for private equity purposes based upon not only its historical performance, but also its anticipated growth. Investors in a publicly trading company, however, typically value their investment based on the trading price of the stock, which may or may not incorporate growth potential in it. This usually results in a higher valuation being placed on a public company than on a similarly situated private one.

When a company goes from private to public with an IPO, the expectation is that the stock will sell at or above the IPO price as soon as the stock starts trading. But a company that starts trading shares after a reverse merger is in a somewhat different situation because its shares are not immediately tradable. This means the valuation has to take into account the anticipated delay between initial investment and liquidity.

Clients can approach these dilemmas in different ways. This particular client took a middle-way approach, essentially splitting the difference between a private and public company valuation, still coming in well below what the company's value was hoped to be once it began trading in a few months. The "public venture capital" concept was thereby further refined by our client. But the venture capitalist was still happy, as this valuation far exceeded his last round of financing and, in fact, exceeded what he had hoped to obtain if another private equity round did take place.

Having completed the valuation analysis, at this point our client learned that a reverse merger financing, even structured as a PIPE, was different from a typical PIPE. Most PIPEs are completed with companies that have been public for a while. Their public SEC filings are scrutinized as the primary form of due diligence. Documentation with the investors consists of a purchase agreement and a few collateral agreements which are basically in industry customary form, with not much to negotiate in most deals. The tough decision is typically for the investor to simply decide whether or not to go forward with a deal; most everything else becomes rather routine with the attorneys and deal professionals at the bank.

As a brief aside, I do not wish in any way to downplay the hard work of lawyers involved in PIPE financings (especially my partners Joe Smith and Rob Charron, who together completed more PIPE deals representing investors than any other law firm in each of the last three years). There is much negotiation that often takes place in completing PIPE deals with seemingly endless conference calls. In addition, the regulatory climate is complex and deal structures continue to evolve, requiring that attorneys adapt and adjust.

As the PIPE market has become more competitive, companies raising money have exacted more concessions from investors, changing the dynamics somewhat and making the process less and less routine. But it is true that many deals are relatively straightforward (as are most venture capital and private equity transactions) if for no other reason than the golden rule of finance: "He who has the gold makes the rules." Investors declare the documents are in the form they require, and accept very few changes. This makes the lawyers' work a bit less onerous once solid deal forms are developed and become industry standard.

Back to our example and the unique features of PIPEs completed contemporaneously with reverse mergers. The first question that was unique to the reverse merger context (and that had to be answered) was: Do the PIPE investors put their money into the private company just before the reverse merger, or directly into the former shell at the same moment as the merger? Logically one would think investing directly in the shell makes sense, since ultimately shares of the shell would be issued to all those who previously owned shares in the private biotech company.

In this case (and many others we have dealt with, but by no means all), the investment bank chose to have investors put their money into the biotech company one moment before completion of the merger. The reason was purely psychological. The bank felt that it would be too confusing to explain to investors that they are investing in a "shell," even if the investment happens at the same time. In other words, it did not want the front of the offering document booklet to say "Shell Co." Instead the bankers wanted it to say, "Biotech Co." In recent transactions, this has been changing, and more deals are being structured as purchases of securities of the shell itself upon closing the merger.

In this case, the decision to invest in the private company created some problems, none of which was insurmountable. First, it meant that, technically, the PIPE investors had to be part of the process by which all shareholders of the biotech company had to vote to approve the reverse merger. This was easy enough to deal with by incorporating into the subscription materials a consent to the transaction. We might have been able to seek shareholder approval of the merger prior to completion of the PIPE investment, which would not then require their approval. But we did not see the need to risk investor ire for not having had the chance to participate in the decision-making process.

Second, administratively, investing directly in the biotech company added a step of actually issuing PIPE investors' shares of the biotech company, then immediately exchanging them upon the merger for shares of the shell. This also was not a big deal, just a bit of a hassle.

The next challenge related to the lack of information. As noted above, in a typical PIPE, straightforward stock purchase agreements are used instead of a full disclosure document, often called a "private placement memorandum (PPM)." It is more common to use a full PPM for an investment bank–led raise for a private company. Sometimes a PPM is used in a private offering for a public company, but this document is usually a bare-bones "wraparound document" that includes a description of the offering, unique risk factors relating to the offering, all wrapped around copies of the company's public filings.

In this case, and in most cases we have encountered, the investment bank decided to complete a full PPM for the PIPE investors putting money into the biotech company upon its merger with the shell. This way investors would receive full information concerning the company to be merged, and the bank would be shielded from a liability standpoint from suggestions that investors were not fully informed of the risks of the investment.

This intelligent decision from a liability point of view caused a fairly significant delay in the deal since the lawyers and accountants took a surprisingly long time to agree on the disclosure language. The old adage "too many cooks spoil the broth" took on real meaning as it simply took time to get all the various players to respond to each successive draft of the PPM. At the same time, the parties were working on due diligence and completing a merger agreement and SEC filing under Section 14(f) of the Exchange Act, which related to the anticipated change of directors.

PRACTICE TIP

A PPM is a good idea when completing a PIPE contemporane-
ously with a reverse merger.

There is also an advantage to the existence of the PPM under the new
SEC rule requiring a Form 8-K filing with substantial disclosure about the
private company immediately following the merger. That is, the PPM can
be used as the basis for this filing, which is essentially a PPM on steroids.
Many components of a PPM are taken right from a typical full offering
prospectus, which the 8-K will effectively mirror. Thus, some of the anticipated delays in deals relating to the new rule will be significantly reduced
to the extent a PPM is already being prepared.

The last challenge in our biotech example involved when to disclose
the existence of the placement agent raising the money. Under SEC rules,
engaging a placement agent to help raise money is generally considered
a material contract, requiring a filing with the SEC and disclosure of
the contract with the agent. But in this case, it was the *private* company
engaging the agent. Also in this case, the public shell had disclosed that
it was entering into the transaction with the private company. Therefore,
a determination was made that it was prudent for the shell to disclose
that the private company with which it might merge had engaged a
placement agent.

The problem then is avoiding a determination that the public disclosure of the offering and the agent might cause a loss of its "private
offering" exemption, which depends on avoiding what is known as
general solicitation. Under Regulation D, to be discussed in more detail later, to ensure that an offering remains private, the company must
avoid advertising and other activities deemed general solicitation. Disclosing the agreement with the placement agent might be deemed to
be such a type of solicitation; however, an SEC rule known as Rule 135
provides guidance as to how to disclose the existence of a placement
agent and a pending private placement without triggering a general solicitation concern, and we followed that rule in making the disclosure.
The key, believe it or not, is to disclose everything without actually
disclosing the name of the placement agent itself.

PRACTICE TIP

When in doubt, disclose the engagement of a placement agent—
but watch out for accidental general solicitation when undertak-
ing a private offering.

Ultimately, though, the transaction was completed, and like a well-rehearsed orchestra, the various pieces of the deal came together and the reverse merger and PIPE closed simultaneously.

Time and Money

Some of the issues that arise in the deal-making process relate to timing. A desire to complete a financing prior to the merger creates disclosure, valuation, and structuring challenges. In these instances I try to encourage clients to wait and complete the transaction in the name of the public entity either at closing or shortly thereafter. In a recent trend, however, a number of PIPE investors have been willing to provide financing to the private company prior to the actual merger, understanding the risk that the merger may never go through. They provide more downside protection for themselves in these transactions and, sometimes, penalties for failure to complete a going public event within a certain amount of time. As deals begin to take a little longer due to the new SEC rules, the opportunity for a private company to complete a financing while waiting for completion of the merger is a very positive development.

This more aggressive financing trend is also helping fuel "self-filings," to be described in more detail in the third part of this book. A PIPE investor funds a private company, which then goes public through a registration statement seeking to allow the PIPE investor to resell his shares in the public market. It is not a public offering by the company, nor is it a reverse merger, since no shell is involved. As will be discussed, these transactions can have some benefits over reverse mergers, but only if certain conditions are present.

As to timing issues, in one case, involving a Rule 419 merger, our client—the operating company—continued to raise money and issue shares after signing the merger agreement and while the SEC was reviewing our "post-effective amendment" seeking shareholder reaffirmation of their investment. This required continued amendments to our agreement to reflect different conversion ratios for our client's shares, and amendments to our SEC filings reflecting the foregoing. A better approach would have been to raise all the money either before or after, simplifying disclosure and paperwork.

In sum, in the majority of cases, financing is the trough at which reverse merger candidates feed. Investors, in particular PIPE investors, continue to develop the best methods for achieving these financings, taking time to study the private operating business along with the shell company with hope of receiving much greater upside potential than with a typical PIPE investment.

CHAPTER 6

Winning Market Support

S o far this book has explained a number of differences between going public with a traditional initial public offering (IPO) and a reverse merger. This chapter focuses on a distinction that many believe is especially critical—the "market support" issue. Some suggest that reverse mergers, specified purpose acquisition companies (SPACs), and other alternatives to IPOs simply are not viable because the post-transaction trading in a stock is often weak and subject to manipulation. The challenge of developing market support in a post–reverse merger company is real, but by no means does the existence of this challenge invalidate these techniques.

Many successful companies went public through a reverse merger. As mentioned earlier, these companies include Turner Broadcasting System, Inc., Tandy Corporation (Radio Shack Corporation), Occidental Petroleum Corporation, Muriel Siebert & Co., Inc., Berkshire Hathaway Inc., and Blockbuster Entertainment, just to name a few. They all managed to develop strong market support and eventually moved up to trade on larger exchanges. Yet there remains a perception in the marketplace that reverse mergers are to be avoided because stocks do not trade with sufficient volume following the transaction. Ultimately, the challenge of building market support is to change the market's perceptions about what is important at specific points in time during the life cycle of a public company.

This chapter reviews the nature of the challenge, summarizes the traditional IPO aftermarket, then discusses methods by which those participating in alternative transactions can earn market support and adjust their expectations about how stocks should trade immediately following a going-public event.

The Market Support Challenge

Because having a liquid trading market is a key variable in the cost-of-capital equation, many private companies use this as an important justification to go public. The more liquid a company's securities, the more likely the company seeking financing will be able to obtain it on favorable terms. Hence, generating interest in a newly public company's stock is important, but should be done with a goal toward building long-term market support.

There is some truth to the notion that post–reverse merger companies face a challenge in developing a trading market for their stock. Many of the reasons for this are discussed below along with ways in which to offset these challenges and in some cases, understand why certain challenges should be of little long-term concern.

Limited Float

Very often post–reverse merger companies have very few shares available to trade. (The number of tradable shares is called the "public float.") Immediately after the merger, almost all the shares are held by the owners of the formerly private company—call these "owner's shares." At least initially, none of these shares can trade. Thus, the trading market is at first limited to those shareholders who held free-trading shares in the shell prior to the merger.

In most transactions, some of the owner's shares are registered with the SEC almost immediately after the merger so that they are available to trade. Some of those shares will be contractually locked up for various reasons and not available to trade immediately, but the rest will be released to help build the public float. Nevertheless, the fact is that trading in shares of a shell whose stock was trading before the merger is very limited immediately after the merger. And even after any owner's shares are registered, they are not released into the market that quickly.

The situation is more pronounced (though, ultimately, equally unimportant) following a merger with a nontrading shell. As we will discuss, the immediate trading market after a merger is not really relevant long-term. But the perception is that the lack of trading following a merger with a nontrading shell is a negative to those seeking to go public.

Concentration of Control of the Float

Even if there are a fair number of shares in the shell's trading float, typically one person or small group controls a large majority of that float.

Usually, this is the individual or group which either purchased the shell previously, or which controlled the former public operating business that is no longer inhabited in the shell.

Even though their shares are free trading, those former control shareholders generally do not seek to sell immediately after a merger. This is because, with a limited float, even a small sale could cause the stock price to drop, hurting the ability for that large holder to sell more shares.

Thus, these holders of large blocks of free-trading shares often wait until owner's shares are registered and trading and, in turn, daily volume has increased. This dramatically reduces the number of "actual" free-trading shares available for immediate activity following a reverse merger or similar event.

Weak Analyst Coverage of Penny Stocks

Larger investors, such as hedge funds and institutions who regularly invest trillions of dollars in public companies, most often rely on market research delivered by major research and brokerage firms in order to make investment decisions. Typically, no research is available on a company completing a reverse merger because analysts who prepare the research usually are not interested in smaller companies or those trading on the OTC Bulletin Board or Pink Sheets. Some analysts will prepare a report for a fee, but that fee—and the conflict it creates—must be disclosed. This makes an issuer-sponsored research report of limited value to larger institutional investors.

In addition, institutional investors must often restrict their investment choices to stocks trading above a certain price, listed on a certain stock exchange, or trading in a certain volume. The point of these restrictions is to prevent the investor from taking a position in a penny stock. Many brokerage firms also prohibit their retail stockbrokers from actively promoting inexpensive stocks or stocks trading on the OTC Bulletin Board, further limiting the stock's exposure to the investment community. Since most post–reverse merger companies' stock trades on the OTC Bulletin Board, not a higher exchange such as Nasdaq or the American Stock Exchange, interest from both large Wall Street firms and retail investors is clearly limited.

Minimal Support from Market Makers

On the OTC Bulletin Board, a brokerage firm serves as market maker, creating an active market for buying and selling a particular stock. That market maker does have an interest in having its clients purchase the stock, but if a market maker is active in hundreds of stocks, it is sometimes difficult for any one to get the attention it may deserve.

In addition, there are fewer and fewer market makers involved in more and more OTC Bulletin Board stocks than in the past. This is because of regulatory changes that have made it less profitable for market makers to be involved with the activity as a stand-alone business. Again, this makes it more difficult to get the market maker's attention for an individual stock, even one that deserves such attention.

Short Selling Pressure

One investment tactic that doesn't win much favor with public companies is to bet that a stock will go down by "shorting" the stock. In a typical short sale, an investor will borrow a stock from its brokerage firm and resell it with the intention of buying it back after the price drops and returning it to the broker. The difference between the price at which the investor sold it and the price at which he or she bought it back is the investor's profit. This technique has many valid uses, such as when an investor wants to send a message of dissatisfaction with management, or determines that a stock likely will go down in the short term.

Unfortunately, in thinly traded stocks such as those of post–reverse merger companies, it is not uncommon for the stock to suddenly take a nose dive because of the actions of one or a few short sellers. The problem with short sellers is that their very presence often sends the stock down, as the broader market may perceive these investors to be knowledgeable, thus causing other investors to flee.

In some cases, short sellers do not believe the stock will go down on its own; they cause it to go down so that their bet will pay off. By aggressively shorting thinly traded stocks, they can force the market to react, causing the very result they were betting on. It may have absolutely nothing to do with the merits of the company or anyone's particular view of the future performance of the stock. It's stock manipulation, plain and simple. When short selling is used for purposes of manipulating the market, it's illegal, but tracking both who is shorting and what their true intentions are is very difficult. The history of successful legal prosecution in this area is minimal and this has encouraged continued manipulative behavior.

Just to add some perspective to this discussion, it's important to note that the bad guys are not just manipulating thinly traded stocks. Are bad guys manipulating larger cap stocks? Yes. Are bad guys manipulating IPO stocks? Yes. Enough perspective?

Thin Trading Reduces Ability to Raise Money Versus Active Trading

Since a major benefit of being public is gaining easier access to capital, one correctly assumes that a company with a heavily traded stock has a much easier time raising money than a company whose stock trades little. But, keeping in mind the "glass half full or half empty" analysis, one can reason that if one weren't public, one's access to capital would be significantly less. By being public, even thinly traded, a company's ability to raise money is still much better than if it was not public.

Does an IPO Guarantee Strong Market Support?

One of the myths that continues to crop up in debates involving reverse mergers is that strong, sustained market support for a stock always follows a traditional IPO, which is what makes it preferable to the alternatives. Nothing could be further from the truth.

Here's how things work in a traditional IPO, in which a company offers shares to the public with the hope of raising a large amount of cash: An investment banking firm serves as lead underwriter of the stock offering. The company and underwriter spend time putting a prospectus together as part of a registration statement, which eventually gets approved by the U.S. Securities and Exchange Commission, National Association of Securities Dealers and, as applicable, the various states.

When the offering is approved and ready to go, the lead underwriter enlists the help of other brokerage firms, who act as part of a syndicate of underwriters who find initial buyers for the stock. Each brokerage firm gets a commission upon the sale of stock to its customer. Technically, the underwriter purchases the shares from the company at a discount from the offering price, and then resells the shares to its customers, pocketing the spread. This is what distinguishes an underwriter of a public offering, who actually purchases shares directly from the company, from a placement agent in a private offering, who simply takes a commission for arranging a sale of stock from the company directly to the agent's customer.

The part that is often kept quiet is this: Brokerage firms historically have been told that if they want to participate in the initial sale and obtain their commissions, they have to commit to continuing to participate in the aftermarket, making sure that people buy and sell the stock for a period of time so that the initial groups of buyers can get out of the stock and make a quick profit. These "pump and dump" schemes were, and to some extent remain, common even in the IPOs of today. Without this aftermarket support, the stock simply tumbles, as it does in a surprisingly large percentage of IPO stocks.

In some cases, the newly public company is so strong that more legitimate support develops. But in the end, it is this manufactured support that drives the stock in its early stages. There is absolutely no assurance that this support will continue beyond the first few months after an IPO, if at all.

FIGURE 6.1   *Recent IPO Deal Activity*

YEAR	MEAN SIZE OF IPOS	RANGE OF IPO SIZES (LOW/HIGH)	MEAN MARKET CAPITALIZATION AT TIME OF IPO
2000	$236.6m	$4.1m–$10.6bn	$1.4bn
2001	$478.8m	$6.0m–$8.7bn	$2.0bn
2002	$319.6m	$5.7m–$4.9bn	$1.1bn
2003	$210.6m	$6.0m–$3.0bn	$672m
2004	$204.3m	$7.7m–$2.9bn	$767m
2005	$169.4m	$2.7m–$5.1bn	$495m

Source: Dealogic. Includes IPOs registered with U.S. Securities and Exchange Commission.

If a company is lucky enough to qualify for an underwritten offering where the stock trades well after the transaction, it may indeed hit the IPO jackpot that so many are seeking. In reality, though, in today's market, an IPO is simply unavailable to smaller companies. As **FIGURE 6.1** suggests, the average IPO fund-raising in recent years remains considerable even as the mean market capitalization of companies going public in a traditional manner has been gradually declining.

So even if an IPO seems like the best way to go public, it is important to remember that, in most cases, small-cap and micro-cap companies simply do not have that option.

How to Build Post–Reverse Merger Support

So how does one deal with the challenge of building market support for a reverse merged company? This section examines the change in attitude one needs, the importance of retaining a strong investor relations firm, the process of *earning* rather than manufacturing support, and how to build the company to a point where trading is possible on a larger exchange.

Get a New Attitude

Patti LaBelle's song "New Attitude" serves as a good metaphor for those seeking to go public through a reverse merger—they need a new attitude. The old-fashioned world thinks the only way to get a company public is through an IPO and an immediate jump in stock trading—activity and buzz. Press reports judging an IPO's success solely by its first day of trading have been hard to counter.

Practitioners of alternatives to IPOs have found Patti's religion and understand that going public is not the end of the process, but the first step in a company's journey as a public company. The first day of trading—or even the first week or month—is not too important. Smart, in-the-know professionals realize that what counts is trading activity one year to eighteen months following the reverse merger (or IPO, for that matter).

A company has to think about the long-term benefits of being public. A heavily traded stock is an important goal, but there is no reason it needs to be an immediate goal. Management must not forget the other reasons it had for going public. It is still possible to raise money even if the stock trades thinly. It is still possible to use stock as currency for acquisitions. It is still possible to use stock options to provide incentives to company managers.

If the stock is thinly traded, it may take a little longer than one might have hoped for investors or founders to be able to cash out of their shares at a fair price. Financings may not be done immediately at the most favorable valuations. Acquisition targets may need an education as to the true value of a company as opposed to value gauged by market capitalization alone. And if these things need to be put off for a year to eighteen months, in the worst case, until the stock is trading better (you hope), so be it. The company should be focused on its long-term goals.

The Importance of Investor Relations

A strong, reliable, and legitimate "IR" or investor relations firm can make all the difference in achieving a solid, long-term trading market for a company's stock. These service providers help attract attention from Wall Street firms and, ultimately, research analysts to improve trading and stock price.

The more capable IR firms do not strategize quick fixes or immediate pops in the stock. They take a measured and longer-term approach to building support. They introduce management to key players at brokerage firms that have the ability to encourage investment in a company's stock. They talk to hedge funds, institutions, and large private investors, arranging "meet and greet" sessions and road shows, which highlight the company's performance and prospects. Some use technology and online tools to enhance the process, directing the Wall Street pros to a Web-based video or other presentation.

Great IR firms go even further and help with strategy and key decision making by offering the Wall Street perspective on any contemplated business maneuver. Sometimes perfectly reasonable business decisions can have a deleterious impact on the trading of a company's stock. For example, a decision to enter a new line of business, which might involve significant, long-term investment whose benefits current investors will not see for years, might be a smart thing to do. But an announcement of this kind could send a stock spiraling downward if investors believe that diverting management attention from current profit-making opportunities is not in investors' best interest.

There are many shady and sleazy IR firms that promise quick and seemingly impressive results. Even if their activities may not be technically illegal, oftentimes, some of the shoddier firms are simply conducting bad business. They create temporary, semibogus support for a stock just long enough to bring in their investor friends, watch the stock rise, get their friends out, and then disappear forever. (This is not too dissimilar from some of the IPO antics that can take place.) After the IR promoter disappears, a company can be left with a big mess to clean up and, sometimes, shareholder and SEC lawsuits. In later chapters, we will cover how to spot and avoid some of these bad players.

Earn Your Support

A famous old commercial for the brokerage firm Smith Barney included the quote, "We make money the old-fashioned way. We earn it." Similarly, the best way to build support for a company's stock, regardless of how it goes public, is to earn it.

Support is earned when a company achieves the things it promises to achieve. Maybe even more important, support is earned when a company does those things that investors and Wall Street want or expect from it. Paying off a market maker (this is illegal) or hiring a sleazy IR firm to hype the stock is not the way to go. Manufacturing events and transactions, as real as they may seem, primarily for the benefit of getting more attention, rarely makes any sense. It is often said, however, that a company must sell both its products and its stock; and proper utilization of an IR firm and making decisions that will yield positive reactions from investors are important steps to take.

In the end, though, sticking to a company's mission and philosophy has a better chance of paying off than tricks and short-term fixes. Of course, the mission and philosophy may need to be adjusted over time, and there does need to be some recognition of the need to "please the Street" in the company's decision-making process. By focusing, however, on running a business to generate profit and create long-term value for shareholders, a company will generally achieve the best results in terms of stock price appreciation and developing a steady liquid market for its securities.

None of this guarantees success, of course. Sometimes, despite the best efforts of management, IR firms, and others, despite sticking to the mission, support simply does not develop. This can happen even if a company is successful and achieving its mission. The time may not be right for the company's industry in the public markets. The IR firm may not have the right connections. The plan may be good but lacking the kind of growth or direction the Street wants to see at that particular time.

These are critical moments in a company's history as a public entity. At these times, it is important to question whether being public made sense in the first place. Sometimes, the difference between profits and no profits is the cost of being public. If the company is not using its public status to its benefit, an honest review of its goals makes sense.

Going public is not without risk. Many who attempt the transition do not succeed. They may end up shutting down or filing for bankruptcy. That is why I recommend careful consideration of the pros and cons before proceeding. Reverse mergers are riskier than IPOs because most of the companies pursuing them are at an earlier developmental stage and, therefore, subject to all the risks of businesses that are hoping to grow.

Many young businesses, whether public or private, do not make it. A company's public status rarely is the primary reason for failure. In other words, these companies are not more likely to fail simply because they are public. In fact, most end up lasting longer than they might have because of additional rounds of financing or other transactions made possible because they were public. An investor views these opportunities through typical risk-reward analysis, determining that the greater risk of being involved in smaller, earlier stage companies is worth the much greater potential upside if a company is even modestly successful.

PRACTICE TIP

Support from Wall Street should be built the old-fashioned way—by earning it.

Movin' on Up

When smaller companies go public, they start out on the OTC Bulletin Board or Pink Sheets, hoping to move up to trade on Nasdaq, the American Stock Exchange, or the "big board," the New York Stock Exchange.

Why is it important for a company to be able to make this move? Because everyone from Wall Street to Main Street pays more attention to the company. As a result, stock prices and market capitalizations generally are higher, financing comes easier, short sellers have a tougher time manipulating the stock, acquisitions are more available, attracting senior executives becomes less challenging, and so on. Basically, all the benefits of being public truly come into focus on the larger exchanges.

FIGURE **6.2**   *American Stock Exchange Listing Standards*

	STANDARD 1	STANDARD 2	STANDARD 3	STANDARD 4
Operating History	N/A	2 years	N/A	N/A
Stockholders' Equity	$4 million	$4 million	$4 million	N/A
Net Income*	$750,000	N/A	N/A	N/A
Total Market Capitalization	N/A	N/A	$50 million	$75 million **or**
Total Assets	N/A	N/A	N/A	$75 million **and**
Total Revenues	N/A	N/A	N/A	$75 million
Minimum Price	$3.00	$3.00	N/A	N/A
Market Value of Public Float	$3 million	$15 million	$15 million	$20 million
Distribution Alternatives	800 public stockholders and 500,000 shares publicly held **or** 400 public stockholders and 1 million shares publicly held **or** 400 public stockholders, 500,000 shares publicly held, **and** average trading volume of 2,000 shares for last 6 months			

*Net income requirement applies to previous year, or 2 out of the 3 most recent years.

Source: DealFlow Media

One obvious way to overcome the challenge of building market support on the OTC Bulletin Board or Pink Sheets is to build a company to the point where it qualifies for listing on one of the major exchanges. **FIGURES 6.2** and **6.3** provide the respective current listing requirements for each of these exchanges.

Each exchange has both qualitative and quantitative criteria it uses to allow a company to list its securities. Each requires hundreds of shareholders, either significant revenues and profits or significant assets, a minimum stock price, corporate governance standards, and other requirements. The qualitative review can be tricky, since the listing committee simply may not like a company and declare it is not in the public interest to allow its stock to trade. This gives the examiners enormous latitude and power.

Most newly reverse merged companies are not at the point where listing is possible on Nasdaq or a higher exchange. This is not a negative. It should

FIGURE **6.3**   *Nasdaq Listing Standards*

	SMALL-CAP MARKET	NATIONAL MARKET		
Operating History	1 year **and**	N/A	2 years **and**	N/A
Stockholders' Equity	$5 million **or**	$15 million	$30 million	N/A
Net Income*	$750,000 **or**	$1 million	N/A	N/A
Total Market Capitalization**	$50 million	N/A	N/A	$75 million **or**
Total Assets	N/A	N/A	N/A	$75 million **and**
Total Revenues	N/A	N/A	N/A	$75 million
Minimum Price	$4.00	$5.00	$5.00	$5.00
Market Value of Public Float	$5 million **or**	$8 million	$18 million	$20 million
Number of Stockholders	300	400	400	400
Number of Publicly Held Shares	1.0 million	1.1 million	1.1 million	1.1 million

*Net income requirement applies to previous year, or 2 out of the 3 most recent years.

**If $50 million market capitalization is satisfied for small cap, then there are no operating history, stockholders' equity, or net income requirements.

Source: DealFlow Media

be considered helpful for the newly trading company to "practice" being public, and for management to get used to all the requirements and obligations of being public before a very close scrutinizing eye is upon them on a larger exchange.

For example, it might take time to assemble a proper board and audit committee. Below the major exchanges, no independent board members or audit committees are required. On Nasdaq and above, a majority of the board must be independent, and a completely independent audit committee is required by the Sarbanes-Oxley Act of 2002 (SOX). In addition, the audit committee must include a "financial expert" who has audited a company's books or served as a CFO (if they do not have such an expert, they have to explain in their SEC filings why they do not have such an expert).

Since these requirements do not exist on the lower markets or exchanges, after trading begins the company can begin putting together a board and audit committee that would satisfy a larger exchange.

Nasdaq and the higher exchanges also require a company whose securities are listed on their exchange to hold an annual meeting of shareholders to elect board members and take other necessary action. This meeting is not required on the OTC Bulletin Board or Pink Sheets. Most states' corporate law (such as the popular incorporation site of Delaware) requires an annual meeting, but in many states (including Delaware) the only penalty for failure to hold an annual meeting is the right for a shareholder to bring a lawsuit to compel the meeting to be held. Thus, as a practical matter, the meeting is not required.

I generally encourage public clients I represent on the OTC Bulletin Board to hold an annual meeting as practice for a higher exchange. The meeting also helps protect the board from any suggestion they are too entrenched and not subject to reelection.

Therefore, a terrific way to overcome the challenge of obtaining market support is to build a company to that point where a Nasdaq, Amex, or NYSE listing is possible. Sometimes a company conducting acquisitions or large financings can satisfy the listing requirements and can get there quicker than they thought.

Ticker? What Ticker?

Companies going public through any means other than a traditional IPO must have patience and understanding. Patience to realize that market support will develop, but only over time, and only when earned. And understanding that there is not a panacea or only one way to develop market support for a stock.

This may seem like strange advice, but I generally advise newly public clients post–reverse merger to ignore the stock ticker they have just worked so hard to obtain, at least for awhile, certainly for a number of months, maybe even up to a year. They need to focus on building the business, achieving their goals, and dealing with the obligations of being public. This includes engaging a strong IR firm, but again, not with an eye toward quickly boosting stock price but rather toward building long-term shareholder value.

An institutional or other investor that just put money into a company as part of a reverse merger transaction may not like this advice, but if they are honest with themselves, and realize why they made the investment, ideally they would agree. An investor betting on the upside of a newly public company should understand that significant trading and liquidity is not around the corner, and a quick flip of the stock will not happen. Ultimately, both the investor and company will benefit if the company succeeds in executing its operating plan and, as a result, builds steady market support.

CHAPTER 7

Shady Tactics

Back in 2003, when I planned the initial structure of this book, it did not seem important to focus on the many obvious issues that surrounded abuses in the shell marketplace. But during the course of the past few years, even as the U.S. Securities and Exchange Commission has been working harder to eliminate shady players through rulemaking and other initiatives, it is getting harder to clearly identify the "bad guys." The dramatic and overriding trend in the reverse merger market is moving to take the high road, and many legitimate players have entered and have joined longstanding industry players with integrity. But as in all things Wall Street, some unsavory types still linger, and of course the hope of those who do take the high road is that we will all learn how to avoid the unscrupulous players and, ideally, send them on their way.

The incentives have never been greater for continuing the bad guys' exit march. Increased involvement of PIPE investors as financing sources creates a unique opportunity to significantly upgrade the quality, reliability, and legitimacy of alternative initial public offering techniques. The challenge is to make sure the shady operators stay out of the business, even knowing they will be attracted by the increasing popularity of alternatives to IPOs.

It can be difficult to identify players of little integrity in reverse mergers. They may seem credible because they have aligned themselves with seemingly legitimate players or because they have intentionally undertaken to hide their fraudulent intent. Some have been involved in shady transactions for many years without any enforcement action against them, allowing them to claim both vast experience and a clean record. Some unsavory players help validate others by providing references which seem to be on the level.

In other cases, dubious promoters find entrepreneurs who will simply look the other way at some of the questionable tactics. Some people don't care whether or not the path to achieving the goals of public status, financing, and growth involves some improper twists and turns. Often these entrepreneurs do not realize that they too can be held liable for the actions of promoters and investment bankers who are acting either directly or indirectly on their behalf.

Worse, there is a cadre of so-called professionals—attorneys, investment bankers, and even accountants—whose business depends heavily on work generated by the activities of questionable players. In some cases, so-called objective professional advisers insist on being partners with their clients, requiring large equity stakes in transactions in lieu of or in addition to cash payments, and this can be risky. As a result, the normal filtering and vetting process undertaken by these professionals, which is supposed to help the company determine the integrity of the players, may not be present.

A Few "Bad Guy" Anecdotes

For what it's worth, I could be rich and retired from all the business I have turned down over the years. But because I represent only those who I believe to be legitimate and fair players, I can sleep at night. I do not expect my clients to be pushovers, since business often requires toughness, but I do expect them to stay within the law, even if they go right up to the line, as long as they do not cross it. And I do expect clients to be forthright with me at all times. If I ever have a concern about either of these, I generally resign from the project.

There is a selfish reason why I have turned down work as well. I have tried very hard to improve the legitimacy, acceptance, and popularity of the reverse merger technique in the face of decades of abuse. As part of this effort, I have worked closely with the SEC and other regulators, and I believe these efforts have borne fruit, including the new SEC regulation passed in June 2005, in which the SEC expressly recognized the legitimate use of this technique. In April 2006, I was invited to Washington to address more than a dozen SEC Enforcement Division staffers on reverse mergers. If the SEC or other industry groups were to believe that I was knowingly working with questionable players, the very ones I have insisted we should seek to eliminate, my status as an industry advocate would obviously be in question.

The following are a few examples of clients I have had to walk away from, and some helpful anecdotes involving shady, but fairly common, business tactics.

Telltale Signs: Not Disclosing Biographical Information or Trying to Avoid Full Disclosure

A new client showed up at my office without a referral. He was interested in raising money in the oil and gas arena. He claimed to have worked with major law firms in the past but wished to work with me now (reason for suspicion in itself, what I call the "why me" test).

He sent me an offering memorandum from a deal he was involved with recently, which included his biography and no mention of anything improper. I took a large retainer, and we began work. Then we researched his background and discovered a number of lawsuits relating to past, alleged securities violations.

I resigned, mainly because he intentionally withheld that information—information that I would have needed to include in his biography. Not only would he be liable for failing to disclose, I might be liable for not investigating him carefully enough.

Do past problems mean I will automatically refuse to represent someone? No. But I do need to develop a sense that previous bad behavior will not be repeated. First, I look for forthrightness. Does the client give me all the facts without my prodding? Second, is the client willing to make all proper disclosure about past problems? And third, do I have a way to independently verify the credibility of the client? If a client passes these tests, I may still represent them.

A case in point: A manager of an operating business asked me to represent his company to raise money privately. At our first meeting, he told me he had been convicted of a crime a number of years earlier. He had been unhappy with the performance of a business associate, went to this associate's place of business, and some alleged bad activities ensued. The associate called the police and my client struck a plea deal to avoid the risk of jail. Both before and after that incident, the client had no legal problems whatsoever.

The client understood that all of this needed to be disclosed and, understandably, he was not happy about it; however, the placement agent seeking to raise the money he needed had a different point of view. The agent felt it showed dedication to protecting his business! Several years after going public, we dropped the reference to the prior conviction because it was old and had been disclosed on numerous occasions.

Another example: One day a very excited gentleman appeared at my office. He had been in the securities business for almost thirty years and wanted to involve me in three major projects after he saw me speak at a seminar.

The transactions he described would, among other things, keep his involvement below the level that would trigger mandatory disclosure. I asked whether there was anything problematic in his background. Sure enough, he had been incarcerated for securities-related problems in the past. "Don't worry," he said, "I learned my lesson, I'm clean now and I want to do things the right way."

I turned down almost $300,000 of immediate business from him. The main reasons were his desire to hide himself in his transactions, and the fact that I had to ask about his background. He had the experience to know I would care about his past problems and he should have been up front with me. So, I felt, maybe he hadn't fully learned his lesson. Even if he had, I wasn't going to take the chance.

One Company's Search for a Clean Shell: A Case Study

A recent experience I had with a client in a service business dramatizes why it is so important to know the backgrounds of all the players in a reverse merger transaction.

I've changed the names and some facts here (to protect my relationship with my client) but none of the important ones. "Shell Shocked," a private business, came to me seeking to go public through a reverse merger. He had engaged an investment banker who was to provide the shell. On its face, the shell appeared fairly decent. It had originally gone public in 1997 through a traditional IPO and had intended to enter a business relating to the art world. The president of the shell had a background in entertainment, but little experience in art.

The stock of the shell had begun to trade on the OTC Bulletin Board after the IPO (which only raised about $100,000), filings were made discussing in detail the nature of the business including the risks, and a small inventory was kept and a small amount of revenues earned. By 2002, however, according to their SEC filings, the company was not able to achieve its business plan and was terminating operations. The result was a public shell, now seeking to acquire another business.

An individual with vast experience in reverse mergers—call him the "Dealmeister"—had become a principal in the shell and acquired some stock with the hope of finding a company to merge with. Shell Shocked was told that no operations had existed since 2002, almost three years, and that little business was currently being conducted, so no liabilities from prior operations existed. This could be confirmed through due diligence.

Shell Shocked had no experience in reverse mergers and believed the Dealmeister's representations that the shell in question seemed to be of very high quality, especially since the investment banker, whom he liked, told him so. The promoters wanted to retain approximately 15 percent of the company through the shell after the transaction and expected to raise between $8 million and $9 million as a condition to the merger, thereby providing an additional 33 percent of the company to the new investors.

Unfortunately, through very little additional research, it became clear that Shell Shocked had to move away from this shell because of a real risk of being in the middle of a serious potential problem with the SEC. Because of the Dealmeister's involvement in at least a dozen other transactions where small businesses went public and then several years later suspended operations in a very similar fashion, we determined that the SEC might declare some of these IPO transactions as frauds intended to avoid the restrictions of Rule 419.

As discussed in detail in Chapter 9, Due Diligence, under the heading "Footnote 32 Shells," the Dealmeister's transactions were very similar. A small business goes public (suspicion #1: small businesses with virtually no revenues rarely go public). It raises a token amount of money, sometimes even less than $100,000 in its IPO (suspicion #2: the costs and hassle of an IPO make raising such small amounts inadvisable). Often the principal of the small business has little or no experience in the industry in question, and often has little experience running a business at all (suspicion #3: no operating experience).

Finally, the Dealmeister, whose business is in fact reverse mergers (not taking tiny companies public through IPOs), had a hand in every deal. It was not always easy to find the Dealmeister in his deals. In some cases, he appeared as a "buyer" of the shell long after the IPO. Although he admitted to us that he played a consulting role in all these companies at the time of the IPO, his involvement was not disclosed. In a few cases, he appeared as a principal from the start.

He virtually admitted to us that he did not want a simple search of his name to bring up enough information about his activities to serve as a road map for regulators (suspicion #4: trying to evade regulators). At the same time, he claimed that nothing inappropriate had occurred in any of his shells. His story was that he had successfully completed a number of reverse mergers and that he would not be willing to suggest that the small businesses he took public were not real, and so on.

When my client decided not to become involved with this particular shell, another was presented. This time, the problem was different. The shell had gone public through a complex "gifting" transaction back in 1990. The promoter apparently had done this many times before and ultimately was indicted and convicted of fraud and served time in jail. In this particular instance, however, he was not charged in connection with this particular shell.

In this case, I had to advise Shell Shocked that legally he was probably safe and could complete a reverse merger with this shell. Why? Clearly, a criminal took it public through a dodgy transaction, so isn't there a concern about liability? In this case, no, because the alleged crime had taken place long ago, so long ago in fact that the statute of limitations likely would bar virtually all claims relating to the bad public offering. The "go forward" suggestion was contingent, however, on an assumption that the original promoter was long gone from the company.

The shell's public filings do not mention the dodgy promoter as an owner of 5 percent or more of the company's stock or as an officer or director of the company, and filings would be required if he fit any of these categories. Indeed, there is nothing in this shell's filings about the criminal conviction of the original promoter. That is not on its face alarming, because this disclosure might not be required so many years later.

During our due diligence process, however, we requested the list of shareholders from the shell's transfer agent. Sure enough, an entity connected to the original promoter still owned more than 6 percent of the company. (We learned about this connection from our examination of other filings.) So the concern was that the promoter still directly or indirectly controlled the company (which would require disclosure). Assurances were given that his ownership would drop below 5 percent after the merger so that it would not have to be disclosed; however, the concern remained that the original promoter was controlling the shell, which led Shell Shocked to look for another shell yet again.

There was another reason this shell was shelved. Shell Shocked had invited several high-profile individuals to join his board upon the merger. He knew that if these individuals saw that the shell he acquired had a checkered past, even if no current liability existed, they would not be pleased. Related to that was a concern that the company's competitors could take advantage of the "crooked shell" acquired by Shell Shocked.

The third shell my client considered was the result of the bankruptcy of an actual revenue-generating business. However, a former principal of that business had sued the shell. The lawsuit was still pending. Assurances were given that the prior shell owner would indemnify Shell Shocked for any costs or liabilities from that lawsuit. But we advised Shell Shocked that we could not assure that he could collect from the prior owner if and when necessary.

As a result, it was determined that the lawsuit should be settled. At this point, we stopped hearing from the shell promoter, which strongly implies they did not actually settle the suit and were hoping to find another sucker to take the shell. In this case, before we stopped hearing from them, we were being pressured for time, to hurry up and take the shell before someone else did, which was an immediate red flag.

We considered a fourth shell. An actual business had gone public and owned some assets. We were told the company wanted to go private and sell the assets back to management, leaving behind the shell. We were told that this agreement was almost completed and that shareholder approval for the sale (requiring a complex proxy statement) was to happen quickly and approval was assured. We were also told that the management buyers would fully indemnify the remaining shell for any liabilities of their business.

Again, we raised caution flags. Why now? Wait, it's a real business, seeking to shed its assets properly, and there's no suggestion of impropriety. The problem here was the recent business activity in the entity. Any creditor of the business that is spun off might be able to sue the shell for liabilities the entity incurred. An indemnity is nice, but as with the case above involving the lawsuit, how can one be sure that the indemnitor will indeed be able to provide the promised reimbursement? Short of money in escrow or a mortgage on the individual's home, nothing is truly assured.

As of this writing, we have reviewed—and our client Shell Shocked has rejected—an additional five shells, and the transaction still has not been completed. This odyssey epitomizes one of the most frustrating aspects of the reverse merger business—finding a clean shell controlled by clean people.

"Bad Guy" Tactics

In general, "bad guy" tactics are used either by the owner or controller of the shell or the financier or the investment banker involved in the deal. In addition, a number of dangerous and shady practices can take place after the merger and relate to trading activities. Some tactics to be aware of are described below.

Inappropriate Expenses and Compensation

Public shells may engage in activities that seem commonplace and appropriate for operating companies, including compensating management, hiring public relations firms, paying rent for office space, issuing press releases that disclose important events, and raising money to cover all these expenses. These are innocuous activities for a public company. But if a shell company (assuming it is not a SPAC) is engaging in them, it is a sign that someone without the highest integrity is in charge.

It is almost always inappropriate for management of a shell to take anything more than zero or nominal compensation for what is an extremely limited role prior to an actual transaction, given that management usually already owns a significant equity stake in the shell.

Shells do not need public relations firms, and they do not need to rent office space. Often the third parties receiving payments for rent or publicity have some business or even family relationship with the controller of the shell.

Strange Money-Raising Activity

It is not uncommon for a shell to raise money for the legitimate costs it incurs (such as to pay lawyers and auditors in order to maintain its public status). But if it raises money to pay management salaries and the like, this should definitely be questioned. In addition, if a shell's stock is trading at a certain price, and money is raised at a much lower price, be suspicious. It is possible, however, to justify the lower price as the only price at which investors are willing to put money into the shell, despite the trading price.

Insider Trading

Another concern is insider trading. Just prior to announcing a reverse merger, trading activity in the shell may increase. A company merging with a shell could inherit potential liability for the actions of a shell principal trading in his individual name. It is not simply the problem of the individual insider trader, and the liability is real (and criminal).

PRACTICE TIP

Monitor trading activity leading up to the announcement of the transaction.

Press Releases and Hype

Sometimes shell operators seek to promote possible mergers at a very early stage. Press releases are issued even when negotiations reach a late stage or when vague and nonbinding letters of intent are signed. The stock price rises, insiders sell on the increase in share price, the transaction falls apart, and the stock heads back down. Again, watch the trading patterns.

PRACTICE TIP

Be skeptical of predeal hype.

Recently, a private company client had reached terms with a shell, and our client submitted their signatures to the shell for the closing, which was to include an exchange of shares and payment of cash to my client. We assumed within a day the shell would send their signatures back along with the cash and other closing documents.

Instead, upon receiving my client's signatures, the shell "inadvertently" issued a press release announcing that the transaction had been closed! Of course, neither our client nor we had seen or approved this release. It took three business days and, of course, no closing or cash delivery to my client, to get the shell to "amend" the press release to indicate that indeed we had not yet closed. Luckily, only a minimal amount of trading took place, but the stock did rise on the announcement. The deal finally closed about a month later.

Time Pressure

Another common practice involves insisting a deal must be consummated quickly. In too many cases, the shell operator pressures a private company's principal to ignore his attorney's entreaties to ensure that full due diligence is completed. "We have another candidate for the shell," or "You know our shell is clean, what's all this need for due diligence?" are common themes in deals. Be suspicious of these tactics.

A letter of intent binding the parties not to discuss a possible transaction with others is the best way to go, giving both sides the appropriate amount of time to complete due diligence and negotiate a formal agreement. Sometimes, if a real concern exists about locking in the shell, a good faith deposit in escrow, which is returned if the transaction ends, helps convince a shell of one's serious intent. Everyone wants deals to be completed quickly, but legitimate players understand the need for focused, efficient due diligence review.

Incomplete Disclosure

Another problem I continuously encounter involves out-and-out fraud. Public filings by the shell sometimes simply fail to disclose all required information. When we insist on due diligence and undisclosed information is discovered, often the response is, "Gee, thanks for pointing that out, you're right." Counsel will suggest they were unaware of the oversight. "My client never told me," they say. To which we then reply, "Why wasn't this question ever asked before?" The principal will typically offer vague claims of being inept at preparing these filings. Be suspicious when this happens.

Incomplete Insider Filings

Sometimes the true ownership of the shell is not disclosed. Anyone who owns more than 5 percent of any public reporting company must file with the SEC disclosing their ownership, and the shell is obligated to disclose the names of anyone that it knows owns more than 5 percent in its annual Form 10-KSB filing. In some cases, shell promoters simply do not make these filings to avoid attention or dicey trading restrictions on large share-holders. This is obviously a bad sign.

Refusal to Back Up Representations and Warranties

A private company receives representations and warranties from the shell about such things as its operations, past filings, and compliance with laws. Without a guarantee or holdback, these become essentially meaningless after the transaction has closed since the merged company can only sue itself. The more strongly a shell promoter refuses to even consider such arrangements, the more suspicious one should be. We'll discuss this further in Chapter 9, Due Diligence.

Messy Isn't Dirty and "Not Nice" Doesn't Mean "Bad"

In some cases, a shell is just plain messy, as discussed in Chapter 9, Due Diligence. It is hard to find documents, confirm status of officers and directors, and so on. Do not mistake a messy shell for a "dirty shell" con-trolled by a shady operator, but be wary of a shell so messy that getting a deal done becomes difficult if not impossible.

Sometimes I hear the following about reverse merger players: "He's a jerk," or "He's a tough negotiator," or "He's not interested in helping our business grow." These may be good reasons not to do business with people, but they do not necessarily indicate evil, illegal, or even shady tactics.

Bad Investment Banker Tactics

I wish I could report that all sources of financing in reverse mergers are paragons of virtue who seek always to protect the long-term interests of their client companies as well as maximize long-term value for the share-holders and investors who they bring to the table. Unfortunately, despite SOX (Sarbanes-Oxley Act of 2002) and other regulatory relief, fraud and greed are alive and well on Wall Street. Luckily, the percentage of bankers doing things the right way appears to be increasing almost daily in the reverse merger world. Here are some of the problems that come up when dealing with investment bankers and financiers.

Lack of Due Diligence

Lack of due diligence is a major problem. This is particularly true when attempting to "scrub" a shell. Too many investment bankers take the word of the intermediaries or shell brokers who bring them a shell and assert that it is already clean. In fact, some investment bankers pony up large cash amounts to purchase the shell themselves only to resell it in the reverse merger.

Every investment banker registered as a broker-dealer with the U.S. Securities and Exchange Commission and National Association of Securities Dealers must conduct due diligence in any situation where they are raising money. Due diligence is the subject of Chapter 9, but suffice it to say that this critical element of deal making is neglected at everyone's peril.

Nonregistration As Brokers

Many investment bankers, especially in the reverse merger arena, are not registered as broker-dealers. Some attempt to claim they operate as "finders," an available exemption from being registered. But if the finder assists in negotiating a transaction, or receives a fee that is a percentage of or contingent on the deal, or provides any investment advice, they probably are not a finder as the SEC or NASD would define it and should be registered.

Some claim they are simply consultants and not brokers. If their compensation is not contingent on their efforts, and not a percentage of the transaction (such as a flat fee), and they are not negotiating the deal, there is a small possibility of obtaining legal advice that they are not required to be registered.

Why are there so many people holding themselves out as investment bankers without registering? Mostly because the SEC has had neither the enforcement dollars nor the incentive to pursue these violators because they receive few complaints about this. Why don't investment banks simply register? The reasons could be many, but generally it's either because of prior problems they would rather not disclose, the burden of SEC and NASD regulation of registered broker-dealers, or the simple cost and hassle of going through the registration process and maintenance of a broker-dealer.

Why should anyone involved in a deal care? Nonregistration isn't just the banker's problem. The company is responsible for representations made to potential investors by its investment banker, and an argument can be made that once a company picks an investment bank to represent it, the implication exists that the investment bank is properly registered. Also, many states that regulate offerings with their blue sky laws will specifically ask if any intermediaries are involved and whether or not they are registered.

Registration also conveys benefits, first by providing some protection for the investor who can complain about a registered broker directly through the NASD's arbitration process. The second benefit is that registered brokers are subject to regular and random reviews and audits by the NASD, which helps keep them honest.

Once the reverse merger is completed, an SEC filing must be made which, among other things, indicates how the company completed its various financings and whether those financings were public offerings that the SEC required to be registered or private offerings exempt from registration. One element of having a proper exemption from registration includes the use of advisers who do not mislead investors and who themselves follow the law. Thus, savvy attorneys for public companies or their later financiers sometimes raise a red flag if prior financings were completed with unregistered brokers.

PRACTICE TIP

Be cautious when working with unregistered brokers.

Accredited Investors or Not?

Another challenge with financiers is making sure they know their investors. Most private offerings in reverse mergers require the company to have a reasonable belief that the investors are accredited, meaning essentially that they meet a certain income or net worth test under Regulation D (more on this in Chapter 8).

The SEC would probably say that nothing short of an investor's certified personal financial statement is enough to demonstrate accredited status. Most practitioners, however, will accept other proof. First, the investor may sign a statement indicating he is accredited and check off or initial the criteria that legally qualify him for accreditation (in other words, not just signing whatever is put in front of him). Second, the company or the investment bank may reasonably believe that an investor is accredited if this information has come from a preexisting business or personal relationship between the investor and either the company or the investment bank raising the money.

Unfortunately, too often investment bankers anxious to complete a deal will accept anyone who is willing to write a check and "help" them fill out the accredited investor statement, even if they do not know the person, or worse, they know the person probably is not accredited.

Looking for Mr. Good Guy

This chapter outlines some telltale signs of the presence of bad guys in a transaction. Chapter 9, Due Diligence, will provide even more detail. In the meantime, here are eleven signs that a shell player or investment banker is legitimate:

❑ No compensation—principals, officers and directors of the shell are not compensated for performing their functions

❑ No unnecessary expenses—a shell should not need to pay rent or hire public relations firms

❑ Limited fund-raising (if any) at reasonable valuations—any monies raised should be at a fair valuation and should be used solely to keep paying lawyers and auditors to make SEC filings and related expenses (This should not exceed $25,000 to $30,000 per year.)

❑ Right type of shell—the shell either was a true, legitimate former operating business that was not intended to be stripped out of the shell or cease business, or was formed as a shell under Rule 419 or as a Form 10-SB shell

❑ No "bad boy" history—it is better if deal players have nothing in their background, even if long ago, indicating criminal behavior, regulatory problems or propensity to being involved in lawsuits

❑ Proper insider reporting and trading—the control shareholders and officers have not traded heavily in the stock, have fully reported their ownership and trading activity, and there is no indication of trading leading up to the announcement of a deal

❑ No inordinate time pressure—everyone wants deals done quickly but a legitimate player understands the need for a private company to do its due diligence and negotiate the merger properly

❑ Backing up reps and warranties—a legitimate shell player will at least discuss the possibility of personal guaranties or holdbacks to back up representations and warranties

❑ Good advisors—ideally, the deal involves well-respected and well-known attorneys, auditors, and investment bankers

❑ Due diligence—an investment banker will insist on proper due diligence before completing the transaction

❑ Broker-dealer registration—the bank involved, if raising money, ideally is an NASD-registered broker-dealer

The rapidly growing acceptance, utility, and legitimacy of reverse mergers, SPACs, and other alternatives to traditional IPOs will continue only if investors, industry players, and regulators are comfortable with the tactics and backgrounds of those putting the deals together.

In brief, the best advice is to work only with those who have been carefully checked out and are deemed to have solid reputations and histories.

PART TWO

LEGAL ISSUES AND
TRAPS FOR THE UNWARY

CHAPTER 8

Deal Mechanics

This part of the book focuses on the unique legal challenges reverse mergers present.

Three sets of issues affect reverse mergers and their aftermath:
- ❏ How to structure and implement transactions
- ❏ Due diligence
- ❏ Regulation

The next three chapters deal with each of these issues in turn.

This chapter discusses two sets of legal issues: those that arise when shareholder approval is required and those that arise in the course of implementing a final deal.

Structural and Implementation Issues Around Shareholder Approval

It is frequently incumbent upon public companies to seek and receive shareholder approval before embarking upon many activities. This can be a time-consuming and difficult process.

If a company is a reporting company under the Securities Exchange Act of 1934, it must complete and file a full proxy statement (or, occasionally, a similar document called an "information statement") any time it needs shareholder approval. This filing can be long, detailed, and complex. Additionally, the filing usually requires SEC approval, which also takes time, anywhere from a few weeks to a few months depending on the content and the U.S. Securities and Exchange Commission's turnaround. Some shell company management teams also are concerned, quite frankly, about ensuring their shareholders actually show up to vote or send in a proxy for a merger. Thus, avoiding shareholder approval is generally considered advantageous.

There are several ways to avoid this encumbrance in connection with reverse mergers. One possibility is to use a nonreporting shell to do the reverse merger. Nonreporting shells have no obligation to file proxy statements, so obtaining shareholder approval for things is a much simpler process. Nor are their officers, directors, and 10 percent shareholders required to file information about their holdings. In addition, the new SEC requirement of significant disclosure immediately after the merger is avoided. It is prudent to remember, however, that if these shells trade, they do so on the Pink Sheets because reporting status is a prerequisite for trading on all other markets and exchanges, including the OTC Bulletin Board.

Companies that report voluntarily are not required to file full proxies either. These companies file quarterly and annual reports with the SEC even though they are not required to do so. This provides some comfort to merging companies in that information has been disclosed, without having other SEC obligations mentioned above such as the requirement to prepare and seek approval of proxy statements.

This advantage notwithstanding, most in the shell marketplace prefer to use reporting companies because they inspire more confidence in investors. Reporting companies must make available high-quality information about their activities, performance, and insider holdings. In addition, a nonreporting company has to become a reporting company after a reverse merger in order for its stock to trade on the OTC Bulletin Board or higher.

Reporting companies must be very careful to proceed in a manner that minimizes the likelihood that shareholder approval and, therefore, filing a full proxy statement will be required. Any number of actions that take place during a reverse merger have the potential to put a company after a reverse merger in the unhappy position of having to complete a full proxy.

These situations include the following (which will be discussed in more detail below):

❑ *Structural approaches to shareholder approval*—If the reverse merger is structured so that the public shell itself is a direct party to the merger, shareholder approval is necessary under most states' laws. A "merger proxy," if required, is extremely detailed and difficult, and rarely gets approved by the SEC after only one or two rounds of comments. Fully audited information on the company to be acquired is required, and information such as a detailed review of every conversation between the parties, the price or valuation at which the discussion began, why it changed, etc., is also typically mandated.

❑ *Forward and reverse stock splits*—If there are insufficient authorized but unissued shares of stock, or in the rare circumstance that it is desired that more shares be outstanding, a stock split may be necessary, requiring shareholder approval in most states and a full proxy.

❑ *Changing the charter to allow for issuance of more shares*— Sometimes this is done rather than engaging in a stock split. It requires shareholder approval.

❑ *Name changes*—In general, a shell needs to change its name after a reverse merger, and this requires shareholder approval, which might be avoided in Delaware.

❑ *Board changes*—If a stock transaction contemplates a change in a majority of the board, a mailing to shareholders is required, though shareholder approval is not.

❑ *Public offerings and private placements*—In general, these avoid the requirement for shareholder approval as long as the securities being issued have already been authorized under the company's charter.

Structural Approaches to Avoiding Shareholder Approval

Reverse Triangular Mergers

Many reverse mergers are structured as reverse triangular mergers. In large part, this is to avoid having to obtain shareholder approval for the merger. The companies involved in a merger are known as the constituent corporations. As mentioned earlier, in a merger, one constituent corporation "survives" the merger and the other is swallowed up and simply disappears with its assets, liabilities, and business taken over by the surviving corporation. In a reverse triangular merger, a shell company creates an empty, wholly owned subsidiary. The shell owns 100 percent of the subsidiary's shares. Then, the subsidiary merges with and into a private company. The end result of this is to make the private company the "surviving" corporation and a wholly owned subsidiary of the shell. The original subsidiary is the nonsurviving corporation and, therefore, it disappears. Shares of the private company are exchanged for shares of the parent company shell. By the way, the "reverse" part of the merger applies because the private company effectively takes over the shell company, yet the shell company survives as the ultimate parent.

In this situation, the two parties to the merger are the private company and the shell's subsidiary. The private company's shareholders must approve the deal; so must the subsidiary's shareholder.

State laws govern how a private company's shareholders are notified of and consent to ownership changes. Generally, those laws require either

(1) written consent by all or a majority of the shareholders, with notice to the others; or (2) advance notice (typically a simple one-page notice) of a shareholders meeting, holding that meeting on at least ten days' notice with at least a majority present and approval of the transaction at the meeting.

The shareholder of the shell's subsidiary is the shell itself. The shell grants or withholds approval through the action of its board. There is no need to seek approval from the shell's public shareholders.

Thus, a reverse triangular merger can typically be completed without the need of approval from the shell's shareholders.

When Non-U.S. Companies Are Involved

Some transactions are not structured as mergers but also achieve avoidance of shareholder approval. For example, most reverse mergers involving foreign companies, which generally cannot engage in direct mergers with U.S. entities, involve a simple exchange of shares. The shell and the private company's shareholders agree that the private company's shareholders will give up their shares of that company in exchange for shares of the shell. The shell, if it has sufficient shares available, approves that issuance through its board. Again, no shell shareholder approval is required.

Why doesn't everyone use this simple technique even in domestic transactions? Because, in a share exchange situation, every shareholder of the private company must agree to swap his or her shares, and sometimes this gives one or two small shareholders enough power to hold up the deal. In a reverse triangular merger, a simple majority vote of the private company's shareholders approves the transaction.

Asset Acquisitions

Another, less popular method of avoiding shareholder approval is an asset acquisition. In this structure, the private company sells its assets (and presumably its liabilities) to the shell in exchange for shares of stock. The private company then liquidates and distributes those shares to its shareholders. Again, the shell's shareholders do not have to approve the transaction as long as there are sufficient shares available. The primary disadvantage of this approach is that the operating company ceases to exist and its contracts, licenses, and customer arrangements need to be assigned or amended in many cases.

Forward and Reverse Stock Splits

Often in a reverse merger, the shell does not have the appropriate number of shares outstanding for the transaction to work. For example, in one recent transaction we worked on, the shell had 10 million shares issued and outstanding, and was authorized through its corporate charter to issue 100 million shares of stock in total. Our client—the private operating company—wished to acquire 90 percent of the stock. This could happen if our client acquired the remaining 90 million authorized shares.

My client believed, however, that after the reverse merger it would be beneficial to have a high per share price in the marketplace. Therefore, he believed that having 100 million shares of stock available to sell was too many. He felt that the right way to get the most desirable share price was to have 10 million shares available in the public float. Ninety percent of 10 million is 9 million, the number of shares that would be given to the private company to complete the reverse merger. This would leave the current owners of the shell with 1 million shares and a 10 percent ownership stake.

To achieve this goal, my client needed the current owners of 10 million shares to complete a "reverse stock split." A one-for-ten reverse split would turn their 10 million shares into 1 million shares. The purpose of the split was to increase the per share stock price by taking the number of shares owned by each person and dividing by ten in order to get the new number of shares. At the time of the split, each shareholder would still own the same total percentage of the company, just with fewer total shares outstanding.

In most states (but not all), shareholders must approve a reverse stock split. Thus, if a shell is fully reporting, a proxy statement must be prepared, then filed with and approved by the SEC. The proxy is then mailed to shareholders at least ten days before a shareholder meeting to approve the split. Generally, proxy cards are included, giving a shareholder the right to appoint a member of the shell's management to vote their shares for them and, therefore, vote without attending the meeting.

Typically, a proxy for a reverse split is short (four to five pages), straightforward, and often is not reviewed by the SEC (if they do not comment ten days after filing, the proxy is deemed approved). However, if the proxy relates to a matter which is a condition to a reverse merger, even one where the shell is not a direct party (such as a reverse triangular merger), the SEC takes the position that this is the same as asking the shareholders to approve the merger itself, and a full-blown merger proxy (the nightmare described above) is required.

There are two ways to avoid this complication. First, in some cases, if sufficient shares are available for issuance in order to consummate the transaction, the reverse merger is closed with the number of shares already existing. In our example, that means the current owners of the shell would keep the 10 million shares they have, and the private company would be issued the 90 million remaining shares. After the merger is completed, the combined company could then seek a reverse split that is not a condition to the merger, and a merger proxy would not be necessary, just the more simple reverse split proxy. Since the private company's shareholders would now control the shell, approval of the reverse split generally would be assured.

The second method for avoiding a full merger proxy is subtler, but we have used it successfully on many occasions. The SEC requires a full merger proxy when the reverse split is a *condition* to the merger. To address this problem, in the example above, we provided in our merger agreement that the parties requested a reverse split, contemplated it, but did not make it a condition to the transaction. We provide for Plan A if the reverse split is approved and Plan B if it is not. Using our example, Plan A was to reverse split the 10 million outstanding shares to 1 million, then issue 9 million to our client's shareholders. Plan B, if the reverse split was not approved, was to leave the current shell shareholders with their 10 million existing shares and issue 90 million to our client's shareholders.

As a practical matter the approval of the reverse split is assured, since as part of the merger agreement we obtained an agreement from a majority of the holders of shares of the shell to vote for the reverse split. Thus, whereas a proxy was necessary for the reverse split taking place before the merger, and the approval was assured, a full merger proxy was not necessary since the reverse split was not technically a condition to the merger. Pretty smooth, eh? Feel free to use it.

Other Problems in Capitalization and Share Availability

Another very common problem in reverse mergers is that the shell may not have sufficient shares authorized under its corporate charter in order to complete the transaction.

Let's change our example to assume that the shell has 50 million shares issued and outstanding, and only 100 million shares authorized. Our client seeks to acquire 90 percent, so without any change in the ownership of the existing shell holders, this would theoretically require our client to obtain 450 million shares. This is because the 450 million would represent 90 percent of that plus the 50 million already outstanding (or a total of 500 million shares). But the shell does not have the authority in its charter to issue more than 100 million shares.

There are several methods to deal with this. The most common approach is simply to implement a reverse stock split in the shell, so that the 50 million issued shares are split into 1 or 2 or 3 million, whatever number is appropriate. The problem, of course, is again the proxy. If that split is a condition to the merger, a full merger proxy is necessary. If it is not a condition, the problem then becomes dealing with Plan B, since in the event the split is not approved, an available number of shares does not exist to issue 90 percent without some sort of split or change in the capital structure.

Even if voting agreements are obtained from shell shareholders to approve the reverse split, the agreement for merger still has to contemplate Plan B if the split is not to be an express condition. And it is not possible to create that plan based solely on the number of shares outstanding. Or is it?

Recently, a public company with operations came to me, with their attorneys, to try to solve this problem. They were making an acquisition that was structured as a reverse merger. The private company merging with their public operating business would end up with 51 percent of their stock. The problem was the insufficiency of available shares. We offered two approaches, one of which was ultimately adopted and implemented.

The first suggestion was to use preferred stock. In this case, the public entity had available but unissued preferred stock. Its corporate charter permitted the board to decide the rights and powers of the preferred stock and to issue it without shareholder approval. This type of security is generally referred to as "blank check preferred."

Thus, their Plan B was that, to the extent its regular common stock was used up, a number of shares of preferred would be issued. Those preferred shares would have the same number of votes as the "missing" common stock. Also, the preferred shares would be convertible into the missing number of common shares; however, those common shares could not be issued until the company's charter was changed to increase the total number of common shares available. A condition at the closing of the reverse merger would be that a majority of shareholders agree in advance to vote for this change to the charter. After the closing, a proxy would be prepared and the charter changed.

There is another approach. In certain cases, a shell does not have preferred stock available in its charter. Thus, it has no means of handling the overage. In such an instance, it is possible to issue a shareholder "rights certificate." The certificate entitles the holder to obtain the number of shares in the overage as soon as the company holds a shareholder meeting to amend its charter and make more shares available.

Again, in this situation, voting agreements are obtained in advance, which require the majority of shareholders to approve the charter change. In addition, the merger agreement requires the proxy for the vote for this change to be filed immediately following the merger. In fact, in some cases the actual form of proxy to be used after closing is approved by both parties prior to the closing of the merger.

In both cases one might ask, why not just wait for the charter to be amended, and then close the transaction? Well, as indicated above, if the amendment is a condition to the merger, a full merger proxy may be required. But even more important, parties want the transactions to be completed quickly. The above approaches allow a merger to be closed with needed financing obtained. In both actual cases, this occurred without the delay of getting a proxy approved by the SEC, the wait while the proxy is then printed and mailed, and the second wait of ten days before the meeting may be held.

Name Change of the Shell

In almost all cases after a reverse merger, aside from its shareholdings, the shell's corporate entity is unchanged. Its name also stays the same. If the name of your shell is ABC Acquisition Company, and its subsidiary merges with the Goodison Steel Company, it is common for the steel company to want to change the name of its new parent public holding company to more closely resemble its name when it was a private company.

Most assume that a name change, which is set forth in a company's corporate charter, requires shareholder approval, a proxy, and the whole drawn out process required by the SEC for a shareholder meeting. In many cases, this is required, and most parties to a reverse merger wait until the next shareholder meeting to effect the change; however, some wish to make this change immediately.

Shells incorporated in Delaware (which many are because of corporate-friendly Delaware law) have another option.

A provision in Delaware law passed in 1998 permits a shell, say it is called ABC Acquisition Company, to establish a new wholly owned subsidiary, called perhaps Goodison Steel Holdings, Inc. Delaware then permits a so-called short form merger—no shareholder approval required when the parent owns more than 80 percent of the subsidiary. According to Delaware law, the shell, ABC Acquisition Company, can "survive" the merger and the subsidiary, Goodison Steel Holdings, goes away as the nonsurviving corporation. As part of the merger, however, the surviving entity can adopt the legal name of the subsidiary. In this example, ABC Acquisition Company would become Goodison Steel Holdings, Inc.

Thus, a name change is effected, without shareholder approval, at least in Delaware.

Schedule 14F: Board Changes

A little known and little used provision of the Exchange Act, Section 14(f), essentially says that if there is an agreement involving the sale or exchange of at least 5 percent of a public company's stock, and as part of that agreement there is an arrangement or understanding to change the majority of the members of the board of directors, then an SEC filing, mailing to shareholders, and waiting period are required. The intention of this law was to prevent those who begin to accumulate a public company's stock from quietly taking over a board without shareholders being aware of the change. (This law follows the familiar lines of those requiring SEC filings from all owners of 5 percent or more of the shares in a public company.)

Most reverse merger agreements include a requirement that, upon closing, the current shell board members will resign to be replaced by designees of the private company. Assuming the owners of the private company will receive more than 5 percent of the public shell's stock upon closing (which in virtually every case they will), this triggers the 14(f) requirement. The document that fulfills this requirement is Schedule 14F.

Schedule 14F is not difficult to prepare. It looks much like a proxy statement for the annual meeting of shareholders in which directors are being elected. This includes biographical information about the proposed new directors and an ownership chart. The SEC does not review a Schedule 14F, which is filed with the SEC at the same time that it is mailed to shareholders. The reverse merger transaction may not close until at least ten days following the mailing of the Schedule 14F or, if later, its filing with the SEC.

The main frustration with this process is the delay. Typically, it is one of the last things the lawyers get around to doing, yet the process takes about three to four weeks from preparation to filing with the SEC to printing, mailing, waiting, and closing.

What is strange about this requirement is that no shareholder vote takes place. Yet shareholders must be informed that directors will be replaced and given biographical information about the nominees. Given that the merger agreement itself will be filed upon signing, one wonders what incremental benefit this truly provides shareholders.

Two techniques can circumvent the 14F filing and mailing. One of these is legitimate; the other is not.

The legitimate way to avoid the 14F filing is to remove the board change as a condition to the merger or anything that is arranged or understood. To some extent similar to the reverse split analysis, those controlling the private company could determine that, since they will own a substantial majority of the stock after the merger, the shell's board members will simply resign on their own and "do the right thing" after the closing. And even if for some strange reason they wish to remain, in a short time the new controlling shareholder generally can cause a shareholder's meeting to take place to replace them (assuming the shell's bylaws permit this). This may cause a thirty- to forty-five-day delay, and assumes the shell board simply does not leave of its own accord (and that there was no prearranged deal or understanding), which is extremely unlikely.

In addition, even if the board does not change, a condition to the transaction can be that the *officers* of the company (as opposed to board members) be replaced so that the president, vice president, treasurer, and secretary are all the leaders of the former private company. Therefore, they can continue to run the business on a day-to-day basis even if the board does not change.

In addition, the operating business itself will be run as a subsidiary of the public "holding company" (formerly the shell). That subsidiary's board can remain as it was prior to the merger, giving the former private company's management effective control over all issues related to managing the operating business that do not require shareholder approval. All these protections assume the worst: that the shell board will try to remain for some reason.

Some practitioners avoid the Schedule 14F issue by not filing the document. They argue, as I did above, that shareholders do not benefit from receiving this information because they have no ability to vote on the merger or anything relating to it. Some attorneys further argue that this omission would not be a legitimate basis for a shareholder's bringing a securities violation claim against the company. This is because the Schedule 14F provides so little information and no ability to vote. I have also heard lawyers argue, "Well, very few people know about this requirement anyway, so who would think to sue claiming we didn't file it?"

If I were an examiner at the SEC, I would have two reactions to these arguments. First, the rules are what they are, and until they are changed, the rules must be followed. Second, shareholders sometimes vote with their feet, by selling shares of the shell in anticipation of a deal they do not support. The 14F includes information that might not otherwise be available prior to a transaction concerning the background of those who will oversee the newly merged company, including any "bad boy" history requiring disclosure. As a result, we always recommend following the rules and either filing the 14F or removing the board change requirement as a condition to the merger or any arrangement or understanding prior to closing.

![PRACTICE TIP]

Just file it.

A Merger Isn't an Offering. Or Is It?

Here's another little known but potentially serious legal problem arising in reverse mergers. In a reverse triangular merger (or share exchange for that matter), the public company issues shares to the owners of the private company. The owners of the private company exchange shares in the private company for shares in the shell. The shell then becomes the sole owner of shares in the formerly private company and the former owners of the private company take control of the shell.

To accomplish this, the public shell issues new shares. Technically, this is a securities offering as much as it is a merger, or so maintain the securities regulators. This may seem strange because it is possible that minority shareholders in the private company could be forced by vote of the majority into this transaction. In such a circumstance, it is hard to see what if anything is being offered to them.

Nonetheless, a reverse merger is considered an offering. This creates a number of potential problems. To explain, here is a short securities law lesson on private placements.

Back in 1933, as part of the Securities Act that was passed following the great crash of 1929, Congress said, essentially: if a company conducts a public offering, a formal process of approval of that offering and disclosure about it needs to be made with the SEC. If the offering is not a public offering, but rather a "private placement," no such registration is required.

This is not as straightforward as it sounds.

Congress neglected to define the term "public offering." From 1933 until 1982, the courts struggled to work out a definition. All they agreed on were the factors to take into account in determining whether an offering was public or private: these included the number of investors, how much capital was being raised, the sophistication and net worth of investors, and how much information was available to them.

This didn't help lawyers advise clients. They knew that it isn't a public offering if Donald Trump is the sole offeree, and he is investing $5,000 in a business. They knew that it is a public offering if three thousand first-time, middle class investors are each investing their last $5,000 in a business. Everything in between was uncertain.

The SEC, therefore, passed the seminal and widely praised Regulation D in 1982. Regulation D, or Reg D, is a safe harbor provision that says: follow the rules we provide, and an offering is definitely not a public offering. Regulation D focuses primarily on two things: the investor and the information being provided to the investor. Within the context of Regulation D, the SEC developed the well-known (and to some extent well-worn) term *accredited investor*.

An accredited investor has an individual income of $200,000 for the past two years (or $300,000 if combined with their spouse) or a $1 million net worth. Brokerage firms, banks, other institutions, or a company or trust with at least $5 million in assets (if not formed for the purpose of doing the deal in question) are also accredited investors. An entity all of whose equity owners are accredited is also considered accredited. My view is some of these numbers should be updated, as a $200,000 income in 1982 obviously is not the same today, but far be it from me to tell the SEC to make it harder for my clients to comply with Regulation D with a tougher standard!

Regulation D warns accredited investors that they are on their own. No one is obligated to provide them with information. This means it is possible to have an offering with one thousand accredited investors and provide them with nothing more than a simple subscription agreement. The SEC accepts this because, theoretically, wealthier people have a greater ability to protect themselves.

Further, accredited investors do not need to actually be accredited to get the benefit of the Regulation D exemption from registration. All that is necessary is that the issuing company has a *reasonable belief* that they are accredited. It is still not totally clear what is an adequate basis for this belief, but most practitioners believe (though I'm not sure the SEC would agree) that a statement signed by the investor indicating by check mark what makes them accredited, combined with some personal or business relationship between the investor and either the company or a representative (such as an investment bank), is probably sufficient.

It is worth noting the existence of Rule 10b-5. This rule prohibits intentionally misleading someone about something important in connection with a purchase or sale of a security. Thus, even in "all-accredited" deals, we typically recommend disclosure be made, even if it is not in the form of a full-blown disclosure document such as a private placement memorandum, or PPM.

Regulation D further indicates that if even one investor is not accredited, that investor must receive all the information about the company that would be provided in a public offering prospectus, minus that which is not considered material to an investor. At that point, obviously it makes sense to provide that disclosure to all investors, even if accredited. This is where the PPM gets prepared and distributed. Regulation D in most cases further limits an offering to thirty-five nonaccredited investors, implying that any more than that essentially involves a public offering.

There are two more key conditions. First, to get the benefit of the Regulation D safe harbor, one must file a Form D with the SEC shortly after the first closing. It is a short form but may end up including asterisks, footnotes, attachments, and the like. (I have heard that the SEC is in the process of streamlining Form D and making its filing electronic.) Second, offerings must follow the laws of each state in which a purchaser lives. Thus, the offering has to be exempt from any filings in each such state. In most cases, a Regulation D all-accredited offering requires no more than a post-sale filing with the state and a filing fee.

A company can have a proper private placement without filing Form D. The old pre–Regulation D analysis (known as a "4(2) analysis" referring to Section 4(2) of the Securities Act) may still be used, but one would assume it difficult to justify a forty, fifty, or sixty or nonaccredited investor offering as not public. Also, states are easier on Regulation D offerings than those claiming exemption under Section 4(2).

A relatively disfavored part of Regulation D provides an exception that allows a company to raise up to $1 million from as many accredited or nonaccredited investors as it wishes, without any specific information delivery requirements. Most states do not allow these offerings (known as "504 offerings" because of the exemption described in section 504 of Regulation D). In general, I decline to be involved as an attorney with 504 offerings. We'll discuss this further in Chapter 13.

What does any of this have to do with reverse mergers?

As mentioned above, the issuance of shares by the shell in the merger is technically an offering. Therefore, the same analysis as in any offering applies. (There are some exceptions from registering an offering that relate to an offering limited to a company's existing shareholders. Unfortunately, this does not apply within the context of a reverse merger since the offering is to *another* company's shareholders, that is, the private company, not those of the shell.)

The first step is to look at the shareholders of the private company, who are the "offerees" of the shell's stock in the merger. If all of them are accredited or there are no more than thirty-five nonaccredited investors, Regulation D can be used. This means complying with Rule 10b-5, filing Form D, and submitting any filings required by the states. If fewer than thirty-five investors are nonaccredited, a PPM must be prepared. Given the new SEC requirements concerning disclosure after the deal, which is done by filing a Form 8-K, this information has to be put together in any event. Then, Form D must be completed, followed by state filings.

A different tack is necessary if the private company has more than thirty-five nonaccredited shareholders. This situation may be encountered in a more developed company that may have many option holders or shareholders who are employees.

In this case the shares to be issued in the reverse merger must be registered with the SEC. The means to this end is filing a Form S-4. The SEC will scrutinize the Form S-4 in depth and that is why it should probably be avoided.

There are three ways to avoid this filing. In some cases, private companies have chosen to repurchase shares from, or cancel options granted to, nonaccredited investors. This is also an offering, but if it brings the number of nonaccredited investors below thirty-five, it is a private one and Form S-4 is not necessary. Alternatively, a reverse stock split can be useful if it brings a number of nonaccredited shareholders' holdings to less than one share. In this event, under most companies' bylaws, the partial shares must be repurchased, eliminating those shareholders.

The second method is to change the deal structure from a reverse merger to a sale of assets (and liabilities). Here, there is no merger or share exchange. A majority of shareholders of the private company approve the sale. Then, the shares of the shell are issued as part of a sale directly to the private company rather than its shareholders. This may avoid the non-accredited problem.

The third approach for companies with over thirty-five nonaccredited investors involves abandoning a reverse merger altogether in favor of a "self-filing" in the manner described in Chapter 11, Self-Filings. Here the company does its own filing to become public without a public offering, and all its shareholders simply continue to own their shares in that event. There is no actual or inadvertent "offering," and thus having more than thirty-five nonaccredited investors is not a problem. Again, the other conditions appropriate for a self-filing should be present, as will be discussed later.

Other Legal Issues

Unique Legal Opinion Issues

In most financings and corporate combinations, lawyers are asked to deliver written opinion letters covering various matters relating to their client and the transaction. A few issues in legal opinion writing are unique to reverse mergers and shells.

A private company may ask for the shell's lawyer to opine that the shell is not an "investment company" as defined by the Investment Company Act of 1940. Most people think of mutual funds as investment companies, but some hedge funds also fit the definition. Essentially, an investment company has to be in the business of investing in the securities of others.

There are certain exemptions, but the most common argument for a shell not to be an investment company is that it intends to become an operating company through a merger. This creates the argument that they are not "in the business" of investing in others. Also, an exemption exists if that intention will be acted upon within one year.

This appears to be consistent with the SEC's point of view, since I have yet to see them even question or threaten a shell with inquiry on the basis of whether or not it is an investment company. Yet shell lawyers typically refuse to give the investment company opinion. This can be frustrating since the implications if it is an investment company are major, requiring much more complex filings with the SEC and many more limitations on its activities.

Shell lawyers argue (usually successfully) that the private company lawyers are as capable as they are of determining whether or not the shell meets the definition of an investment company.

A group of shell operators have taken things a step further. They own a public shell and use it to acquire company after company. After each acquisition, the shell spins off the new business through an SEC registration process. SEC staffers have begun to quietly ask if these companies are indeed investment companies. I have discouraged clients from operating their shells this way.

Another unique opinion often requested of shell counsel is to affirm that, to counsel's knowledge, the shell's filings with the SEC are complete and comply with the SEC's disclosure rules. Shell counsels generally resist this as well, arguing that they were not fully knowledgeable of the shell's affairs.

Sometimes, the shell has not completed its annual state franchise tax filings in the state of its incorporation, causing it to lose its "good standing" as an official corporation. Obviously, this is a problem because one cannot close a merger with a company that technically does not exist.

In the opinion process, virtually all shell lawyers are willing to give the "good standing" opinion and typically they pull a report to confirm that the shell is indeed in good standing. The problem is that this is often done a day or two before closing, and if it turns out the company is not in good standing, a mad scramble occurs to prepare the filings and pay any back taxes, sometimes delaying a closing with millions of dollars sitting in escrow waiting for this ministerial issue to be resolved. I typically request that shell counsel review the good standing of its client early in the process so this last-minute scramble does not occur.

Are Reps and Warranties from a Shell Meaningless?

In virtually every business combination or financing transaction, each party provides "representations and warranties" to the other parties. A representation is simply a statement of fact. For example, "The Company has 10 million shares of Common Stock outstanding." A warranty, similar to the warranty on a car or refrigerator, is a promise that something is in a certain state or condition. For example, "All of our inventory is in saleable condition," or, "We have complied with all applicable laws concerning our pension plan."

The "reps and warranties" are often carefully negotiated and an important part of the comfort-building process in completing a transaction. It is not uncommon to have thirty or more reps and warranties on such issues as intellectual property, litigation, employee matters, environmental matters, capitalization, authorization of the transaction, and so on.

Reverse mergers, similar to many acquisitions, cause a challenge in the area of reps and warranties, in some respects in both directions. Why is this so? Well, take the shell side first. The private company will receive reps and warranties from the shell. But what if, after the transaction, it turns out that one of the reps was false? Let's say it turns out the company had 20 million shares of stock outstanding instead of 10 million (not likely but just use this as an example). Since the shell is now owned 90 percent by the former owners of the private company, who would they sue for this breach of a representation? In essence, themselves. Would one sue a company in which one now owns 90 percent? Thus, as a practical matter, without more teeth, the reps and warranties are meaningless.

From the point of view of the shell, a similar but much less dramatic effect is true. If a rep from the private company turns out to be untrue, the shell still sues itself—in other words, the former shell. But the former owners of the shell now own only 10 percent of that shell, and the former shell now has all the assets from the former private company; therefore, one can sue something with some value. Thus, this issue is a much more pronounced risk for the private company.

What happens in most normal acquisitions not involving reverse mergers? If an acquirer is provided with reps and warranties from his target, and then he acquires it, he also really has no one to sue. Thus, it is very common in acquisitions for personal guaranties to be provided by principals, promising that the reps are true and backing them up if not, and usually involving a reasonable limitation on the guaranty. Alternatively, or in addition, part of the consideration for the acquisition is sometimes placed in escrow for a period of time (maybe six months or a year) to be used against any claims of breaches of reps or warranties.

How do practitioners in reverse mergers deal with this problem? Not very well, in fact. In the 1990s, a number of shell principals were willing to personally guarantee the reps and warranties. In the next chapter, in the "messy shell nightmare" described there involving an unimplemented reverse stock split, the nightmare was resolved in part by those personal guaranties. Personal guaranties are especially common if there are particular concerns or "hair" on the shell. Why give personal guaranties? For the reason described above. Private companies simply feel that the reps were meaningless if given by a company that they were about to take over.

The new millennium has changed everything. Part of the reason is the great demand for shells, giving shell operators more leverage in negotiations. In some cases, legal opinions from shell counsel serve as insurance policies for breaches of some reps by the shell. But very few deals that I have been involved with in the last three to four years have involved personal guaranties or holdbacks of cash or other consideration to back up reps and warranties. Private companies simply are "going bare" when it comes to protection against misrepresentation.

Shell operators say, "Do any due diligence you want and get comfortable and don't worry about the reps." Or they say, "Our shell is owned by your investment banker. Don't you trust him to have done careful due diligence?" Or they say, "We're a shell, not an operating business. There's nothing important to give a rep about that you can't independently verify." Or they say, "If we commit fraud and intentionally mislead you in any way, you can sue us all individually regardless." Or they say, "We just bought this shell and, unfortunately, have no ability to provide comfort for what the shell did before we purchased it." Predictably, some of these explanations hold water. Some don't.

I believe it is good practice to have reps that have meaning and can be enforced. My response as a private company's counsel would be, "Well, don't you know these reps to be true? If so, you should have no problem standing behind them." Or, "If we take 15 percent of the cash you are getting and put it in escrow for six months, if your reps are true you should have nothing to worry about." Or, "As between you and us, if you just bought the shell, who should take the risk regarding things that happened in *your* shell before you bought it? Us or you?" Sometimes a middle ground can include a pledge of the shell operator's stock, so that he relinquishes his ownership if he has misrepresented anything. Or one can provide for an adjustment in the terms of the deal, such as an increase in one's eventual ownership, if a rep turns out to be untrue. Often money held back or personal guaranties are capped, so that the shell operator knows the extent of his potential exposure.

Why is this so important even if one is comfortable that the shell operator is legitimate? Even assuming the best of intentions, if there is no or little incentive to make sure everything is indeed as it is being represented, problems will almost certainly arise. This is also true for operating without legal opinions. One assumes the lawyers will be diligent, but there is no question they are that much more careful when they have to opine as to an issue.

PRACTICE TIP

Try your best to make sure the reps have meaning.

Issues Relating to Fairness Opinions

In some cases, one party to the reverse merger is concerned about ensuring that the value placed on the deal is fair. They may not have enough experience to be sure about the price. Or they may have a conflict of interest and seek independent verification of the deal structure. Or a board may simply wish to purchase an insurance policy, so that if their shareholders complain later about the price and value, the board can point to the expert review of the transaction.

What is a fairness opinion? As mentioned earlier, an independent firm, having no involvement in the transaction whatsoever, issues an opinion that almost always says that the transaction is "fair to shareholders, from a financial point of view." This differs from a valuation. In a valuation, an independent firm comes in and tries to determine the actual value of a company or asset. A fairness opinion is not necessarily saying that this is the *best* price or the most accurate, but merely that it is fair.

Firms that issue these opinions include most investment banks and some independent firms that specialize in valuations and fairness opinions. Opinion prices vary widely. Investment banks may charge several hundred thousand dollars, whereas valuation consultants may issue an opinion for less than $50,000.

What do they do to determine fairness? They research comparable companies in the public arena. They interview management, the investment bankers, and so on. They examine the financial statements of the company. They may even do a mini-audit of certain aspects of the financials. After a few weeks of work they generally are in a position to issue an opinion.

As indicated above, the opinions may be worthless if an investment bank thinks it will get a nice fee for taking a risk certifying fairness without any independent research. Be careful of opinion givers whose relationship to the parties may not be officially affiliated, but where close business ties might strain their objectivity. Also be sure the opinion is really necessary. If one is extremely comfortable with the valuation in question, the extra cost and delay to obtain a fairness opinion may simply be unnecessary if there are no conflicts of interest and the like.

One way to spot a bad guy: He strongly resists getting a fairness opinion, even if he is not paying for it. Always wonder what he may be trying to hide. He will argue that it will take too long, they are too conservative, whatever. The more he resists, the more necessary the fairness opinion.

PRACTICE TIP

Use real firms that are experienced in these matters, and make sure they do real work and provide real help in making sure a transaction is structured properly. And there generally is no need to spend more than $50,000 for such an opinion in the typical reverse merger context, at least based on today's market.

Above All Else:
Seek Competent and Experienced Advisers

Who knew there were so many unique features of reverse merger transactions? I certainly did not when I started representing clients in this area. There are many tricks and traps that are easy to fall into even if one is an experienced securities attorney, auditor, investment banker, or operating company executive. *If there is one overarching practice tip to everything in this book, it is this: If one is considering a reverse merger or other alternative to a traditional IPO, make sure to work with practitioners experienced in doing these types of deals.*

In structuring a reverse merger and getting it done, the well-trained eye of those who have been through these deals many times before is always recommended. As the next chapters on due diligence, SOX (Sarbanes-Oxley Act), and the new SEC rulemaking indicate, keeping up with current trends and practice approaches requires being involved in transactions and the industry of alternative IPO financings on a fully engaged basis.

CHAPTER 9

Due Diligence

There's enough material to write a book just on the challenges of due diligence in reverse merger transactions. In corporate transactions, law firms generally assign due diligence work—reviewing a company's legal documents, lawsuits, intellectual property, and the like—to the most junior attorney on the team. In reverse merger transactions, due diligence is so critical that it probably should be completed by the most senior person. On the other hand, due diligence is extremely dull and time-consuming, and the senior partners tend to gravitate toward the golf course rather than actually reading stuff.

Due diligence is so important in reverse mergers because it is the means by which shells, private companies, and investors learn the true facts of the deal. Information uncovered through due diligence investigations can cause changes in the structure of the transaction or even its termination.

Yet, unfortunately, in many cases clients do not want to spend time and money completing due diligence. They prefer to work on trust (big mistake) or accept a greater risk (another mistake) in exchange for completing a transaction quickly. (This is even more important given the concerns about the reliability and enforceability of reps and warranties discussed in the last chapter.)

Some clients perform *some* due diligence, requesting only the most important documents. This may be adequate, if the company being scrutinized is public; however, the approach is not without risk. If, for example, a seemingly unimportant agreement includes potentially serious consequences for its breach, it may be inadvertently overlooked. If a broker-dealer is involved, he has an affirmative obligation under NASD (National Association of Securities Dealers) rules to complete a due diligence review of any company he may raise money for or be involved with in the context of an acquisition.

The Basics

What follows is a list of the major areas to investigate when performing due diligence on a public shell.

❑ Corporate structure and history, including certificate of incorporation, bylaws, stock records, and stock issuances;

❑ Current management, prior management, and consultants, their backgrounds and involvement in other blank checks, extending backward for the whole life of the shell;

❑ SEC filing history of the shell, with an eye toward learning whether filings are current and complete according to SEC rules, whether the shell is a reporting company or is only claiming to be one (I have seen this happen), whether there are any SEC investigations past or present, and the whole story of how the shell went public in the first place;

❑ The history and details of any operating business within the shell, how recently that business ended, and what potential liabilities could still haunt the shell;

❑ Any litigation or threat of litigation by or against the shell;

❑ Whether the company attempted or succeeded in completing any other reverse mergers and what the results were;

❑ Any intellectual property owned or used by the shell and any potential benefit or liability relating to that property (patents, trademarks, copyrights, and so on.);

❑ Any contracts the company had entered into for any reason which might still be technically in force;

❑ What compensation if any is being paid to shell management, whether any questionable expenses exist such as payments to public relations firms or "rent" for offices, and to what extent and how often money has been raised in the shell and at what prices;

❑ Identity of the auditors, and whether the company changed auditors at any time, whether or not due to a disagreement;

❑ Recent and historical trading patterns in the stock if the shell is trading;

❑ Review the list of shareholders to attempt to garner information about who they are and what long-term interest they may have in the company post-merger;

❑ Required SEC filings by officers, directors, and 5 percent and

10 percent shareholders of their interest in the company to see if all necessary filings were made and are current;

❑ Review of press releases by the shell including frequency and purpose.

Clean, Dirty, and Messy Shells (and Footnote 32 Shells)

Chapter 7 offered suggestions for spotting and avoiding shady promoters and fraudulent deals. Due diligence requires a slightly different and somewhat broader perspective, demanding not only a determination of the integrity of players but also whether even legitimate promoters have properly documented their actions and followed all their legal obligations.

Most clients want "clean" shells—companies with well-kept, organized records and no history of unsavory activity. These are few and far between and can only be identified after investigation. Form 10-SB shells being formed as blank checks (see Chapter 15 for details) must be examined, even though they are as close to 100 percent clean as is available in the marketplace.

Shells are more likely to be "dirty" or "messy" than "clean." A messy shell is one in which no shady activity is suspected but record keeping is disorganized, and it is difficult to determine what actually has been going on in the shell. A dirty shell is one in which involvement of some questionable players and/or occurrence of some questionable actions is suspected. Here are some of the distinguishing characteristics.

Messy Shells

In a messy shell, although certain agreements may have been made (they may even have been mentioned in public filings), no one is able to locate a copy of the agreement, or the only copy is not signed by the parties. It may or may not be clear that the company's bylaws are the ones actually provided. Older records of when people acquired shares may not be available or may be incomplete. Information comes in from the shell owners in dribs and drabs and is not organized.

On one occasion, for example, a messy shell had previously entered into a reverse merger but unwound the deal after about six months, selling the assets back to the owners. Each owner, in giving up his or her shares of the shell, signed seemingly identical agreements releasing the shell and ceasing to be a shareholder. But, one of the agreements contained a hidden clause indicating that if the shell were to complete another reverse merger, the former shareholder would receive a cash payment equal to 5 percent of the value of the reverse merger!

Some law firms would not have reviewed all fifteen agreements as thoroughly as my associate did, instead presuming them to all be identical. I'm proud of my team's work in this instance. My client approached the controller of the shell to find out more about this arrangement. The controller said that this individual had been "long gone" and was unlikely to resurface to claim his prize. My client (now defunct and bankrupt) decided to take the risk and closed the deal anyway.

PRACTICE TIP

Review every document carefully, and more than once.

Some messy shells are behind in their SEC filings. They may promise to get current before the merger closes. Often these rushed filings turn out to be incomplete or just plain incorrect and presented at the last moment prior to a closing.

PRACTICE TIP

Be cautious if filings are not current. It is better to wait for the filings to be completed, and then enter into a transaction.

In other cases, it is impossible to identify the board and officers of a shell. People claim to serve in those roles and sign SEC filings with those titles, but nothing in the due diligence shows when and how they were elected. In such instances, it is usually necessary for the shareholders to elect a new board and for that board to elect new officers. This prevents another group from later claiming to be the "real" board, thereby negating the authority of the board that closed the deal. It may be possible to argue that the board that completed the deal had so-called apparent authority, thus perhaps avoiding penalty. But I would generally not recommend a client take that risk.

PRACTICE TIP

Be sure the board and officers of the shell were properly elected.

Sometimes messiness relates to the ownership of shares. A large shareholder may have returned his shares, but the documentation is not convincing or is not available. Don't worry, we are told, he really did it. That's not good enough. It may be necessary to go back to the shareholder and reconfirm his forfeiture of shares. All share owners must be tracked down and verified. Shares may have been recently issued with scanty documentation or without full compliance with SEC filing requirements. Small offerings of shares may have been completed without proper Regulation

D filings, disclosure, or blue sky compliance. All these messes must be cleaned up.

Even well-intentioned shell promoters sometimes get in their own way. In one case, we requested that a shell change its name prior to closing on a reverse merger. In most cases (except for my Delaware trick mentioned in the last chapter), this would require shareholder approval. The shell promoter went ahead and filed a name change in Delaware without the requisite proxy and shareholder vote. My client chose not to worry about it and closed the deal anyway, reasoning that no shareholder would claim to have been harmed by an unapproved name change. They further reasoned that the SEC was unlikely to investigate. I grudgingly agreed that these risks were low, but not without reminding the clients that if something major happened later, the one or two minor things would become another part of the class action complaint which would then read along the lines: "Look at all the things they did over the years..."

Pending lawsuits make a shell messier. As briefly mentioned earlier, in one recent deal, the person who had been CEO of the shell when it had been an operating business sued for several hundred thousand dollars after he was terminated. The seller of the shell indemnified the buyer by promising to pay all expenses, including lawyers and any judgment, relating to the lawsuit.

When the shell was presented to us, we were told, don't worry, so-and-so has agreed to indemnify the shell. Our response: Who is this person, where is the indemnity agreement, and what assets does he have so that if we sue him to collect on the indemnity he will stand behind it? If these things cannot be provided, we suggest settling the lawsuit and making it go away.

Clearly the shell operators were surprised, thinking we would grab the shell and accept the bare indemnity. After some hemming and hawing, they agreed to settle the case and supposedly were prepared to do so for $25,000. After that we never heard from them again, despite repeated requests to provide background on the litigation, information about the settlement, and other due diligence. This caused the investment bankers on the deal to move on to another shell. Let someone else grab the shell with the pending lawsuit and indemnity.

The hope with a messy shell is that it can be "scrubbed," as we say, and become cleaner. Whether that is possible depends in large part on the cooperation of the shell's management, attorneys, and auditors. In many cases, that cooperation does not come because many shells are operated by individuals seeking the simplest, quickest, least complicated transaction they can find. In some cases, they send out a purchase agreement with instructions to counsel to have a client sign the document and return it. In other words, no negotiation! That alone is almost reason to walk away, but we let them know that we intend to review, comment on, and revise the document if necessary (it is almost always necessary).

The Messy Shell Nightmare Scenario

This story is worth telling in detail even though it caused me personal pain. A number of years ago (in other words, all statutes of limitations have passed!), I represented a shell that needed to catch up on several years of missed SEC filings. I took over from a big firm that had stopped working because they weren't being paid, which is always understandable.

The shell had been a real operating business with a retail component. It didn't work out as a public company, so the owner agreed to sell the business back to its founder in exchange for the founder's return of his stock of the shell. In addition, as part of approving the sale back to the founder, the shareholders (prior to my involvement) had approved a one-for-twenty reverse stock split to help prepare the company for a possible reverse merger after reverting back to a shell.

In both cases, though the sale and reverse split were approved, they were never formally implemented. So in addition to catching up on the filings, we were going to close the sale of the business and effect the reverse split. The sale went relatively smoothly, as, we thought, did the reverse split. We sent a notice to every shareholder that this was the record date for the split and that they could send in their stock certificate for a replacement. We notified the transfer agent to reflect this on its records as well, and assumed they would inform Nasdaq and the securities clearinghouse known as Depository Trust Company (DTC), so that people holding shares in "street name" electronically would have their holdings automatically adjusted.

The notices to Nasdaq and DTC were never delivered (we found this out much later). About a year after all this work to implement the sale and the split, we finally completed a reverse merger, along with another reverse split, this one with all the proper notifications. In part because of the mess involving the prior operating business, three key shareholders of the shell agreed to personally indemnify the private company for any problems relating to the shell.

Several weeks after the merger, the CEO called and said there was a problem. Apparently, people from the shell were now seeking to sell hundreds of thousands more shares than they actually owned. Of course, he blamed me and directed me to "fix it." I said, wait—every shareholder got a notice, the transfer agent knew, and the notices should have been sent, and so on. It was not clear whose legal responsibility it was, but here I was in the middle of it.

This is the call that every professional, certainly every lawyer, dreads. The problem potentially involved over 100,000 shares of a company now trading at over $10 a share, in other words, over $1 million. Yes, my malpractice insurance would cover it, but who needs such a claim? (Ultimately, no claim was ever brought against us, and my record—knock on wood—remains perfect in that no client has ever brought a claim or gotten a penny to settle any potential claim against me. In fact, this client ultimately rehired us to do additional work in later years!)

We spent three very long months not knowing what would happen. Nasdaq agreed to allow us to simply respond to shareholder complaints, rather than make everyone whole who might be affected. My clients, the former shell owners, and I donated 21,000 shares to help solve the problem. I set up an elaborate procedure for claims to be made, and ultimately just over 20,000 shares had to be paid out. Not a bad solution, given that my clients collectively kept 60,000 shares each and only had to give back 5,000 each but, of course, we all would have preferred it didn't happen.

The moral of this story is that despite everyone's best efforts on due diligence, some things can still be missed. We assumed the transfer agent had sent the notices but we probably should have checked. They assumed we did it. The very capable lawyers for the company that ultimately merged with the shell probably also should have checked the method by which the reverse stock split was actually implemented. Would I have checked the Nasdaq and DTC notices if I were he? At the time, I'm not so sure but, of course, now I would!

Also, what about the shareholders? They all got notices and went ahead and traded anyway. Even though we made them whole, don't they bear any responsibility? This is the part that frustrated me. A number of these people got a windfall they knew they did not deserve and simply took advantage of a loophole that went in their favor.

PRACTICE TIP

Check everything, check it twice, and never assume people do what they are supposed to do.

Dirty Shells

Dirty shells are more challenging to dissect. In these circumstances, we believe that possible abuses have been taking place and bad guys are either present or lurking in the background. The challenge, of course, is whether the unsavory ones have covered their tracks well enough, which usually they have not. And, of course, the general advice is: when you find a dirty shell, run, don't walk, away from it.

The telltale signs of a dirty shell are very similar to those discussed in Chapter 7, Shady Tactics. I won't repeat that information, but will add a few extra tidbits to think about when taking a look at a shell. But first, a bit about the SEC's recent targeting of so-called Footnote 32 shells.

Footnote 32 Shells

The now infamous Footnote 32 is part of the SEC rule passed in June 2005 to require a detailed disclosure filing four days after a reverse merger with a shell company (much more about this in the next chapter). First, it had to define *shell company*, which it did by essentially saying that it is any company with no or nominal operations and no or nominal assets (other than cash). The footnote is short and worth repeating in full:

> We have become aware of a practice in which a promoter of a company and/or affiliates of the promoter appear to place assets or operations within an entity with the intent of causing that entity to fall outside of the definition of blank check company in Securities Act Rule 419. The promoter will then seek a business combination transaction for the company, with the assets or operations being returned to the promoter or affiliate upon the completion of that business combination transaction. It is likely that similar schemes will be undertaken with the intention of evading the definition of shell company that we are adopting today. In our view, when promoters (or their affiliates) of a company, that would otherwise be a shell company, place assets or operations in that company and those assets or operations are returned to the promoter or its affiliates (or an agreement is made to return those assets or operations to the promoter or its affiliates) before, upon completion of, or shortly after a business combination transaction by that company, those assets or operations would be considered "nominal" for purposes of the definition of shell company.

By my estimation, this one tiny footnote sweeps aside a large percentage of the public shells in the marketplace and deems them worthless. For years, since the passage of Rule 419 in 1992, savvy promoters have been completing tiny initial public offerings of supposed operating businesses or start-ups. "We are going into the book business," they would say. Or, "We will be a beverage distributor." A number own mining or mineral rights or have options on entertainment properties. I saw one in which a former entertainer said she was going into an art business.

They seek to raise a small amount in their IPO, maybe $50,000 or even only $10,000. In most cases, they don't even raise anywhere near that.

They do this because Rule 419, which governs the IPOs of blank check companies, is very restrictive. But operating businesses or start-ups are exempt from Rule 419. Those who comply with Rule 419 are at a disadvantage because, under this rule, the stock issued in an IPO of a shell cannot trade, and promoters believe it is important for their shells' stock to trade.

These filings are creative. Flowery language about a shell's intended business, the risks involved, and so on is very impressive. The untrained eye will see nothing suspicious when presented with a shell that says it went public hoping to develop a business that has not materialized, or mineral rights that they will hand back to the promoter because they couldn't raise money to do the exploration. Rather, the unaware will think, "A business never really happened here, so there is not much in the way of liability exposure. A pretty clean shell." We know better.

Footnote 32 shells are problematic even though some promoters believe all they are doing is making a victimless end run around Rule 419.

There are two sets of victims of these shells. First is every purchaser or seller of the stock in these shells who thinks they really are going to develop those mineral rights and hit it big. Suddenly, they find themselves being reverse split one-for-twenty and merging with a biotechnology company—not what they signed up for. Now, in truth, most of these shells trade, as they say, by appointment. In other words, they don't trade with much liquidity. But there generally is some trading and those buying the stock presumably have no idea what the promoter's real plans are.

The second set of victims is every legitimate player who seeks to form shells the right way, either by using Rule 419 or a Form 10-SB shell or a SPAC (specified purpose acquisition company). Why are they victimized? Because they are trying to do things as the SEC would prefer, and they still end up with a shell that cannot trade, or in the case of a SPAC a shell which still has a number of Rule 419 restrictions, whereas the Footnote 32 shells manage to trade, increasing their value in the marketplace (at least prior to the appearance of Footnote 32).

Footnote 32 shell promoters seek to parse the language and question the intent of the footnote. They argue it only applies if a promoter or an affiliate puts the assets in himself. So if they get their friend to put the assets in, that is okay. They argue the footnote only applies if the assets are to be removed upon a merger. What if we leave the assets in but declare ourselves out of the business we were intending? That should work, right? We had real revenues, they will say, so it was a real business that just didn't work out.

They also argue that the footnote does not suggest these are frauds (although it uses the term *scheme*), but simply states that they should be categorized as shell companies for purposes of the new rule requiring disclosure. That means a full disclosure document (the super Form 8-K, to be discussed in the next chapter) has to be filed after the merger. They also argue that the SEC allowed the company to go public, which, they believe, indirectly blesses it. The SEC would certainly be embarrassed to come back and say, "Oh no, you were a fraud all along and we didn't spot it." Therefore, the SEC will leave the company alone, or so the promoters argue.

That being said, I still strongly advise my clients to stay away from transactions with all Footnote 32 shells. At the end of the day, they are frauds and hurt legitimate shell players. Also, SEC staffers have told me they are stepping up enforcement efforts against these operators. I advise each client considering a merger with a Footnote 32 shell that they may find themselves in the middle of an SEC investigation that could bring down the company.

The best legitimate way to avoid Footnote 32 is to take a real, actual small business public, maybe even one that shouldn't be public just on its own, with the intent of growing by acquiring other businesses in the same industry. Bring real management with knowledge of the industry on board. The small business will continue to operate after those acquisitions as part of the continuing public company; it will not be spun off or shut down.

Trying to do a "roll-up" in an industry is not a fraud. It is a legitimate way to avoid Rule 419 and the new SEC disclosure rule on merging with a shell, as long as the operations of the original small business cannot be deemed "nominal."

How does one spot a Footnote 32 shell, since on the surface it looks like a real company struggling to make it? First, look for the five telltale signs of Footnote 32 shells, and then check for the final confirming clue. The five telltale signs are as follows (not every company with these characteristics is bad, but these are certain indications):

❑ A start-up or very early stage company is doing an IPO or other "going public" filing and allowing shareholders to resell their stock in the public market.

❑ The IPO is seeking to raise very few dollars and may be structured under SEC Rule 504 (to be discussed in Chapter 13, Form 10-SB).

❑ Management of the "company" has little or no experience in the supposed business they are entering into or has experience in the securities or consulting business or other area of Wall Street.

❑ Sorry to say this, but the company claims to be based in Utah, Nevada, or Canada.

❑ Sorry to say this, too, but the company intends to be engaged in a business relating to oil, gas, mineral rights, or to own rights in entertainment projects that are not yet developed.

And now the final clue: The officers, directors, large shareholders, or consultants of the company have done it multiple times before. This usually takes literally five minutes to check online, though at times the promoters are fairly cagey about bringing in nominees to run each little shell (another indication that they think they might be doing something wrong). But in the end, they have to have their interest somewhere, so names do appear and do repeat (sometimes they are buried as "consultants" or selling shareholders in a resale registration, so look closely). Sometimes they think they are being careful by doing one only every year or two. A simple search reveals them.

When I see Footnote 32 features, I immediately check the background of the individuals involved. Unfortunately, I almost always find nearly identical filings for other companies and, sure enough, each of them completed a reverse merger not long after going public with a supposed business.

One would hope that, now armed with Footnote 32, thanks to the sharp folks at the SEC Office of Small Business Policy who recognized and sought to address the problem by including the footnote, we all will be on the lookout for these disguised shells.

I will continue to steer clients away from these shells. In my view, the only way the former shady image of reverse mergers can be erased is by removing as much gray from the black and white world as possible. If it looks like it may be sort of bad, stay away. As mentioned in Chapter 7, it might be easier for me to take whatever business comes in the door and not try to elevate this technique to the high road where it belongs. But I care about my reputation and integrity. I know that the only way reverse mergers will continue to blossom is if Wall Street and Main Street become completely convinced of the legitimacy of the players and their tactics.

Post-Deal High Jinks

Sometimes the dirty shell operator doesn't show his colors until after the deal. How? He enlists unsavory investor relations people to illegally pump the stock so his shell owners can reap the rewards. It is almost always a problem when a $10 million company finds its stock trading at a $300 million market valuation, not to mention a likely SEC investigation.

PRACTICE TIP

Check out the aftermarket performance of previous reverse mergers completed by this promoter, and always work with reputable IR firms.

Hiding Control Status

Some underhanded promoters seek to hide their ownership of the shell. Why? Either they have had some prior problems with regulators, they want to be under the radar to avoid a problem, or they are hiding from a Footnote 32-type situation. They hide in various ways. If they own more than 5 percent of the company, they have to disclose their owner-ship, but in some cases they simply don't do the filing. In other cases, they try to spread their ownership over various entities, relatives, and trusts so each shareholder individually stays under 5 percent, which may or may not work ("groups" are supposed to aggregate their ownership for purposes of determining whether they own 5 percent). They do this repeatedly.

Another reason they hide relates to owning more than 10 percent. Of-ficers, directors, or 10 percent owners of public companies face restrictions on their trading under the SEC's "short swing profit rule." This rule pro-hibits buying and then selling, or selling and then buying the stock within a six-month period at a profit. Should this happen, with limited exceptions, that profit is disgorged back to the company. It is permitted consistently to buy, or consistently to sell, but not one and then the other. This certainly restricts an active shell promoter seeking to trade in and out of his stock. These individuals reason that by not filing, they can avoid the short swing profit rule. Of course, that violates SEC rules and may even be a crime.

If a company merging in asks about all this, unscrupulous shell play-ers may reply, "It's my problem not yours, so don't worry about it." And they don't file, they argue, because after a merger they will own less than 5 percent or 10 percent, so who's hurt? The fact is this can initiate an SEC investigation and any SEC investigation hurts the company. When a shell promoter turns up on a perp walk on Court TV, shareholders get mad at their advisers.

PRACTICE TIP

Always get a list of shareholders from the shell's transfer agent and carefully scrutinize who owns what, asking questions about relationships and making sure all appropriate filings were made.

Hurry, Don't Worry

In some cases, private companies and their investment bankers face tremendous pressure from a shell operator to complete a deal quickly. "We have someone else ready to take it," he says, "Hurry up, don't worry about due diligence, everything is fine, if you don't take this by tomorrow you lose it."

This hurry-up attitude is almost always a sign of dirty shell she-nanigans. Any legitimate shell operator should patiently encourage due diligence. Tim Keating of Keating Investments, a well-known reverse merger investment banker, sets the standard. If Tim is selling a shell, he sends beautifully organized binders containing everything necessary for a due diligence review, and other information as well.

PRACTICE TIP

Stick to your guns and insist on proper due diligence, which you promise to complete quickly.

Due Diligence Review of the Private Company

Due diligence is as important for shell owners as for private companies—in fact, in some ways more important. Directors of a shell have a fiduciary responsibility to the shell's public shareholders to carefully review the private company, especially when shareholder approval of the proposed transaction will not be obtained (most of the time). If the shell's controlling shareholder has another interest in the deal—if the shareholder is also the investment bank that will seek to raise money for the merged company, or if they have an ownership interest in the private company merging in—fulfilling this responsibility is even more crucial.

I do not need to spend much time talking about the process of reviewing due diligence of an operating business, as it is not dissimilar to the process in any private offering or acquisition. One reviews all the legal documents, corporate structure, intellectual property, litigation, press releases, and so on, along with checking out management, financials, and so on. Any capable corporate lawyer should be able to complete this process with the assistance of financial professionals trained in the skills of deal-making. Of course, investment bankers also generally play an important role in this review process.

Due diligence of the private company includes assessing whether or not it is "ready" to be public. This includes determining which of the company's contracts will have to be disclosed once public, whether the company's financial team has the background to work for a public company, who the company's board members are, and whether a full five-year biography might include some negative disclosures, and the like.

Minimize Surprises

In sum: Complete due diligence. This means withstanding the pressure to cut corners that inevitably comes during the heat of trying to complete a transaction.

A well-known celebrity considered participating in a transaction that had not been fully checked out. I advised him: "A bad deal can often be worse, much worse, than no deal at all." Due diligence is no guarantee that a deal will ultimately be successful, but it goes a long way toward ensuring that there are no ugly surprises once the deal is done.

CHAPTER 10

The Regulatory Regime

The Sarbanes-Oxley Act of 2002, commonly referred to as "SOX," is the biggest change in securities regulation since 1934. It was passed as a response to the alleged malfeasance at Enron, World-Com, and the many other companies caught up in accounting and related scandals when the stock market boom went bust in the early 2000s.

Politicians in Washington began discussing corporate reforms in July 2002. Usually, new bills wind their way through months or even years of committee meetings, conferences, lobbying efforts, and the like before they're enacted. Not so with SOX. By the end of July 2002, just one month after the initial hearings, Congress passed the bill and President George W. Bush signed it. While most of us were on summer vacation, many of the sweeping changes included in SOX were implemented.

Implementation of SOX

One of the biggest changes was to require CEOs and CFOs to personally certify, under penalty of civil and criminal penalty for perjury, that, to the best of their knowledge, the financial statements in their company's public filings are materially correct. Companies had to provide these certifications almost immediately—in their very next filing. In some cases this occurred in August 2002, almost immediately after the bill went into effect. I know of at least one company that simply went private before this date because their executives refused to certify.

SOX also changed the timing of filings. Eventually, all public companies will be required to file their quarterly reports thirty-five days after the end of a quarter, rather than forty-five days. Annual reports on Form 10-K or 10-KSB for these companies will be filed sixty days after the end of the year rather than ninety days. Insider reports of changes in holdings by officers, directors, and 10 percent shareholders of all public companies now must be completed within two days of the change. In the past, these filings could sometimes be delayed by as much as five or six weeks.

SOX created a new cause of action: securities fraud. The U.S. Securities and Exchange Commission and private parties can now bring charges of securities fraud against alleged bad actors in public companies. At one time, cases were brought for wire fraud, mail fraud, and the like. This is no longer necessary. Statutes of limitations on these cases also were broadened.

SOX prohibits public companies from loaning money or extending credit to their senior officers. Apparently, many companies loaned money to senior executives, then forgave the loan as a way to hide compensation.

SOX also changed accounting and auditing practices.

Companies on larger exchanges (not including the OTC Bulletin Board and Pink Sheets) are required to have audit committees on their board that are totally independent of management. Those committees are required to hire, fire, and set compensation for auditors without management involvement. Theoretically, this will make auditors less subject to bullying by management.

In addition, all accounting firms that wish to audit public companies now must register with a new organization known as the Public Company Accounting Oversight Board, or PCAOB. If an auditor has more than one hundred public clients, the PCAOB will send in its own auditors to audit the auditing firm at least once a year. All other accounting firms are subject to random audits. This scrutiny has made auditors more conservative in their approach, to the point where many in public companies now consider auditors to be their adversaries.

According to Section 404 of the bill, companies must hire a separate accounting firm to establish financial controls, which their auditors must then monitor and update every year.

This is probably the most difficult and costly change SOX requires because it involves hiring a second accounting firm. As of this writing, the SEC has delayed the day on which these rules will apply to smaller companies (also known as "nonaccelerated filers"), but the day is expected to come. The SEC Advisory Committee on Smaller Public Companies has recommended all but eliminating Section 404 obligations on companies with less than approximately $125 million in market capitalization (though this number would adjust), and reducing them for companies with less than approximately $700 million in market capitalization. It is

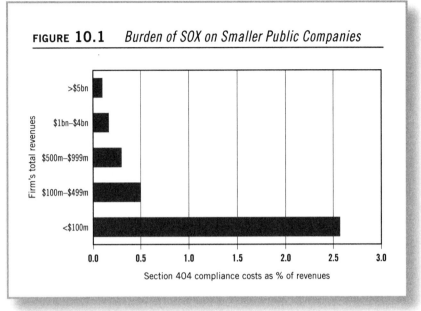

FIGURE 10.1 *Burden of SOX on Smaller Public Companies*

not clear what the full SEC will do about this recommendation.

SOX defines *nonaccelerated filers* as those with a market capitalization of less than $75 million (market capitalization is determined by multiplying the number of shares outstanding by the per share stock price). As of this writing, these companies have until the first fiscal year ending after July 15, 2007 to implement the financial controls described above. They are also currently exempt from the new rules regarding accelerated filings.

As mentioned throughout this book, this sweeping set of changes has had a disparate impact on smaller public companies. If the small business lobby had had a chance to be heard before SOX was passed, there might have been changes to the final legislation. That said, the law is what it is and small companies continue to deal with it. **FIGURE 10.1** illustrates the extraordinary burden small companies must shoulder when it comes to compliance with SOX as measured by compliance costs as a percentage of revenues.

After more than three years of experience with SOX, in general we have found that compliance has been less of a burden on smaller companies than most people had expected. The main reason for this has been the fact that 404 compliance has not yet been mandated. The rest of SOX, while somewhat annoying, has simply become "the new normal" and, in fact, is pretty manageable for most companies.

In the end, SOX largely provides a positive set of changes that will reduce the opportunity for shenanigans in both big public companies and small. The fact that the pendulum had to swing farther in the direction of regulation than I feel was probably necessary is sometimes the cost of reacting to a real problem. Between the SEC Advisory Committee and attention it receives in Congress, it is hoped that some of the more extreme provisions in the Act can be altered or revisited to reduce the impact on smaller companies.

June 2005 SEC Rule Changes: Reverse Mergers Are Further Legitimized (but Tougher to Consummate)

In April 2004, the SEC advanced a set of proposals that were intended to close several loopholes widely used by those pursuing reverse mergers. These rules were made final in June 2005 and published under the name "Use of Form S-8, Form 8-K, and Form 20-F by Shell Companies." (Throughout this text, we refer to these rules as the June 2005 SEC rulemaking.)

Prior to this proposal, a private company merging with a public shell had seventy-one days from closing to submit any real information about itself in the form of audited financial statements. During this time, investors in the newly merged company had no reliable information on which to buy or sell shares and were effectively left in the dark.

Even after the release of financial statements, the disclosure of other information could be delayed. For example, details of executive compensation, a comparative analysis of the company's year-to-year performance and risk factors relating to the company, all could wait until the company's next annual report filed on Form 10-K or Form 10-KSB. Depending on the timing of the merger, this could take place as much as a year later.

In some cases, companies voluntarily released this information; indeed, some lawyers felt there was SEC guidance requiring this disclosure (I respectfully disagree with that interpretation). Others simply felt that the rules are what they are and since they do not require this disclosure, there is no need to do it. Prior to the June 2005 SEC rulemaking, we typically encouraged as much disclosure as early as possible. But we certainly couldn't force clients to prepare a full year end–type disclosure when the SEC was not requiring it.

One negative aspect of the historical lack of disclosure is a trading restriction. Anyone with information about the merged company that had not yet been publicly released is prohibited from trading in the company's stock. In certain cases, this restriction encouraged companies to make the disclosure sooner rather than later.

Genesis of the June 2005 Rule Changes

In February 2004, I was invited to visit with about a dozen SEC staffers in their Washington offices to discuss the reverse merger business. I summarized the information I generally provide in my seminars so they could see how the private sector and the corporate bar were dealing with the various issues of the day.

We discussed, among other things, three major areas in the business that were subject to abuse by unscrupulous players. One was the seventy-one-day vacuum of information following most deals that is described above. The other was the popular use by public shells of Form S-8, normally used for registering securities involved in a company stock option plan, to dole out tradable stock like candy to consultants, intermediaries, investor relations firms, and others doing work for shells. Last, I talked a bit about "Footnote 32 shells." (For details, see the previous chapter.)

Shady dealers used the seventy-one-day window as an opportunity to manipulate the stock price by issuing press releases about the company after the merger but before the seventy-one days had passed. Often those press releases, even if factually correct, were misleading because they lacked the context of other information that was not yet public. For example, what if a company in dire financial straits needs a financing very soon, but nobody knows it? Then the company releases an announcement that it had hired a CFO, or obtained a new customer, or launched an exciting new product. Again, good news, but what value is it if neither of these was sufficient to keep the company afloat?

Form S-8 is not technically illegal (neither is the rosy press release in the prior example), but the form was not really designed to register securities for use as compensation for consulting work. In some cases, "consultants" are actually affiliates of market-making firms trying to build support for a shell's stock. Using stock to pay market makers is illegal. On the other hand, stock is an appropriate (and entirely aboveboard) way to compensate actual shell managers, such as officers and directors, who can benefit from getting stock as a reward for their efforts, especially where a shell has not generated any cash to pay them for their admittedly limited services.

In our meeting, we also discussed the fact that more and more legitimate players were entering this field for reasons mentioned throughout this book. The hope was to encourage the regulators to adopt a carrot-and-stick approach—to come down hard on abusers but encourage those who wish to do things the right way.

In April 2004, the SEC proposed changing its rules to take care of these problems. It proposed defining a *shell company* as a company with no or nominal assets (other than cash) and no or nominal operations. It proposed requiring an SEC filing within four business days after a merger with a shell company that makes it no longer a shell company or where there is a change in control of the shell company. This filing would include essentially all the information that a company completing an IPO would disclose, including audited financial statements. The filing was to be made on a Current Report on Form 8-K, and would include all the "Form 10 information"—information that would be in a Form 10 or Form 10-SB for the merged company. Second, the SEC proposed eliminating the use of Form S-8 in a shell company.

Interestingly, in one public SEC hearing to announce the proposals, which I attended, the commissioners, normally well briefed and prepared with statements and comments, seemed a little surprised by the proposal coming from their staff in the Division of Corporation Finance and the Office of Small Business Policy. SEC Chairman Donaldson asked, "Well, are there any legitimate reverse mergers?" Another commissioner commented that it seemed as if enforcement hearings were consistently involving reverse mergers gone bad and didn't quite understand why these transactions were to be encouraged.

The staff calmly and patiently retorted that the technique itself is valid and legitimate, but some have abused it, and that there are a growing number of honorable finance professionals seeking to use this method as an alternative to an expensive, risky, dilutive, and time-consuming IPO.

The comment period followed. (The public must be allowed to comment on any proposed rule from an administrative agency before it becomes final.) This short six-week period was quite frenzied, and around forty people weighed in on the proposed rule. My main comments suggested a longer period before this major SEC filing, or perhaps dividing the filing into portions. I also suggested delaying the filing if the post-merger company's stock is not trading and that the use of Form S-8 should be allowed solely for issuance of stock to officers, directors, and employees. The full text of my comments may be found on the Web at http://www .sec.gov/rules/proposed/s71904/dnfeldman1898.htm.

The Rule Is Adopted

In the last public hearing before Chairman Donaldson's departure, held on June 29, 2005, the SEC adopted new rules, almost exactly as proposed, without incorporating changes made during the comment period. New requirements included: a major filing four days from closing, the definition of a shell company given above, the prohibition on the use of Form S-8 to provide compensation to consultants, and the famous Footnote 32.

Most encouragingly, this time each commissioner had a prepared statement proclaiming the merits of the legitimate use of the reverse merger technique in corporate structuring. They all felt that the new rules would further discourage questionable characters from entering into these transactions. The final rule as adopted and accompanying release can be found on the Web at http://www.sec.gov/rules/final/33-8587.pdf.

Specifics of the Rule

The following sections discuss the overall requirements of the new rule along with a little commentary.

Shell Company Definition

A *shell company* is a public reporting company that has no or nominal assets (other than cash), and no or nominal operations. A merger with a shell company after which it is no longer a shell company or another transaction pursuant to which there is a change in control triggers various new disclosure requirements. Alas, as you recall, Rule 419 defines a *blank check* to be a development stage company with no business plan or whose business plan is to merge with or acquire another company. Clearly, shells and blank checks are similar. But there are distinctions that make a difference.

For example, a legitimate start-up company with an idea to develop new software, if public and a reporting company, would qualify as a shell company (because it has nominal assets and operations) but not a blank check (since it has a real business plan). On the other hand, a dormant company that used to have operations but maintains significant assets (perhaps valuable patents, third-party claims, or maybe even a significant net operating loss carryforward) could qualify as a blank check (plan is to merge) but not a shell company (it has more than nominal assets). So, is the SEC confusing things here? I don't think so.

As things stand, the legitimate software start-up can bypass Rule 419 to effect a public offering without the investor protections offered by that rule but would still be subject to the disclosure requirements upon any reverse merger (if it still maintains nominal assets and operations). The dormant company with assets could not effect an IPO without the Rule 419 restrictions, but could complete a reverse merger without complying with the new disclosure rules, since it did not have "nominal" assets.

One can only surmise that the SEC set out to broaden the scope of activities it seeks to regulate either with the Rule 419 restrictions or the new disclosure rule, if not both. But why the start-up software company is deemed a shell company is still confusing to me. I believe the SEC's view is that the only negative consequence for being a shell company is the requirement to file a Form 8-K with Form 10 information (if it changes control or effects a transaction where it ceases to be a shell), and that this is not a major burden. And maybe, indirectly, this was a way to seek to deal with the Footnote 32 problem. By forcing "start-ups" into complete disclosure, people with unethical intentions would be less interested in completing an IPO of a fake start-up just to get past Rule 419, since they will be subject to the new disclosure rules.

Another challenge to contend with when considering the SEC's shell company definition is the use of the word *nominal*, as in no or nominal assets (other than cash) and no or nominal operations. What does *nominal* mean? The SEC was aware of this concern, since in the rule proposal it included a request for comment on whether the word *nominal* is too uncertain and whether there should be more specific numerical definitions of a shell. In the end, however, it left the language and seems to have adopted the approach the U.S. Supreme Court used in trying to define *pornography*: "I can't define it, but I know it when I see it."

Apparently, the SEC wanted to allow individual practitioners the flexibility to determine the definition rather than having a specific quantitative cutoff. As indicated at the hearing when adopting the rule, if the SEC were to suggest, for example, a minimum of $100,000 in assets, a glut of shells would be created with $101,000. But how does one determine what constitutes a shell? Are the assets of a barbershop nominal? What about a consulting firm with three employees and $200,000 in billings?

Unfortunately, the answers here are unclear. One thing is certain: Those who like to live at the edge of the law will surely test what *nominal* means, and one can imagine a number of SEC "no-action letters" being requested to clarify some of this. (A no-action letter is a response from the SEC staff to a letter from a specific company seeking the staff's confirmation that it will seek no action against the parties if certain actions are taken.) I have been unofficially advised, for example, that maintaining a website probably constitutes nominal operations. In the meantime, much as in the time leading up to the development of Regulation D in private securities offerings, legal opinions on whether borderline situations are shell companies will be hard to come by.

Form 10 Information Required

The new rule requires a Form 8-K, known as a "current report," be filed within four business days of closing a transaction with a shell company if the transaction either effects a change in control or changes the shell company into a nonshell company. Usually, Form-8-Ks are not reviewed; all one has to do is file them. However, the SEC always reserves the right to review any filing, and it may indeed do so.

The Form 8-K is to include all information that the merged company would have put into a Form 10 or Form 10-SB to voluntarily subject itself to the SEC reporting requirements, much like the Form 10-SB shells or, as we will see later, the filings sometimes undertaken in "self-filing" alternatives to reverse mergers.

This includes all the information that would be in a prospectus for a traditional IPO: two years of audited financial information (or three years for a company not able to benefit from the Regulation S-B disclosure scheme), full business description, risk factors, affiliate (related party) transactions, executive compensation, comparative period-to-period analysis of financial results, description of capital stock, discussion of prior securities offerings, and the like.

All material contracts and other key documents, such as the company's charter and bylaws, must be included and filed as exhibits. Full five-year biographical information needs to be provided on all officers and directors and their ownership information as well as all 5 percent shareholders. All this needs to be put together and ready to file within four days of closing a reverse merger.

The 8-K also needs to be filed if there is a change in control of a shell company, even if it still remains a shell. Interestingly, this provision applies if a shell simply issues a controlling interest to a new third party. If control changes to another shell promoter or banker, the new rule requires a Form 8-K filing. Presumably, however, that filing will be rather straightforward, saying something like, "We are still a shell, our mission has not changed, only our ownership."

Prohibition on Form S-8

A shell company may no longer use Form S-8 to register shares for those who are employees of or consultants to a shell company. In fact, a former shell company must wait sixty days after its change in status before it can use Form S-8. This means, among other things, that our start-up software guy with nominal operations who goes public may not use Form S-8 until his operations and assets (other than cash) are not nominal. Our example of a blank check with significant assets but no plan other than to merge into another company can use Form S-8 because, technically, it is not a shell company.

This is a step forward because underhanded actors who once used Form S-8 as a quick and easy way to reward their friends can no longer do so.

The New Check-Off

One change in the rule affects every single public reporting company, from General Motors and Microsoft on down. The front cover of every quarterly and annual report to be filed by every public reporting company with the SEC now includes a check-off box to indicate whether or not the filer is a shell company under the definition.

Look forward to a turf battle among those who are likely candidates for making this determination, including securities legal counselors and valuation experts. It is not clear whether the company's attorneys or accountants should decide whether a company's operations or assets are "nominal." Time will tell.

PRACTICE TIP

Don't try to define nominal *at home. Get good professional advice.*

One Nice By-Product: Information

Here's one major benefit of all these changes, including the Form 8-K to be filed after a merger with a shell company (the industry has begun calling it the "super Form 8-K" or just "super 8-K" filing) and the declaration of shell company status through a check-off on SEC filings. For the first time ever, shells and reverse mergers will be accurately tracked and information about these transactions gathered and disseminated. Before this, it has been impossible to get accurate answers to the questions I am frequently asked: How many reverse mergers are there? How many shells are there? How many have cash? How many do foreign deals?

DealFlow Media, Inc. publishes *The PIPEs Report*, which provides detailed rankings and other information regarding the PIPE (private investments in public equity) market. After all, filings relating to PIPEs are relatively easy to find given many common words and phrases in their filings. Unfortunately, prior to the implementation of the June 2005 SEC rules on reverse mergers, the same information was not available for reverse mergers. Even though DealFlow Media, Inc. now publishes *The Reverse Merger Report* every quarter and attempts to catalog as many deals as possible, it still can't be sure it has captured every transaction.

Now that the information will be available thanks to the check-offs and 8-K filings, it will be interesting to see just how many deals and shells are out there. Most of us speculate that hundreds of reverse mergers are done each year, but none of us really knows. We suggest that hundreds of shells exist, but again we do not know. The new check-off requirement will go a long way to adding transparency to the business via the use of quantifiable metrics.

Of course, this information will not be perfect. Nonreporting shells trading on the Pink Sheets still will not need to disclose their status. They are not subject to the new SEC 8-K reporting rule and their deals also would not be disclosed. In addition, some shell companies will try to claim they are not shells because their operations are more than nominal.

Who Is Exempt?

The new 8-K requirement only applies to SEC reporting companies. Those who do not trade or trade on the Pink Sheets and are nonreporting need not comply with the new rule, though it may be advisable in any event to do so, at least upon the commencement of trading in the merged company's stock if the shell is nontrading. In a strange way, this may actually improve the value and desirability of Pink Sheet shells (at least among those less interested in providing full disclosure or desiring to delay it).

Another transaction that is made exempt by the rule is a merger with a so-called business combination related shell company. If a real operating business sets up a shell solely to reincorporate or complete an acquisition, that entity will not be deemed a shell company for purposes of the new rule. Obviously, some commentators raised a concern that the proposed rule would inadvertently thwart major, legitimate merger transactions, and the SEC took care of that with this change. Certain asset-backed issuers also are exempt from the rule.

Any reverse merger involving a nonshell company also is exempt, even if there is a change in control. So the New York Stock Exchange's takeover of public company Archipelago Holdings, completed in March 2006 with much fanfare, was technically a reverse merger, since the NYSE acquired 70 percent of Archipelago and took over its board. Since Archipelago had more than nominal assets and operations, however, it was not a shell company, and the super 8-K requirement did not apply.

Blank check companies with substantial assets are also exempt because they are not shell companies under the definition. They are subject to Rule 419 whenever they try to register new shares but do not have to file the super 8-K upon a merger or change in control.

A Little More on Footnote 32

In the last chapter, we discussed Footnote 32. All I will add here is a mention of the importance of the fact that the SEC acknowledged, addressed, and sought to deal with these troublesome shells and the fact that maybe it did not go far enough. All the footnote says is (I am paraphrasing here), "If you are a Footnote 32 shell trying to get around Rule 419 by putting in a business to be taken out, we consider you to be a shell company right from the start."

Under the June 2005 SEC rulemaking, when that shell merges with an operating business or changes control, it must file a super Form 8-K just like everyone else; however, it does not otherwise penalize what I consider to be fraud on behalf of these promoters. In fact, it arguably emboldens them to do IPOs of these types of shells, start trading (unfair to legitimate shell creators not allowed to trade), do a merger, and then simply do a super 8-K filing under the rule. Despite my entreaties to my clients that the SEC is making a statement that these machinations are bad, it has not actually done so directly.

I am hopeful the SEC will consider even further regulatory action to stop the proliferation of Footnote 32 shells.

So, Is It Good or Bad?

So, are the new SEC rules good rules or bad rules? The answer is, they are good—or at least a lot "more good" than bad. I expect the murkiness of the definition of a shell company will be ironed out over time through interpretations and no-action relief from the SEC. The amount of new information will probably be very eye-opening. The elimination of the seventy-one-day no information zone has been intelligently addressed. The prohibition on use of Form S-8 was a positive change, and very few legitimate players will be hurt by it. Creation of Footnote 32 was a very important start at eliminating a real abuse.

Most important, the declaration of this technique as legitimate and valid in corporate structuring has rather dramatically and yet subtly changed the entire industry. Those of us doing things the right way feel somewhat vindicated. Those who may have been on the fence have been helped over it. Those who may still believe only unscrupulous operators are involved in the reverse merger business may begin to think differently.

PART THREE

A Few Other Simple Ways to Go Public

CHAPTER 11

Self-Filings

The self-filing approach is a way to take a company public without either an initial public offering or a reverse merger. By self-filing, an operating company can go public without the use of a shell. The techniques described in the following chapters have long been available to private companies. But only recently have these companies begun to explore them with a high level of interest.

A number of factors make self-filing increasingly attractive. First, the quiet IPO market, increase in shell prices, and decrease in shell quality and availability make reverse mergers more difficult. Sometimes, self-filing is the only option because an acceptable shell is not even available for a merger. (Specified purpose acquisition companies offer a valuable alternative for some private companies, but in truth many companies considering going public simply are not big enough or growing fast enough or in the right industry or sector for SPACs to be interested.)

Second, the problems associated with due diligence and scrubbing shells and the hassle of negotiating with shell promoters—who demand greater equity interest, and offer less in terms of protection and indemnity in the event of misrepresentations or liabilities remaining in the shell—seem to increase every day.

Third, many private companies dislike having to give away between 5 percent and 20 percent of their company's equity just to acquire a shell to use as a merger vehicle.

Last, some CEOs and their advisers still have negative attitudes toward reverse mergers. I have come to expect this attitude from more traditional venture firms and venture-backed companies. Self-filings offer these people a way to go public without the "taint" that they believe accompanies a reverse merger.

Introduction to Self-Filings

A self-filing is the choice by a private company to begin the process of voluntarily becoming a reporting company under SEC rules. By so doing, a company assumes the obligation of filing quarterly and annual reports, and becomes subject to proxy and other rules. The remainder of this chapter will review the three conditions necessary for a self-filing to make sense. The next two chapters examine the most common methods for an operating business to go public through a self-filing: Form SB-2 and Form 10-SB.

When Does Self-Filing Make Sense?

Three factors determine the wisdom of self-filing instead of completing a reverse merger with a shell company. One, does the private company already have a large shareholder base? Two, can the private company take care of its own financial needs during the lengthy self-filing process? Three, does the private company have on tap a capable investment bank or Wall Street adviser to help "build" a public company from the private one?

Shareholder Base and Shareholder Status

To understand if self-filing is a better choice than a reverse merger, a company must first analyze what it will give up by not having the resources of a shell at its disposal.

Shells offer private companies two critical assets: public company status and a preexisting shareholder base. The shareholder base is important because it increases the likelihood of a trading market developing sooner rather than later. If a private company has a small handful of shareholders, it can use the shell's base to create a larger float after the merger.

Many market participants also believe that a shell has two other valuable assets: a trading symbol and a trading market. I respectfully disagree.

An active trading market in a shell's stock may be a negative characteristic, as would be the case when there is a very large shareholder base consisting of many investors who have a low cost basis in their shares. In such instances, many shareholders dump their stock into the market post–reverse merger, ultimately depressing the stock price. If during due diligence of a shell it becomes difficult to discern who the shareholders actually are, then there is a risk that many of these shareholders will be "share sellers" once the merger is announced and the stock becomes liquid.

Each private company will value a shell's shareholder base differently, depending on its specific situation.

When a private company already has a strong shareholder base—as it may if it has gone through a number of rounds of venture capital or private fund-raising—it may not benefit much from a shell's shareholder base. Some private companies have forty or fifty shareholders. Many shells have only fifty or sixty; few shells have more than several hundred shareholders. (SPACs, however, often have thousands of holders, but are limited in the types and sizes of companies they are interested in.)

Sometimes, a private company with just a few shareholders can work with an investment bank that may be able to raise money and simultaneously increase the shareholder base. This reduces the value of shareholders offered by the shell.

The number of accredited shareholders is also important. If a company has more than thirty-five shareholders who do not meet the "accredited investor" test described in Chapter 8, Deal Mechanics, it may be more difficult to pursue a reverse merger.

As described earlier, the issuance of shares during a reverse merger constitutes a securities offering by the shell. Therefore, it must meet the standards of Regulation D or Section 4(2) in order to avoid having to register with the U.S. Securities and Exchange Commission. If the company has more than thirty-five unaccredited investors, it falls outside the purview of Regulation D and Section 4(2) and will probably have to file a Form S-4 with the SEC. This is a complicated and time-consuming filing and may require some of the techniques described in Chapter 8 to avoid this filing. One of those techniques is pursuing a self-filing, where no shares change hands and, therefore, no offering takes place to existing shareholders, even if there are more than thirty-five unaccredited shareholders.

Timing of Financing

Most companies seeking to be public are doing so at least in part to raise needed financing. The timing of that financing is often important to a company's growth and, in some cases, its survival.

Some companies need a large funding to take place in the very near term. For example, a biotechnology company may need to fund a large-scale research study. A growing business may want to acquire another in part with the payment to that company of cash. Or a business may need to purchase equipment or real estate. In each of these cases, small amounts of funding may not do the trick, even in the short term.

Self-filings make sense for companies that can defer new financing until the process is completed. The self-filing process usually takes between five and eight months, but it can take longer, depending on the speed of in-house financial staff, auditors, and counsel, and the SEC's review of the filing. Indeed, it can take more than a year. It is generally not possible to complete a large financing during this time.

But, of course, there are exceptions. Venture-backed companies may continue to receive funding from their original investors while they self-file. This is an infrequent occurrence because in most cases venture-backed companies decide to go public because their venture or private equity funding source has dried up or is unable to provide additional financing. (Many private equity funds have limitations on the amount they may invest in a single company.)

A PIPE (private investment in public equity) investor who is normally only willing to invest in public companies may invest in a private company that is in the process of self-filing. But often the PIPE investor, if interested at all in investing in a private company, is willing to invest only a small amount until the company is public.

Therefore, in general a self-filing only makes sense for a company that has the ability to receive, at a reasonable valuation, whatever funding is necessary to continue to operate until the company is public. In some cases, self-filings occur with the assistance of an investment bank that intends to conduct a large PIPE once public. These banks often will provide interim or "bridge" financing to the private company while it awaits going public.

In some cases, no interim financing is needed. The company may wish to conduct a PIPE when it is public for a specific growth or acquisition opportunity, but this financing can wait until the process is complete. In this instance, or where a company has a source of interim financing, a self-filing can make sense.

PRACTICE TIP

Whatever amount of time one thinks it will take to complete a self-filing, multiply that by 150 percent.

Remember: Self-filings take time. If advisers and auditors estimate that the process will take six months, plan on at least nine months. Some even recommend doubling it. Keep that in mind when talking to investment bankers and others about the company's capital requirements and the time period for which funding must be provided.

Another warning: As will be discussed in the next chapter, there are two main approaches to pursuing a self-filing—a Form SB-2 resale registration and a Form 10-SB filing. During the waiting period after the Form SB-2 filing and before its effectiveness, the SEC staff takes the position that no private financing can be undertaken, except in limited circumstances involving very high-end institutional investors. Thus, only companies that are fully financed while waiting for SB-2 to go into effect should pursue that route. If interim financing is desired while waiting for the filing to be approved, a Form 10-SB may make more sense. There's more on this in the next chapter.

Wall Street Savvy Needed: Building a Public Company

Recently, my wife hired a construction manager to begin a construction project on our house. He took a percentage of the overall cost but coordinated everything, found the vendors and subcontractors, got the best deals from them, and made sure they did the work carefully and fast. We were smart enough not to try to be our own general contractor, since we know very little about construction.

In contrast, a self-filing is a "do-it-yourself" version of going public. In an IPO, an investment banker pretty much takes care of everything. In a reverse merger, usually the shell promoters or investment bankers are experienced enough to deal with many of the details.

It is inadvisable for a private company to pursue a self-filing unless members of senior management have significant Wall Street experience, or the company engages a capable investment bank or financial consultant to walk it through the process of transforming a private company into a public company. An important part of this process is hiring the right outside professionals. What follows is a discussion of the services these professionals perform.

Auditors

Public companies need capable auditors. Most investment bankers know where to find efficient, responsive, cost-effective firms to conduct the private company's financial audit. The firm must be registered with the Public Company Accounting Oversight Board (PCAOB). In some industries, in particular those that are highly regulated, it helps to use a firm that has knowledge and experience in the industry. For example, biotechnology, telecommunications, defense contracting, and other industries deal heavily with government regulation, and an auditing firm with industry-specific experience is a real plus.

It is not that easy for a private company to "vet" different auditing firms and to understand the differences between them. Experienced Wall Streeters know the reputations, strengths, and weaknesses of the various firms, and often have existing relationships that make the selection process smoother.

Although I recommend appropriate in-house or engaged expertise to help make this selection, here are a few things to consider when hiring an outside audit firm.

First, get a solid cost estimate for the project in question. Some firms will even complete a project for a flat fee, which may be preferable. Second, evaluate their understanding of the business. Ideally, they will have some experience in representing similar companies.

Third, get a sense of what kind of team will work on the project. How involved will the partner-level people be? How accessible are they? Who will the day-to-day liaison be? Someone junior? Senior?

PRACTICE TIP

If the primary contact in a firm is below the "manager" level, it might be wise to consider another firm. In smaller firms, regular contact with the partner is often possible, which of course is great.

Fourth, the size of the firm matters. In general, the larger the accounting firm, the stronger their reputation and more dependably ethical their practices. The so-called final four of the once "big 8" firms (Ernst & Young, Deloitte & Touche, PriceWaterhouseCoopers, and KPMG Peat Marwick) all represent many public companies in many different industries, including the world's largest companies, and have stellar reputations, even after the Enron debacle and its impact on the accounting industry.

That being said, it rarely makes sense for a smaller public company to use a final four firm, even if one of them is willing to take the company on as a client. For starters, their client intake procedures are overwhelming, and with all of the interviews and background checks, it takes quite awhile to be accepted as a client.

Next, as a result of SOX and the obliteration of large accounting firm Arthur Andersen thanks to the Enron debacle, larger firms tend to be extremely conservative. If there is a judgment to be made, rest assured it will be made in the safest possible way to protect the auditor. Keep in mind that the PCAOB audits each final four firm every single year, and there's little doubt that the auditors are making decisions to impress those that audit them.

At these auditing firms, things not checked in the past are getting checked. Things checked in the past are checked twice. "Cold reviews" of auditor work within the firm are much more extensive than ever, and each approval or consent for anything that will be included in an SEC filing goes higher and higher up the line, adding delay and cost.

Several of the final four firms are making an effort to strengthen their presence in the middle market. They have set up special groups to take care of smaller clients. What success they have had is due to the cachet that comes with using a final four firm. Many companies, particularly venture-backed ones, believe that final four representation helps them bring in top-quality board members, lenders, investors, and so on, and they are probably right. So the analysis of which firm to work with involves a balancing of costs and benefits, as do most decisions.

Also, companies with operations in multiple countries may benefit from using one of the final four, since they all have offices or affiliations in virtually every country. But, depending on the location, it may be possible for a smaller or mid-sized auditing firm in the United States to develop a comfortable relationship with a firm on the ground in another country. The deals I have worked on in China did not involve final four firms.

Middle and smaller-sized auditing firms often have strong reputations as well, and can be more flexible and cost-effective than the final four.

Attorneys

After engaging auditors (or maybe even before), the self-filing company should seek a competent securities law firm. Most private companies do not retain lawyers with securities offering experience. In some cases, counsel has this experience but has little expertise in reverse mergers or the going public process. Finding a firm with deep experience and a good reputation on "the Street" can be difficult. Again, having the advice of an experienced Wall Street professional is important when choosing the right firm.

Market Makers

In order for its stock to trade, every public company requires brokerage firms to serve as market makers if quoted on the Pink Sheets or OTC Bulletin Board, or specialists if listed on the larger exchanges such as the American Stock Exchange or New York Stock Exchange. Market makers literally "make a market" in a stock and are required to ensure that every desired purchaser or seller can complete a transaction. If someone wishes to sell and cannot find a buyer, the market maker is obligated to purchase the stock. Market makers also have tremendous influence over a stock's trading price, and can bring in their own clients to buy and sell the stock.

To find a market maker, consult an investment bank or financial consultant, either of which would have relationships with these firms.

It's worth noting that there has been a tremendous decline in the number of firms willing to make markets in Bulletin Board stocks in the last few years. This resulted in part from changes in the amount of spread a market maker can apply between the "bid" and "ask" price of a stock, which ultimately reduces the profitability of serving as market maker. And very few of those that are in the business are willing to make markets in more than a handful of stocks, so the market is truly controlled by only three or four large firms.

In general, the ability of a newly public company to simply take a stroll down Wall Street and find willing market makers is slim. If management has stock market experience, that's great. But if not, an outside adviser is most helpful.

PRACTICE TIP

At the slightest hint of sleaze, quietly slip away from a market maker. Some market makers try to get compensated for their efforts, which is illegal. The only money they can make is in commissions or their own profits trading the stock in question or by performing certain advisory services. In truth, it really doesn't make sense that market makers cannot be compensated. They benefit when a stock trades more, so why not also pay them when that happens (and, of course, disclose this to the public)? Alas, however, as of now the NASD has seen fit to maintain an appearance of objectivity, which is not borne out in reality. The SEC Advisory Committee on Smaller Public Companies has recommended developing a method to compensate a market maker for filing the necessary documents to get a newly public company trading.

ANOTHER PRACTICE TIP

If it seems the market maker is involved with small, newly public companies' stock shooting to the moon way too quickly, again slip away. A money-losing company generating $3 million in revenue should not be trading as if its value was $300 million, yet this happens. When it does, count on an SEC investigation and, ultimately, shareholder litigation. Obviously, this should be avoided.

Public Relations and Investor Relations

I (and many others) lump both public relations and investor relations into one category, although most professionals in this space would prefer we did not. Public relations and investor relations (PR and IR for short) can be critical for a growing public company to build public attention and investor interest.

Many private companies engage PR firms to help build their customer base. PR firms generally help a company with big announcements and press releases, do damage control when things are not going well, and advise what strategic and tactical moves may be well received by the public at large. Great PR firms can be true marketing gurus helping with broader issues like branding, targeting the corporate message, and the like. They provide opportunities for press coverage and arrange for company executives' appearances on key broadcast outlets; however, these firms are not necessarily experienced in working with public companies. It is necessary to find one that is.

Investor relations firms, by contrast, concentrate on existing and potential shareholders, other investors, and Wall Street in general, by "selling" the company to them. They do not typically deal with press releases and other PR functions. Rather, they focus almost exclusively on how to get a stock trading with more liquidity and at higher prices. Good firms also help in other ways, such as introducing sources of capital for the company, and providing broader financial consulting services.

IR FIRM PRACTICE TIP

Stay away from guys who will promote your stock by sending mass unsolicited e-mails or pushing a company to do press releases when the company's CEO gets over a cold. The legitimate, albeit old-fashioned way to do IR is by wearing out shoe leather, pounding the pavement on Wall Street to tell the company's story to hedge funds and other institutions that have the ability to make or influence investments in companies. As mentioned earlier, more IR firms are employing the Internet and technology to create online presentations available to many more potential investors, which can have a great benefit.

Transfer Agent

Every public company needs a transfer agent. A normally ministerial function, transfer agents keep the company's stock records, issue stock certificates when appropriate, help conduct a company's annual meeting by providing inspection services and current lists of shareholders, help with stock splits, stock dividends, and similar changes, and (at a relatively low cost) prevent such administrative functions (and some liability exposure) from being undertaken inside the company.

Transfer agents also are involved in three dicey areas of securities law: the placing and removal of legends on stock certificates, transfers of restricted securities, and the issuance of new stock. As will be discussed in more detail below, the two principal ways a share of stock becomes tradable in the public market (if a trading market exists) are (1) by being individually registered with the SEC or (2) by being held long enough that the SEC allows it to trade under Rule 144 even if not registered (assuming Rule 144 can be used). Shares that are not registered or held long enough are called "restricted" securities and generally carry a written legend on the back of the certificate restricting transfer other than through registration or an exemption from registration.

When a share becomes tradable—usually because it has been held long enough under Rule 144—this legend can be removed so that trading can take place. Typically, an investor asks her broker to arrange for the legend to be removed, and this request is forwarded to the company. A transfer agent then generally requires an opinion of counsel that the shares may be sold under Rule 144, along with other paperwork. At this point, the transfer agent will issue a new unrestricted stock certificate representing shares that can now be sold publicly.

Similarly, transfers of stock that are restricted require involvement of the transfer agent. Some transfer agents insist on legal opinions for these transactions and others do not. This is also true with regard to new issuances of stock, whether upon completing a PIPE or other financing, or issuances to advisers, consultants, and the like. Again, some transfer agents require opinions and others do not. The process of obtaining the opinion slows the process of getting a company's shareholder the appropriate certificate, but in a post-SOX environment, it is understandable for the transfer agents to seek to protect themselves.

Ultimately, transfer agents' reputations relate to their size, their flexibility in borderline situations where their help is needed most, and overall quality. Some of the larger firms work to develop a broader relationship, helping a company raise money or attract investor interest, or even serve as investors themselves.

PRACTICE TIP

Don't immediately go with the cheapest firm; quality is very important. Also, as with all vendor relationships, check references. Ask questions about what requirements apply for different transactions.

Internal Staff

Every private company finds that upon going public it needs to strengthen its financial staff, including bookkeepers and a controller. In addition, the company must make sure it has a competent chief financial officer (CFO). It is very important that a public company have a CFO or senior financial person who has specific experience working with public companies, especially since the passage of SOX. There are headhunters who specialize in finding these people, and investment banks, law firms, and auditing firms are familiar with the best ways to find these internal team members.

When looking to hire senior financial people, there are two critical points to consider. First, of course, as is true with any hire, check references and make sure the person is capable and experienced in the job at hand.

Second, the person should not have been associated with any questionable Wall Street players. Like it or not, guilt by association is unfair but not unreasonable given the vital nature of the role this person plays. A CFO has the greatest opportunity to cook the books and do what is necessary to please his superiors or shareholders. Obviously, the ideal CFO is above reproach. It is true that many who have worked for dubious players are themselves aboveboard. Often they claim to have left a company upon discovering problems. But for that small percentage that played a role in bad behavior, it may not be worth the risk.

There Is No "I" in Team

The classic phrase, "There is no 'I' in team," sums up this introduction to self-filings. The various firms and people described above must work together like a well-oiled machine.

No one member of the team can facilitate a streamlined self-filing process without hard work and cooperation from others. As counsel, I find myself frustrated if the auditors are not up to par or if the IR team is being too aggressive or if I get the impression that someone involved is causing interference. When the process goes smoothly, a self-filing can be a pleasurable and rewarding experience for the team and an effective way for a company to become public.

As they say on TV, "Don't try this at home." No one should attempt a self-filing without a group on board that can build a team that is competent and works well together.

CHAPTER 12

Form SB-2

This chapter describes how to complete a self-filing through the use of Form SB-2. The next chapter continues with the mechanics of a self-filing with Form 10-SB, and then finishes with a discussion of a few other techniques in the category of what some are now calling "alternative public offerings" or APOs.

Self-filing with a Form SB-2 may be appropriate for companies that do not wish to go public by merging with a shell and that will not need financing until the filing has become effective (at least five to eight months). Companies that will need financing during the pendency of the SB-2 registration should consider self-filing by means of Form 10-SB, explained in the next chapter.

Self-filings through an SB-2, or Form 10-SB for that matter, are emerging techniques. The discussion here serves not so much as a guide, but as an informed suggestion of what's to come in the expanding universe of alternatives to IPOs.

How Do Shares of Stock Become Tradable?

Once a company is public and has a trading symbol, its shares can be traded publicly through a broker if the appropriate U.S. Securities and Exchange Commission regulations are followed. The basic rule is that the shares to be sold must be registered with the SEC unless an exemption from registration applies.

Registration of Shares

Companies and shareholders with stock to sell publicly can register their shares with the SEC. A company's first public stock issuance is called an initial public offering (IPO). Subsequent registrations are called "follow-ons" or, sometimes, "secondary" offerings.

Shareholders whose shares were not registered when they acquired them can complete a registration—known as a "resale registration." They undertake to register the shares when they need liquidity and the ability to sell the shares publicly and cannot wait long enough for an exemption to apply (for example, one exemption, under Rule 144, allows public sale without registration after shares have been held for either one year or two years, depending on certain circumstances, and another exemption permits public resale without registration if shares were issued pursuant to a bankruptcy reorganization).

In most PIPE transactions, investors acquire unregistered shares (which bear a legend prohibiting transfer except upon registration or an available exemption from registration), with the understanding that the issuing company will effect a resale registration on the investor's behalf, generally within ninety days. This is usually preferable to a secondary offering because it can happen more quickly with fewer regulatory hurdles. The resale registration generally is not reviewed by the National Association of Securities Dealers (NASD) and has much less stringent state securities, or blue sky, review than an IPO. Of course, in exchange the company generally raises money in the PIPE at a discount to the stock's trading price, since the investor takes a short-term liquidity risk.

Registration takes time. Someone must write the public offering prospectus or offering document, which is included as part of the registration statement filed with the SEC, making sure to include the information the SEC requires. The prospectus includes at least two years of audited financial statements, a year-to-year comparison of results, executive compensation, business description, review of litigation, risk factors, a full capitalization chart, a detailed discussion of dilution, related party transactions, and a whole host of exhibits including material contracts, corporate charter, and bylaws. Other elements of the registration statement include a summary of prior securities offerings and certain undertakings the company must make to the SEC to complete the registration.

This registration statement (including the prospectus) is filed and then reviewed by the SEC's staff of examiners in their Division of Corporation Finance. The SEC must respond to the filing of an original or amended registration statement within thirty days. The SEC examiners may request more time (like everyone else they occasionally get backed up with work). One should always accede to this request. It is not unusual to go through three or four iterations of the filing before it is approved, upon which the SEC declares it "effective" and then it can be used to sell shares publicly.

In an IPO registration, a prospectus must go to the buyer the first time each newly registered share is sold; however, SEC rules stipulate that shares sold in *resale* registrations do not have to be accompanied by a prospectus as long as one is publicly available. The registration must be kept "current" until all shares registered under that registration statement are sold by the selling shareholders. This may require quarterly and other updating but is usually easy to do.

The SEC review process can vary greatly from deal to deal. Much depends on the particular examiner or group within the SEC's Division of Corporation Finance. What one group identifies as a major problem can pass through another group with no comment.

Exemptions from Registration: Rule 144

As mentioned above, stock must be registered with the SEC before it can be sold publicly, unless an exemption applies. A number of exemptions are available, depending on the circumstances and facts of a particular situation.

For example, certain issuances in connection with a bankruptcy reorganization are exempt from registration, and shares issued can be immediately resold if there is an existing trading market for them.

In fact, some reverse merger practitioners are creating shells through these issuances in bankruptcy. The small but ardent group doing this, led by Tim Halter of Halter Financial Group, has honed a series of valid techniques to create clean shells by taking usually dormant businesses through bankruptcy and issuing shares to creditors, creating hundreds of shareholders and a very clean shell with shares that can trade immediately following a reverse merger. The main challenge, it seems, is finding the dormant companies that are right for this bankruptcy option. In addition, although these shells have the benefit of a large group of shareholders and free-trading shares, they are not reporting companies. Therefore, a company merging in must complete a registration on Form 10-SB or similar form after a merger before the shell can become a full reporting company. This delays a listing on the OTC Bulletin Board or higher exchange until the public entity is a full reporting company.

The most popular exemption from registration is Rule 144. As discussed in Chapter 4, Introduction to Rule 419, shares can become freely tradable without registration as long as they are held for a certain period of time. In general, a shareholder must hold unregistered shares for one year. After that, the holder, if not an affiliate, can sell up to 1 percent of the company's outstanding stock (or average weekly trading volume, whichever is higher) during each ninety-day period during the second year of holding. After shares have been held for two years, they are freely tradable without these volume restrictions.

If the holder is an affiliate of the company, meaning an officer, director, or other control person (this is generally presumed if one owns over 20 percent or has the ability to effect policy change in the company), no shares become freely tradable for one year. After the one-year period, the volume restrictions described above (1 percent every ninety days) apply not just for an additional year, but for as long as the holder remains an affiliate, and for ninety days thereafter. If shares are purchased from an affiliate, a new holding period begins as if the affiliate never started his own holding period. Thus, an affiliate cannot allow a purchaser to "tack" his holding period.

Another Rule 144 wrinkle relates to derivative securities such as warrants or options. If one receives an option on a certain date and holds it for a year, then exercises the option for the cash purchase price, a new holding period begins after that cash purchase. But an exception in the rule allows what's known as "tacking" of the holding period from the day the option or warrant was issued if the option or warrant is simply traded for common stock. In other words, in so-called cashless exercise transactions, the holding period relates back to when the original derivative was received.

Cashless transactions work as follows. Say a warrant to purchase 100 shares of stock has a $3 per share exercise price and is issued on January 2, 2006, when the stock is trading at $2. This warrant is known as being "out of the money" because the warrant exercise price is above the current market price. A year later, on January 2, 2007, the stock moves up to $6 a share, making the warrant "in the money," since the holder can exercise the warrant for $3 when the stock is at $6.

A holder can exercise the warrant for cash at $3 per share, upon which a new holding period begins, and he must wait at least another year under Rule 144 to sell the shares. Alternatively, if permitted by the terms of the security, the holder can exercise a warrant for fifty shares by turning in the warrants for the other fifty, in other words, by returning fifty warrants which now have a net value of $3 per share after the purchase price, which becomes the purchase price for the other fifty.

The negative side of the cashless event is that the holder must give up a portion of his holdings. The positive side, besides avoiding the use of cash, is tacking the holding period and the immediate ability to sell the underlying shares under Rule 144. In general, PIPE investors receive cashless exercise warrants as part of their investment. They prefer this cashless exercise feature to protect themselves from the risk that the company will not succeed in completing the registration of their primary stock holdings purchased from the company (after a registration Rule 144 would not be needed), and at least they know that one year after closing the PIPE transaction they will be able to sell some of their warrants as long as they are in the money and there is a liquid market.

This same analysis applies to preferred stock or convertible debt. In both cases, the security usually can be exchanged for common stock on some basis, without payment of additional cash. Under Rule 144, because one security is exchanged for another, the holding period relates back to the date of acquisition of the preferred stock or convertible debt. Again, in PIPE transactions involving these securities, an investor utilizing this cashless feature has some protection if the resale registration is not completed.

Self-Filing Through Form SB-2 Resale Registration

Prior to 1992, SEC Regulation S-K set out the disclosure rules for all public companies. Some smaller companies complained that the requirements were too onerous. At the same time, politicians pressured the SEC to make it easier for small businesses to access the capital markets. (This was during the administrations of U.S. Presidents Ronald Reagan and George H. W. Bush.) Thus, as part of a package of reforms, a new set of disclosure rules called "Regulation S-B" (for small business), were passed.

As part of this reform, smaller businesses received their own set of SEC forms, almost all of which end in the suffix *SB*. So an annual report, normally made on Form 10-K for larger companies, is Form 10-KSB under Regulation S-B. The quarterly report on Form 10-Q becomes Form 10-QSB. The basic registration form for shares is S-1 under the S-K large company rules and SB-2 under the S-B smaller company rules.

The major difference between S-B and S-K is that an S-B filer only has to provide two years of audited financial statements, whereas an S-K filer has to provide three years. There are some other differences, but they're considered minor within the context of the discussion herein.

Under the SEC rules, a company fits the S-B system if it has revenues of less than $25 million, is a U.S. or Canadian issuer, is not an investment company or asset-backed issuer, and its parent (if a subsidiary) is also a small business issuer. Also, if the company has a public float (held by nonaffiliates) of $25 million or more, it would not fit into the small-business filing system.

With some exceptions, most companies pursuing reverse mergers or self-filings fit the definition above for a small business. So if they are completing a self-filing through a resale registration, it will be on Form SB-2.

Using the Form SB-2 resale registration method of self-filing, a privately held operating business "goes public" by effecting a resale registration of shares that have been distributed but, under Rule 144, cannot yet be sold. Assuming the company qualifies under the SEC's small-business disclosure system, it will file Form SB-2, which includes two years of audited financial statements.

The SEC Advisory Committee on Smaller Public Companies has proposed expanding the availability of the S-B system to larger companies, but combining it with the preexisting S-K system and simply providing for relief under that system for certain filers.

Private Offerings During Registration

One of the basic no-no's of a primary offering or resale registration is that, with narrow exceptions, one cannot pursue a private offering of company securities when a registration is pending with the SEC. In a famous no-action letter, the SEC ruled that the only private placement one can pursue during a registration is an offering to qualified institutional buyers or QIBs, as defined in SEC Rule 144A.

Technically, this no-action letter, known as "Black Box," only applies to company registrations. It does not address resale registrations; however, over the last year the SEC staff has been applying the Black Box analysis to pending resale registrations anyway. This means that one may not pursue a private placement other than to QIBs while either a company or a resale registration is pending; those who do will incur SEC ire.

QIBs are entities that, acting for their own account or others, own or invest on a discretionary basis at least $100 million in securities of issuers not affiliated with the company selling securities to the QIB. So basically, if an entity does not regularly invest over $100 million, it is not a QIB. Also, securities dealers who own and invest at least $10 million in securities not affiliated with the company are QIBs. Securities dealers are presumed to be more sophisticated than others who may invest larger amounts and, therefore, are permitted the lower threshold. Individuals cannot be QIBs.

Therefore, many usual sources of financing—angels, venture firms, and accredited investors—are unavailable while a registration statement is pending. This blackout period while pursuing a self-filing can last between five and eight months—sometimes longer. Occasionally, depending on circumstances, the SEC will allow an exception.

This rule, prohibiting most private placements during a pending offering or resale registration, exists to make sure that one of the provisions of Regulation D is not violated. The provision says that when a company wishes to complete a private placement, it may not engage in a "general solicitation" of investors. The offering documents filed pursuant to the registration are publicly available during the SEC review process. The SEC's position is that this very public availability of information in connection with an offering (even if a different offering from the proposed private placement), whether filed by shareholders seeking a resale or a company seeking an initial registration, constitutes a general solicitation of a non-QIB private placement. As a result, the two offerings are "integrated" or joined together. The determination that the two offerings are integrated results in the company's failure to meet the requirements for a valid private placement and would cause the company to be required to register the securities offered in the private placement as well.

The SEC will make other exceptions, however, besides offerings to QIBs. In one case we worked on, the staff allowed a small private placement to a principal of a brokerage firm while the company in question was in registration for an IPO. The reasons this was permitted included the fact that the investor, though not a QIB, was an experienced Wall Street veteran; the security he was purchasing (debt with warrants) was very different from the IPO security, thereby increasing the argument that the IPO prospectus does not constitute general solicitation for the private placement; and the fact that the offering of $500,000 was relatively small compared to the much larger IPO.

Companies that pursue an SB-2 resale strategy must ensure that either (a) they obtain any financing they need for the duration prior to the filing of the SB-2, (b) they have connections to obtain financing from QIBs or some other possible exemption under which they can obtain financing, or (c) they do not need financing until the SB-2 is effective.

PRACTICE TIP

If financing is necessary while a registration is pending, consider going public through Form 10-SB, which is discussed in detail in the following chapter. Most practitioners believe that the restriction on private placements during registration does not apply to a Form 10-SB filing, since no public offering is taking place to be integrated with the private offering.

One major benefit of the SB-2, however, is that if the company has many shareholders whose shares would not become publicly tradable under Rule 144 if it goes public through Form 10-SB (which does not register individual shares and relies on enough shareholders being able to sell under Rule 144 without registration), the SB-2 effects the removal of all trading restrictions on the shares being registered.

PRACTICE TIP

If many holders have held stock for less than a year or are considered affiliates of the company, don't run too fast from an SB-2. Or, consider my strategy below of a Form 10-SB with contemporaneous financing, followed immediately by an SB-2 resale registration.

Mechanics of Form SB-2 Self-Filing

The beauty of the SEC's integrated disclosure system is that almost regardless of the type of filing being undertaken, much of the same information needs to be prepared, just in a different context. The basic process of completing an SB-2 resale registration involves first, engaging the necessary professionals to assist; second, identifying the shareholders whose shares will be registered; third, preparing and filing the document; fourth, dealing with SEC (and possibly NASD) comments and revisions; and fifth, establishing a trading market. A detailed examination of each follows.

Engaging Professionals

A cadre of professional assistants is necessary for the timely completion of an SB-2 filing. Necessary experts include auditors, legal counsel, a transfer agent, and so on. As stated earlier, it is a good idea to engage an investment bank or other Wall Street veteran to assist in selecting these professionals. Indeed, the professionals may advise that an SB-2 is not the most advantageous route for a particular company. It is helpful if the various members of the advisory team have worked together on other matters, but it is far from essential. Any experienced professional knows how to develop a working relationship with new people. The most important thing they should have in common, besides skill and experience, is an attitude of determination to make the project a high priority in their shop.

Identifying Shareholders

The next decision, given that this is a resale registration, is determining which shareholders will have their shares registered. The first question to ask is which of the company's shareholders may already have the ability to sell his or her shares publicly under Rule 144. (Remember, technically a resale registration is made on behalf of the "selling shareholders," not on behalf of the company.) Some shareholders—not affiliates of the company—will have owned their shares for two years. Under Rule 144 these shares may be traded without prior registration.

Equally, the company or its investors may wish to restrict which shareholders will have the right to have their shares registered. For example, a key member of management who may have held shares for a short time may wish to have his shares registered, but investors may feel it is not desirable for a member of management to have the ability to cash out of his company ownership.

At this time, an analysis of the timing of financing makes sense. If the company is considering a PIPE or other financing before it goes public, that would have to be completed either prior to filing the SB-2 or after the SB-2 has gone into effect. (See above for the reasons for this.) If the financing is completed before the filing, then the investors' shares can be included in the SB-2 registration and will be tradable as soon as the registration becomes effective. Those who invest early, however, take a risk that the SB-2 or other going public event will never occur and they will be left with illiquid securities.

In fact, in a number of recent transactions handled by our office, PIPE investors have been willing to invest in a private company, as long as its very next step is to go public through an SB-2 resale registration that registers their shares and allows them to trade upon effectiveness. This is a departure for PIPE investors, who previously had only been willing to invest in private companies as part of a reverse merger.

In many cases, though, companies and their investors wait until after the company is public to conduct a financing. By waiting to complete the PIPE until after the company is public, the investor assumes less risk but must then wait for an additional registration to be filed to include their shares after going public (or await an applicable exemption). Nevertheless, if the SB-2 registration takes the company public and shortly thereafter a PIPE is closed, and then an additional SB-2 is filed almost immediately to register the PIPE investor's shares, this second SB-2 filing is likely to get a much quicker review by the SEC.

The flip side of limiting who gets to register has to do with the float. The larger the number of both shares and shareholders available to resell in the public market, the stronger the potential that a robust and liquid trading market will develop, thereby creating a reasonable float in the outstanding shares of the company. Unlike an IPO, where lockups are common to restrict insiders from unloading their shares, in alternatives to IPOs such as a self-filing, the only people who can create the float are those very insiders. Some companies limit how many shares key insiders may sell over certain periods of time (through what is known as a "lockup" or "leakout" arrangement), but still allow the shares to be registered. This is generally a more logical approach than excluding people from the registration.

Preparing and Filing the Document

The preparation of the contents of the document is similar to the preparation of the new super Form 8-K, which is required after a reverse merger with a shell company. Usually, the attorneys, with help from management, take the lead in putting the document together. The basis of the filing is a well-written business plan prepared by management that is transformed into a prospectus. Before writing the registration statement, my associates and I typically spend most of a full day with management, understanding their business, its opportunities and challenges. Then we research similar companies and develop risk factors (a key section of the prospectus that outlines specific risks to the company and its business) from that and from information we receive from management.

The auditors must complete their two-year audit, as well as assist management in preparing a section of the document known as "management's discussion and analysis." In this section, they must describe, line item by line item, what changed from year to year and quarter to quarter (if in the middle of a year), and why it changed. They also must review the company's liquidity situation as well as its capital resources. The auditors also fully review the SB-2 filing and must sign off on all its contents before providing their consent for the audit to be included in the document.

Once the filing is ready, it is sent for what is now known in the trade as "edgarization" under the SEC's Electronic Data Gathering, Analysis, and Retrieval system (EDGAR). EDGAR is the electronic filing system fully implemented by the SEC in 1996. EDGAR allows review of any SEC filing by anyone with an Internet connection and access to the SEC's website at www.sec.gov.

EDGAR was set up pursuant to a complex SEC rule known as "Regulation S-T." Specialized firms, including most financial printers, will convert a document for SEC filing. They will then return it for proofreading and final approval. Since the filing is electronic, yet includes a signature line, the filing must include a "conformed" company executive's signature (in other words his or her name is simply typed in above the signature line) and the actual original signature must be kept in the company's records. At one time, some larger law firms were offering an edgarizing service to their clients, but most abandoned it as either unprofitable or inefficient.

PRACTICE TIP

Leave extra time to obtain EDGAR codes—the IDs and passwords needed to file with EDGAR. A filing service typically can obtain them, but it can take one to two days, and occasionally more, for the EDGAR filing support people at the SEC to issue the codes.

Once all the approvals are obtained, a company authorizes the EDGAR service to push the button and file. The filing date is the same as the day the files were sent, as long as this was before 5:30 p.m. Eastern time. The filing date can be important, as the financial information in the filing must be current. If the financials go "stale," it may be necessary to input updated information and then file.

SEC (and NASD) Comments and Revisions

After filing comes waiting. Sometimes the response arrives in fewer than thirty days, but not usually. The company typically receives a formal comment letter from the SEC examiner who reviewed the filing. This letter states who at the SEC is in charge of the filing and gives the company and its registration an SEC file number. If the filing includes selling shareholders who are affiliated with brokerage firms, the NASD may need to review the document as well, to determine if any interest held by those individuals or entities violates their limits on underwriting compensation. The NASD's review has no specific time frame and can take quite a bit of time.

Most professionals rank SEC comment letters by the number of comments received. "We only got forty comments" is not an unusual happy response on a first filing. I think, though, that quality of comments is more important than quantity. I once received seventy-two comments on an initial filing, and felt very unhappy. But as I went through the comments, it was clear that very few of them were substantive, the great majority cosmetic or minor. That, to me, is better than receiving forty difficult comments to address.

An SB-2 allows a reasonable and flexible amount of response time (unlike a Form 10-SB filing which, as will be discussed in the next chapter, comes with a ticking sixty-day clock); however, a response to the SEC is mandatory. If no response is received, the SEC will eventually decide that the registration has been withdrawn and abandoned (although it will usually warn you before doing this).

The SEC reviews an SB-2 filing thoroughly because it involves a public offering by the selling shareholders, whereas Form 10-SB simply requests that the company voluntarily subject itself to the SEC reporting requirements. Therefore, an SB-2 filing can take longer than a Form 10-SB filing.

Comments tend to be divided between financial and nonfinancial and, therefore, must be reviewed with auditors as well as company officials. The team then responds to the comments. In some cases, agreeing with a comment is no problem (such as when they suggest that a risk factor is too "generic" and must be removed). In some cases, agreeing with a comment is a project (such as changes to the financial statements or altering a business description). In some cases, the company simply disagrees with a comment and wishes to express its view (occasionally the examiner misunderstands a disclosure of some kind or the SEC is requesting disclosure that is not required and which the company prefers not to make).

At this point, a decision is made whether to simply file an amendment with such changes as the company wishes to make, along with a letter responding point by point to the SEC's comments (even if the response is "see our change on page x"), or to contact the examiner with regard to any larger issues. Comments for which the company and its advisers believe its response may cause a problem with the examiner might be better discussed before filing an amendment. Professionals help companies make these judgments based on their experience.

Ultimately, an amendment is filed, along with responses to the comments, and then the SEC takes another round to review and provide another comment letter, ideally with fewer comments than the previous letter. This continues, essentially, until they are out of comments. The number of rounds of filings this takes is a function of the company's willingness to play ball with every SEC comment, the capability of the SEC examiner, and, frankly, the SEC's apparent comfort level with the filing or transaction in question.

If the SEC staff is concerned about players involved in a transaction, they can delay and add more comments, not officially stopping the process but certainly slowing it down. Heel-dragging may not be official policy, or officially condoned, but any fair-minded practitioner would admit it does occur from time to time.

Once the SEC has completed its comments, it declares the registration statement "effective" and it can be used to resell the securities that were registered through that process. Typically, effectiveness is accelerated by a formal request asking for a certain effective date.

The NASD can be more difficult, and some filings can't go ahead without their approval. And in general, there is simply no way to predict how long it will take. Comments in the third round of communications can be brand new and of the type that should have been raised in the first round. It can take forty-five or sixty days to get one round of comments.

PRACTICE TIP

Wherever possible, try to avoid NASD review. (The Form 10-SB filings do not involve NASD review, but the SB-2 might, if a broker-dealer or affiliate is registering its own shares for resale.)

Establishing a Trading Market

Once the SB-2 is effective, the company is public. No IPO. No reverse merger with a shell. Financing has been obtained either before or right after the filing becomes effective. There are now enough shares in the public float to qualify for, say, the OTC Bulletin Board, which unofficially requires at least thirty-five to forty nonaffiliate shareholders with at least one hundred tradable shares (Note: This requirement is not on any official list of rules, but as a practical matter the regulators will bury your application to trade if you do not meet this criterion.)

All that's missing is a listing on an exchange or market, without which the shares may not be traded through brokers. On the Pink Sheets and OTC Bulletin Board, the company cannot apply for a listing; the market maker must do so. On the Nasdaq, American Stock Exchange, and New York Stock Exchange companies apply for listing, not market makers.

Most companies going through a self-filing do not yet qualify for the higher exchanges, so market makers will be needed to get trading going. I generally recommend that a company encourage market makers to start the application process while the SB-2 or other filing is pending so as not to waste time. The process of getting approved can take a few months, so the sooner the process starts the better.

In general, the OTC Bulletin Board will begin reviewing an application for a company that is not yet public, as long as the company has initiated the process. Running these two processes in parallel gives the best chance the company will have a listing by the time the SEC clears the registration statement so that the shares can begin trading.

Wrap-Up on SB-2

For a company that sees a self-filing as appropriate, an SB-2 resale registration generally is a quicker and cleaner way to go than a Form 10-SB—unless the company needs financing while waiting for the filing to take effect. In that case, consider the approach described in the next chapter.

In general, investors willing to finance a company prior to the filing will prefer an SB-2 as the quickest way for their shares to become tradable, and as long as they provide all the money needed to get through the filing process, it is typically preferable over the Form 10-SB approach.

CHAPTER 13

Form 10-SB

M uch of the self-filing process discussed in the last chapter applies to those who use Form 10-SB. (This includes engaging competent professionals to assist in the process and preparing the actual filing.) This chapter describes the situations in which a Form 10-SB may be preferable to a Form SB-2, the form itself, and how it differs from a Form SB-2. We'll also look at the process of a Form 10-SB filing and effectiveness, and finally, how to develop a trading market for securities.

To avoid confusion, I wish to distinguish between the subject of this chapter, where a private operating business uses Form 10-SB as its method of going public, and the use of Form 10-SB, as described in Chapter 15, as a method to create and take public a shell company that seeks to merge with a private operating business.

Self-Filing Through Form 10-SB Registration

When is it preferable to use Form 10-SB instead of Form SB-2 for a private operating business to go public? Since a Form 10-SB filing does not contemplate an offering, a company can use it and at the same time raise money privately from sources other than QIBs. (Remember: companies waiting for a Form SB-2 filing to become effective can only raise money from qualified institutional buyers.) In addition, if the company has a number of shareholders who have held securities long enough to be able to sell publicly under Rule 144, filing an SB-2 resale registration may not even be necessary. If a PIPE (private investment in public equity) investor wishes to have securities registered, an SB-2 can be filed after the 10-SB.

Form 10-SB Versus Form SB-2
(Exchange Act Versus Securities Act)

Form 10-SB is remarkably similar to the SB-2, except it does not describe a securities offering. The company description and other sections are basically the same as on an SB-2 or any public offering document. (Again, the integrated disclosure rules mean disclosure is often the same, even though the purpose is different.)

SB-2 is a form created under the Securities Act of 1933, and 10-SB is a form under the Securities Exchange Act of 1934. As a refresher, following the great stock market crash of 1929, Congress sought to regulate the ailing securities markets. The '33 Act, as it is often called, or the Securities Act, as we will call it here, established guidelines for companies conducting public offerings, requiring them to register any such offering with the U.S. Securities and Exchange Commission.

The '34 Act, frequently referred to as the Exchange Act, set up the integrated disclosure system and series of periodic and current reports required by reporting companies, the regulation of securities brokers, the proxy rules, and the causes of action for violations, and insider trading and reporting mechanisms. If a company is subject to the reporting requirements of the Exchange Act, it may be able to list its securities on the OTC Bulletin Board, Nasdaq, American Stock Exchange, or New York Stock Exchange. Nonreporting companies' stock may only trade on the Pink Sheets.

When a company goes public through a public offering by it or its shareholders (for example, on Form SB-2), it is automatically subject to the reporting requirements through the end of its first fiscal year after the offering (this is pursuant to Section 15 of the Exchange Act). After that, continuing to be a reporting company is by choice (pursuant to Section 12 of the Exchange Act). Some companies simply cease reporting after this one year, and their stock trades on the Pink Sheets.

Most companies completing a public offering immediately become reporting companies through a very simple filing known as Form 8-A. If this is filed within the first full fiscal year after the offering, a company automatically becomes permanently subject to the reporting requirements.

After this time, or if a company has not yet conducted a public offering, if it wishes to become a reporting company, it files a more complex form known as Form 10-SB (or Form 10 if it is not under the Regulation S-B reporting system). As mentioned above, this form is very similar to Form SB-2 and other registrations involving securities offerings; however, this form, like Form 8-A, is filed simply for the company to have a class of its securities (typically its common stock) registered with the SEC, rather than individual shares. No offering is involved and no shares become tradable by virtue of this filing (unless an exemption from registration applies like Rule 144).

There is a little known SEC staff telephone interpretation from 1997 that essentially says, if after one fiscal year of filings under Section 15 a company voluntarily keeps up all periodic quarterly and annual filings, and all the information that would be in a Form 10-SB is in those filings, even though the time may have expired to use simple Form 8-A, a company is permitted to use it anyway.

Some shell operators purposely use this approach, keeping their filings up, trading on the Pink Sheets, then pursuing a reverse merger and filing Form 8-A right before the deal is signed. The reason for this is, while periodic reports are made, the company is not subject to any other Exchange Act requirements such as insider reporting and proxy rules while waiting to enter into a merger. I know from SEC insiders that they are not thrilled with these "voluntary filers," in part because of the lack of other information the public generally likes to see.

Form 10-SB is typically used in two situations. One is when a company has conducted a public offering, its stock is trading, and it is beyond its Section 15 mandatory filing period. Now it seeks to become a reporting company either to complete a merger or move up to a higher exchange, and it has not kept up all its filings, or those filings do not include all information that would be in a Form 10-SB, and thus cannot use Form 8-A.

In the other case, a company "goes public" through a Form 10-SB filing. This is how the form can be used within the context of a self-filing. A private company wants to voluntarily subject itself to the SEC's reporting requirements. But if no shares are individually registered, how can trading commence? This can be done in one of two ways. Either enough shareholders have held their shares long enough under Rule 144 to allow them to become tradable once the company is reporting and has a ticker symbol, or the company intends to file an SB-2 resale registration to release some shares from restriction immediately following the 10-SB filing being completed and effective.

The question then becomes: Why file an SB-2 after a 10-SB rather than just go public through an SB-2? The answer, as mentioned above, is timing of financing. If a company needs to complete private placements and raise money while waiting to become public, it can do so while a 10-SB is pending but not while an SB-2 is pending, other than to QIBs.

If it seems a little tedious to deal with two different filings, consider that the second filing, taking place right after the first, is likely to get much less SEC scrutiny (assuming they have carefully reviewed the Form 10-SB before its effectiveness, which is likely). And this way, a company is able to finance itself while waiting to go public, can close a PIPE when the 10-SB is effective, and then file the SB-2 resale registration with its money already in the bank.

Filing Form 10-SB and Automatic Effectiveness

The process of preparing and getting the Form 10-SB filed is basically the same as with an SB-2. The difference comes into play after the filing is made. Under SEC rules, Form 10-SB is *automatically effective* sixty days after it is filed. In other words, if the SEC chooses not to comment, the form is effective and the company is thereupon public and subject to the Exchange Act reporting requirements. If the SEC does comment, the form still becomes effective sixty days after its original filing date provided the amendments have been filed and all comments have been cleared before sixty days pass. Miss this deadline and the SEC will either allow the form to go effective and treat future responses to the comments as a so-called post-effective amendment or insist that the form be withdrawn and re-filed, starting another sixty-day period. Which way they go does not seem always to be predictable, but there appears to be a trend in allowing these to go effective with amendments filed after the form is effective.

At times as it nears the end of the comments, the SEC will announce that it does not intend to review the final amendment. In this case, the filing becomes effective on day sixty.

None of this guarantees that the comment/revision process will be completed in sixty days. Yet, the process is still generally less laborious than with an SB-2, since the SEC tends to review securities offerings more closely.

Developing a Market After Filing a Form 10-SB

As mentioned above, the process of obtaining a ticker symbol and getting trading started is a little more complex with a Form 10-SB approach. Hopefully, the company has at least thirty-five to forty nonaffiliated shareholders with more than one hundred shares that have been held a sufficient time to be tradable under Rule 144. If so, trading on the OTC Bulletin Board could commence immediately upon the form being declared effective. If not, an SB-2 needs to be filed and brought to effectiveness before trading on the OTC Bulletin Board can begin. In the meantime, if there are some shareholders with tradable shares, a ticker can be obtained and trading can commence on the Pink Sheets.

Brief Overview of Other Methods
to Become Public

The securities laws permit a number of other methods for going public. Currently, however, none of these is in wide use, and a number of states prohibit some of the techniques discussed below. Although the reverse merger technique has, for the most part, overcome the bad rap it acquired during the 1980s, some of these other techniques have been unable to shake their shaky reputations.

That said, going public through Regulation A, Rule 504, an intrastate offering, or through Regulation S is technically legal. As discussed below, however, Regulation A is rarely used, Rule 504 is prohibited in most states, it is very difficult to properly use an intrastate exemption, and the wild days of Regulation S have been tamed by regulatory reform. Nevertheless, a full account of these techniques is provided in order to understand the context in which they exist along with reverse mergers, specified purpose acquisition companies (SPACs), and self-filings.

Regulation A

Regulation A, also referred to as simply Reg A, was passed to help small companies raise money. In general, it permits an offering of up to $5 million in any twelve-month period to an unlimited number of investors, whether or not accredited. An offering circular is prepared and approved by the SEC, but the form is a bit more streamlined than a full registration statement and does not require audited financial statements. It includes a method to test the waters with potential investors, even using general solicitation, before going through a filing with the SEC. Shareholders also can use Regulation A to sell up to $1.5 million in securities. Blank check companies are not permitted to use Regulation A.

The process does not permit a company to become a full reporting company without a complete Form 10-SB and audited financials, but it does permit a safe harbor for an offering which otherwise might not be public, and permits trading of the stock issued in the Regulation A offering.

Some have used Regulation A to take themselves public and begin to trade on the Pink Sheets as a nonreporting company. In part because of the reduced disclosure both at the time of the going public event and afterward, Regulation A has been used by some unscrupulous players to use these public entities to manipulate trading and give the public virtually no information about the company.

Most securities lawyers cannot remember the last time someone they know has used Regulation A, but it is out there as an option. Although I don't have specific experience, I assume the individual states where such offerings are taking place are not too thrilled with Regulation A either, and that may be one of the reasons for its limited popularity—the inability to "clear" blue sky review to let an offering be completed.

I have heard from SEC insiders that a potential overhaul of Regulation A is in the works, and an increase in the amount allowed to be raised may be coming. It is not clear at this point whether that will entice investment banks and others to come back to Regulation A (if they were ever there in the first place).

Intrastate Exemption

The SEC and federal agencies are only able, generally speaking, to regulate interstate commerce. This means that a transaction occurring wholly in only one state may be outside their jurisdiction. In fact, the securities laws contain an express exemption from registration for an offering that takes place wholly within one state.

Some have gone to states where regulation of securities is light (these are becoming fewer and fewer) and completed offerings solely within that state to avoid the necessity of SEC registration. The company also must be physically located and incorporated in that state. The key is being in a state whose regulation would somehow allow for an easier time than SEC registration.

Most states provide that an offering which would otherwise be public for SEC purposes requires the preparation and approval by state regulators of a full disclosure document. It is also not clear whether shares are restricted after being offered in an intrastate transaction. If they are restricted, although the offering itself is exempt, the shares still must be held for the requisite Rule 144 period before trading can commence.

These offerings are hard to pull off and have not been widely used to my knowledge.

Rule 504

An SEC exemption from registration under Rule 504 of Regulation D can be a dangerous transaction to get involved with. Here's how it works: Rule 504 allows an exemption from registration if an offering is below $1 million in total. Thus, these smaller offerings were somehow deemed to not need stringent regulation. This had the effect of allowing the tiniest companies to raise money and go public without significant transactional cost.

Other Regulation D offerings require significant disclosure to any nonaccredited investor and limit the number of nonaccredited investors participating in a deal to thirty-five. In a Rule 504 transaction, an offering can be completed to any number of accredited and nonaccredited investors, all without any specific information delivery requirements.

Thus, one thousand nonaccredited investors could each invest $1,000 under Rule 504 and all the company needs to provide is a simple subscription agreement and no other disclosure. SEC Rule 10b-5 prohibits misleading someone in connection with a securities offering, but it assumes intentional fraud. Mere failure to provide information, unless shown to be done with the intent to hide something, is not necessarily actionable by an unhappy investor.

The clincher is, unlike other Regulation D offerings, the stock issued in a Rule 504 transaction is immediately tradable if a ticker exists and the stock may be traded, typically on the Pink Sheets. Thus, companies will complete a small offering, obtain a ticker, and proceed to have a trading stock without ever providing full disclosure, becoming a reporting company or, frankly, ever intending to become a reporting company.

The obvious advantages to company management and the deal promoters is the ability to begin to cash out of their stock (assuming the availability of Rule 144 for other shares issued in the company outside the Rule 504 offering), all without providing any sort of public filing or public information.

During the 1980s and 1990s in particular, Rule 504 caught on as a way to take companies public, especially after the passage of Rule 419 in 1992 restricting the initial public offerings of blank check companies. Unfortunately, many players in this field were unsavory types looking to engage in improper, illegal, and fraudulent activity, and many SEC investigations and actions resulted from Rule 504 offerings gone bad.

Rule 504 is still on the books, but as a practical matter its use has been all but eliminated. In many cases, the SEC responds when shady operators gather in one particular part of the financial world. In this case, it was the state regulators overseeing securities matters who one by one essentially said, "Don't try to do a Rule 504 offering in our state, we will not permit it." I believe only about eight states still allow 504 offerings. So as a result, only the hardiest promoters can move forward with this type of transaction. Unfortunately, as was the case with reverse mergers for a long time, most people associate Rule 504 offerings with players to be avoided, and I continue to count myself among them.

Where could Rule 504 have been practical in the legitimate capital market environment? In a private placement for $1 million for an already public company that is reporting, and where a full disclosure document is prepared and/or there is a desire to bring in more than thirty-five unaccredited investors. Then, tradable shares would immediately result in an already existing trading market, no one would question the information delivery process, and money could be raised. Unfortunately, again the baby was thrown out with the bath water when the states all but killed this exemption even though there were some valid potential uses. I have represented legitimate players trying to use Rule 504 in this manner, only to be shut down by the states. So, although once popular, this technique is effectively unavailable.

![PRACTICE TIP]

Avoid Rule 504 offerings unless one is very, very careful.

Regulation S

In 1990, the SEC passed the now infamous Regulation S, or Reg S. After several court cases, the SEC had to admit it had no jurisdiction over events outside the United States. Then it came up with a way to regulate foreign companies and offerings as long as some U.S. connection existed. Regulation S originally exempted from registration securities offerings by U.S. companies if the investment was completely or partially from foreigners or by a foreign company if raising money completely overseas when some directed selling efforts took place in the United States.

The clinchers were, first, that no information delivery or accredited investor status mattered, and second, that the original rule seemed to suggest that shares issued in a Regulation S exempt offering could be resold publicly without restriction within forty-one days of being issued. So one could offer to any number of offshore investors, whether or not accredited, without any information, all without requiring SEC registration by a U.S. company.

There were some who argued the SEC had no right to regulate this kind of offshore offering in any event, but since the regulation focused on U.S. companies, the SEC won the argument.

Resell after forty-one days? Doesn't Rule 144 require a one-year waiting period? And doesn't everyone else have to be registered if they want to sell before that? The SEC says they meant the shares could be sold publicly *outside the United States* in forty-one days. But the rule neglected to make that distinction. So savvy promoters, with extremely well-paid lawyers in tow, went forward doing these deals with solid legal opinions as to the shares' ability to be resold in the United States in forty-one days.

Very quickly, commentators began to do what they do, highlighting the obvious issues. About half of them said the SEC could not have meant resale in the United States, and the other half said that since there is no precedent, anyone is free to interpret the regulation in any reasonable way. Unfortunately, the SEC could not simply change or amend the rule quickly, since that type of change involves a lengthy rule-making process, not to mention the embarrassment of admitting what appears to have been a simple drafting error that created a cottage industry.

I'll give you the end of the story and then we'll go back to talk about how Regulation S involved the birth of PIPEs. In 1998, the SEC finally got its act together and, rather than admit the mistake, it simply amended the rule to say you can resell publicly after one year—in other words, the same basic time period as in Rule 144. This effectively mooted the question of whether or not it meant sale in the United States. That was pretty much the end of the use of Regulation S in the manner I am about to describe.

So what happened when Regulation S came along? Offshore hedge funds and investors had a field day. Company after company went public through a Regulation S offering where the offshore investors resold their shares in the United States after just forty-one days following what was basically a private offering permitted under Regulation S. Investors loved that they could invest privately, then have a public market almost immediately. Sound familiar? Yes, these deals were the predecessors to modern PIPEs, and indeed many PIPE players got their start doing Regulation S deals in the early and mid-1990s.

What was good and bad? Well, lawyers giving Regulation S opinions were very well paid. Why? Because it was clearly controversial to provide such opinions and it involved a little risk for the attorney. As for me, after talking to SEC experts on Regulation S and hearing them say privately, "Do not view our silence on this issue as acquiescence," I decided to not represent clients on Regulation S deals where I was being asked to provide a forty-one-day U.S. resale opinion. This did not mean that anyone who did represent these clients was bad; it was just a choice I made.

Some unscrupulous actors clearly took advantage. They made no disclosure, got foreign investors in, and then out in forty-one days. The company got its money, the original investor made a tidy profit, and shares traded after that based on essentially no information. Good guys made disclosure prior to the investment. Some became reporting companies voluntarily. Some took the conservative approach and only allowed resale outside the United States.

But for experienced hedge fund investors, Regulation S created a real opportunity to help growing companies and make a quick profit. They had no interest in being investors, just arbitrageurs. This same attitude pervaded the PIPE market in the late 1990s and early 2000s. Deals were structured to maximize the incentive for the investor to sell quickly after his shares were registered.

Since 2002, life is much different in the PIPEs world. Transaction structures have changed, the hedge fund investment community has grown more crowded, and PIPE investors truly are more like investors now, betting on the longer term upside potential of a company's stock.

This is the main reason why many PIPE investors have discovered reverse mergers, as a more risky opportunity to invest in a company's future but with much greater upside potential.

These days, about the only real benefit Regulation S has is for a foreign company to raise money from foreign investors, but possibly through a U.S. investment bank. The forty-one-day exemption still applies in that circumstance. But for some, it was quite a ride there for a while.

Which Way to Go?

As should be clear at this point, I favor reverse mergers, SPACs, and self-filings as the most regulator-friendly, efficient, and currently popular techniques for going public without an IPO. A reverse merger with a nontrading shell is probably more preferable in most circumstances than a merger with a trading shell. Self-filings provide a way to avoid the dilution from merging with a shell, and hopefully still raise money, but the process takes longer and developing a trading market may be more challenging. The self-filing process also requires a steady hand from a Wall Street veteran.

Although the guidance provided here should be useful to help determine the circumstances in which each of these transaction structures make sense, each company and financial adviser must look at the unique situation in which a company finds itself and analyze which approach is the most logical given all the facts specific to the individual company.

PART FOUR

Manufacturing Shells and Current Trends

CHAPTER 14

SPACs

As mentioned in previous chapters, there are two ways to create a shell. One is by using the public entity remaining after an operating publicly traded company either goes out of business or gets sold or liquidated. The other method is to create a shell from scratch, as many players have chosen to do, especially in the last few years.

The major reasons for the proliferation of newly formed shells are the high cost of purchasing trading shells from former operating businesses, combined with the difficulty of finding a clean shell even if cost were not an issue. By creating a shell, a deal promoter structures it according to his needs and ensures that it is clean. This part of the book focuses on creating shells and other current trends and is intended to supplement the discussion of Rule 419 shells in Chapter 4, Introduction to Rule 419.

A significant development in the shell creation business since 2000 has been the proliferation of both specified purpose acquisition companies (SPACs) and Form 10-SB shells (discussed in the next chapter), which together constitute by far the most popular current methods for creating shell companies.

Both techniques have been around since the 1990s. In the mid-1990s about a dozen SPACs were formed. They stopped being popular as the initial public offering market boomed later in the decade. SPACs returned with a vengeance in 2003 when the IPO market hit the doldrums and remained inaccessible to smaller companies. As of this writing in early 2006, over eighty SPACs have gone public or are in registration, with more planned.

The popularity of Form 10-SB shells increased in the late 1990s when the U.S. Securities and Exchange Commission stopped trying to halt the formation of these shells. In the last few years, more and more legitimate players and PIPE (private investment in public equity) investors have turned to Form 10-SB shells as both the SEC and Nasdaq (in its oversight of the OTC Bulletin Board) have suggested they have no problems with them.

One brief note on names and categorizations: Often, outsiders and industry professionals alike talk about SPACs and reverse mergers as if they are separate topics. In truth, a SPAC is a shell like any other, and it engages in a reverse merger like any other shell. It is simply a special type of shell. Therefore, SPACs should be considered part of the reverse merger landscape, not something separate from it.

Introduction to SPACs: The GKN Experience

David Nussbaum of boutique investment banking firm EarlyBirdCapital is essentially the founder of the SPAC movement.

In the mid-1990s, while heading up brokerage firm GKN Securities, Nussbaum saw an opportunity. The IPO market was suffering. The Internet boom had yet to occur. The nation was just coming out of a recession, but things were beginning to look up. President William J. Clinton was balancing the federal budget, the economy was starting to improve, and companies were growing to the point where being public could provide some benefit. Yet they had no way to get there through traditional means.

Nussbaum took advantage of an exemption from Rule 419. This exemption provides that any company with $5 million in assets, or that seeks to raise $5 million in a public offering (the SEC views this as requiring a "firm commitment" underwriting), need not comply with any of the restrictions of Rule 419. The thinking, apparently, was that 419 was meant to harness smaller players, and those who can raise $5 million are more likely to have other methods of protection for investors.

This exemption from Rule 419 means one can complete an IPO of a shell with $5 million much like during the pre-419 days. This means there is no money in escrow or restrictions on use of the money, no time limit to complete a deal, no shares in escrow (so there can be trading in the shell), no shareholder reconfirmation prior to closing a reverse merger, theoretically allowing for a quicker transaction.

But Nussbaum saw a different opportunity. He would conduct a firm commitment underwriting for a shell that his firm would complete of $5 million or even more (most of his SPACs in the 1990s raised between

$15 million and $20 million). But instead of being free of the Rule 419 restrictions, he voluntarily adopted a number of them, primarily to help attract investors to his shell vehicles.

So, even though the SEC did not require it, his SPACs (as he started calling them) put all the money raised in escrow, except a small percentage for operating expenses and commissions paid to the investment bankers. They required investor reconfirmation with a full disclosure document approved by the SEC. They put a time limit on finding a merger partner, but they allowed more time than Rule 419, up to two years instead of eighteen months to close a merger. But, most important, Nussbaum arranged for a trading market for the stock of the SPAC, as well as for warrants sold to investors in the IPO. This would not be permitted in a 419 shell that did not raise at least $5 million.

In addition, as a twist for marketing purposes, Nussbaum declared that each shell would specialize in an industry or geography—one for telecommunications, one for entertainment, and so on. Then he would attract a blue ribbon management team who would be in charge of finding the right deal for the SPAC. The management would be compensated primarily with a hefty chunk of stock, but their experience and eye for deals would be valuable, and in some cases each would invest their own money into the SPAC's IPO as well.

Investors snapped these up. Why not? They purchased a unit consisting of a share of stock and a warrant to purchase more stock later, or sometimes two warrants. Ninety percent of their money would not be touched and would earn interest while the SPAC searched for a merger target. If investors did not like the eventual deal that was proposed, about a year or two later, they would likely receive 92 percent to 95 percent of their original investment back.

Or, when a deal was announced, and the stock moved back up, in most cases they could simply sell their shares and make 100 percent of their money back, holding the warrants to see how the deal would ultimately go. Others would sell the warrants and hold the stock. Others might like the deal and simply let their money ride.

Although the investment was in a blank check, the money was protected and the investor had a legitimate means to opt out when the deal was presented. In other words, he offered many of the protections that 419 offered, but stock was permitted to trade in the SPAC.

In the meantime, Nussbaum and his firm earned commissions on the money raised. He also earned commissions on the trading of the stock while waiting for a merger.

Companies also liked the SPAC concept as a way to get public. In general, a company that otherwise might have considered a smaller IPO saw the SPAC as guaranteed cash, less risky than an IPO in which there is always a chance that the underwriter will not be able to raise the desired amount of money. Plus, some companies took advantage of the self-imposed expiration date on the SPAC and cut favorable merger deals in the waning days of the two-year time limit. All in all, the companies that merged with these initial SPACs generally fared well, and the technique worked.

Some companies preferred a SPAC to a more traditional reverse merger for several reasons. First, the SPAC has cash (although some traditional shells have cash, too). Second, the SPAC has a relatively active trading market, which most shells do not. Third, the SPAC is totally clean and not burdened, as are many trading shells, with a history from a prior operating business in the shell.

In the late 1990s, as the IPO market picked up, Nussbaum moved away from SPACs. Also, some state regulators were beginning to have problems with allowing the aftermarket trading of SPAC stocks. As mentioned, SPACs seem to move countercyclically to the IPO market for small- and mid-cap stocks. Thus, as the IPOs of Netscape and America Online helped usher in the gold rush now known as the Internet boom, GKN moved back to more traditional IPO work.

The SPAC Resurgence

In 2003, Nussbaum, now running EarlyBirdCapital, determined the time was right to bring back SPACs. I don't think he could have known what he was starting. Although he is still one of the most prolific players in the market, he has helped create a cottage industry. Many brokerage firms specializing in small- and mid-cap stocks either are planning a SPAC, have already completed one, or are actively participating in one. **FIGURES 14.1** and **14.2** illustrate the variety of investment banks, investors, and attorneys active in the recent SPAC movement.

Nussbaum's biggest challenge in the new millennium was convincing Nasdaq to allow the stock of the first new SPACs to trade on the OTC Bulletin Board. In the 1990s, shells routinely were granted the right to trade over the counter. In the early 2000s, however, an unofficial ban on allowing new shells onto the OTC Bulletin Board went into effect. We hear, however, that some shells (other than SPACs) recently have been permitted on, which is a positive development.

Although I do not know the details of Nussbaum's discussions with Nasdaq, my understanding is that it required quite a bit of high-level arm-twisting to convince Nasdaq that, primarily because of the large amount of money being raised and the high quality of management, the legitimacy

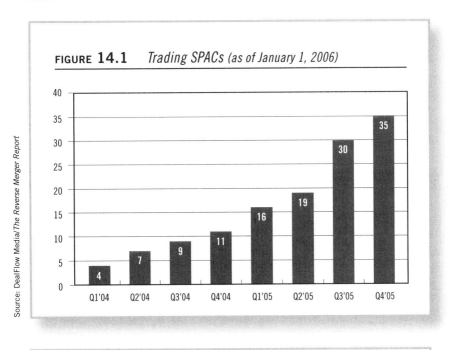

FIGURE 14.1 *Trading SPACs (as of January 1, 2006)*

Source: DealFlow Media/The Reverse Merger Report

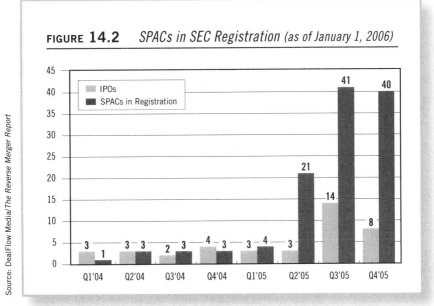

FIGURE 14.2 *SPACs in SEC Registration (as of January 1, 2006)*

Source: DealFlow Media/The Reverse Merger Report

of the SPAC and its anticipated trading market should be respected. To his credit, these discussions opened the door for all others to follow. More recently, a number of SPACs have been permitted to trade on the American Stock Exchange as well. This is significant because no state blue sky review of an IPO is required if a company is going to trade on the Amex (or Nasdaq or the New York Stock Exchange for that matter), since Congress preempted that regulation in legislation passed in 1996.

In Chapter 16, we will talk more about current trends in the SPAC market. Some things have changed in the SPAC market of today versus Nussbaum's one-man industry in the 1990s. First, SPACs are now raising significantly more money. Some now raise well over $100 million. Second, SPAC investors are becoming savvy and are forcing bankers to retool the commissions they receive for raising money. As a result, more underwriters of SPACs are now agreeing to back-end a portion of their commissions until a merger with the SPAC is actually consummated.

Third, as Figures 14.1 and 14.2 show, major players including Deutsche Bank, Merrill Lynch, and Citigroup have begun to get active in the SPAC market, bringing greater legitimacy and, perhaps, a greater sense that this technique will be useful over the long term. Fourth, SPAC management teams are beginning to look like business A-lists. People like Steve Wozniak, one of the founders of Apple Computer, have joined SPAC teams. Is it just a matter of time before Jack Welch runs a SPAC?

The SEC has made life a little difficult for the new so-called SPAC-meisters. The examiners of SPAC registration filings have tried different tactics to put roadblocks in the way of this technique. All registration reviews were temporarily halted in early 2005 when a SPAC by the name of International Shipping Enterprises announced a merger deal only a couple of months after having gone public. The SEC believed that this meant conversations must have taken place with the target company prior to being public. Since SPACs must confirm in their filings that they have had no discussions with possible merger candidates before going public, this raised red flags at the SEC. If the SPAC had had such a target picked out in advance of going public, then disclosure of the target, its business, risk factors and so on, might have been required.

In addition, the SEC recently tried to question the treatment of warrants which are purchasable by management, potentially creating another barrier to getting such deals public, although the rules for handling these warrants ultimately were resolved with an SEC no-action letter.

Nevertheless, the bankers and their attorneys generally have fought off attempts to stand in the way of SPACs, and the industry has survived the various regulatory setbacks. The recent involvement of larger banks, and the simple fact that the SPACs are legal and permitted under SEC rules, means that, in the end, the SEC must allow them to continue. Maybe, as they did with other types of reverse mergers leading up to their June 2005 rulemaking, the SEC will begin to accept that there are many legitimate players in SPACs who should be encouraged just as the elimination of any bad guys should be aggressively pursued.

Who wins in the SPAC deals of today? Underwriters, of course, who may see as much as 7 percent of the money raised wind up in their pockets, along with commissions from trading the stock of the SPAC. Service providers such as lawyers, auditors, EDGAR-filing preparers, and transfer agents, also benefit. The lawyers get a double hit—first a fee to bring the SPAC public (this involves two law firms, one for the underwriter and one for the SPAC itself), then another fee when the SPAC negotiates a merger and prepares a disclosure document that has to be approved by the SEC.

SPAC management teams benefit as well. They receive some stock for their efforts, but they also often put their own money into the SPAC in order to have some skin in the game, as Wall Streeters like to say.

Investors also can win in the SPACs. They have very little downside risk prior to a merger. Hedge funds and institutions appreciate this facet of the structure. Also, there is real potential upside, as the few SPACs in the current market that have completed deals have generally seen good post-deal stock performance. Of course, the real test will come in the next few years, as the many SPACs now in registration or looking for merger deals watch the ticking clock and complete transactions.

Private companies looking to merge with SPACs can win because they see the ready cash. They also often benefit from the guidance and advice of the SPAC management team. Many times the company merging in will retain some people from the former SPAC management to assist in building their company.

The next section provides a more detailed discussion of the structural components of a SPAC and then the pros and cons of this rapidly growing technique.

Anatomy of a SPAC

Following are highlights of some of the core components of a Form S-1 filing, which is the primary registration statement for a typical SPAC.

As is customary on the cover of Form S-1, the issuer and issue are indicated, along with the amount being raised in the initial public offering. In the case of SPACs, it's also noted that this is a blank check company formed for the purpose of acquiring an operating business. Typically, as mentioned, a specific industry or a certain type of business or geographical area is listed as the target for an acquisition or business combination.

Also included on the cover is the public offering price of the units, along with the underwriting discounts and commissions, and the underwriting syndicate.

The Prospectus Summary of Form S-1 makes the case for investing in the IPO and sums up the investment opportunity in a particular business sector. Highlighted are management competencies as deal generators since the success of the SPAC ultimately depends on management's ability to identify and close an acquisition. Investment bankers assembling the management team favor dealmakers and operating executives who have created value for public shareholders. The Use of Proceeds section frequently lists consultants or advisers who might also be called upon to assist in executing the business plan. Understanding who is involved with the SPAC (and how they're paid) goes a long way in assessing the investment opportunity.

Also in the Prospectus Summary is a key reference to the IPO's mechanics: The SPAC must complete an acquisition of a certain size within a specified time period after the offering or else the SPAC will be forced to liquidate. As these specified purpose vehicles raise greater assets in the $100 million to $200 million range, the possibility increases that a contemporaneous closing of multiple acquisitions will be necessary to meet this size requirement. Skepticism about the viability of such a complex transaction—in which one target might gain considerable leverage at closing—paired with the practical reality of the SPAC finding value in target companies, creates a real challenge for very large SPACs.

The Offering section identifies the term sheet. The prevailing issuance structure during the latest SPAC boom consisted of a $6 unit comprising one share of common stock and two warrants with an exercise price of $5 each. After the registration has gone effective, the units begin trading on the OTC Bulletin Board (or, in some cases, the American Stock Exchange) and each of the common stock and warrants begins to trade separately on the ninetieth day after the prospectus date unless the lead underwriter determines that an earlier date is acceptable. Generally, the date the unit components begin to trade is determined by when a current report on Form 8-K is filed reflecting the financial condition of the SPAC post-funding.

Because of the unit structure, the common stock and warrants can be traded separately to create a hedge. Although some SPACs do boast a roster of fundamental investors, a SPAC is really viewed as a structured finance product designed to attract low-cost capital from investors with expertise in the primary securities market. As an IPO surrogate, a mixed syndicate of investors that includes long-term equity funds and hedge funds with a shorter-term focus is perhaps ideal in terms of speed to market and trading liquidity.

A significant appeal of the structure is the downside protection afforded by the portion of IPO proceeds placed in an escrow account. In this example, slightly below 92 percent of the post-offering proceeds are placed in this account and are not to be released until the earlier of the completion of the business acquisition or the SPAC's liquidation in the event no acquisition is consummated within the allotted time period. The amount held in trust comes to $5.50 per unit or 92 percent of the offering price without taking into account offering fees. The remaining proceeds of approximately 8 percent are used by management as operating capital to find and effect the proposed business combination. More and more current deals are distinguishing themselves in the investor marketplace by offering to retain even higher percentages of invested funds in the escrow account.

Warrants typically cannot be exercised until the later of the consummation of a business combination or one year from the date of the prospectus, which for all intents and purposes means that until an acquisition is completed, investors shouldn't count on exercising their warrants.

The remaining portions of the Offering section address the terms under which shareholders must approve a proposed business combination. An acquisition by the SPAC can only proceed if a majority of the shares of common stock voted by public shareholders are voted in favor of a business combination and shareholders owning less than 20 percent of the shares sold in the initial offering exercise rights to convert their stock into a pro rata share of the trust fund if the business combination is approved and consummated. Shareholders who convert their stock into their share of the trust fund continue to have the right to exercise any warrants they hold.

If no business combination is completed within a specified time period after the offering (usually either twelve or eighteen months) or within eighteen or twenty-four months, respectively, after the offering if a letter of intent has been executed within the initial time frame but the combination not yet closed, then the SPAC is forced to liquidate. This includes a complete dissolution of all trust funds plus any remaining net assets.

Advantages of SPACs

The advantages of the SPAC to investors are simple. First, they take limited risk in investing, because almost their entire investment is placed in an escrow account immediately and earns interest while awaiting a merger. Thus, after the cash earns a year or two of interest, the worst case for an investor might be a 5 percent or 6 percent loss if they choose not to participate in a merger.

The second advantage for investors is the opportunity to trade their stock and warrants, which is not available to investors in Form 10-SB shells. If a unit comprising a share of stock and two warrants originally is purchased for $6, because of expenses taken out of the investment, the stock often trades around $5 or $5.25 while awaiting a deal. In typical cases, however, once a merger deal is announced, the stock moves right back up to the original $6 price. At this point, an investor could choose to sell the stock and get 100 percent of his original investment back, while still holding warrants that could benefit him on the upside, with absolutely no risk.

The third advantage for investors is the time limit. They know that one way or the other, the key decision will be made no later than two years after they put their money into the deal. If no deal comes along, they get almost all their money back. If a deal does materialize, they get to look at it and decide if they want to approve it. But management does not get an open-ended time frame.

Fourth, investors like having the high-level management team, and are betting on their ability to find good deals. The bet can be compared to investing in a venture capital fund, where the management of the fund is relied upon to find good deals. The difference here is that venture capital funds are blind pools of money, since an investor generally has very little say over what deals the fund invests in. Although the investor in a SPAC does not choose the deal, he can opt out and get his money back or vote not to reconfirm his investment when it is presented to investors. But most investors would tell you that a major benefit to this deal structure is having the ability to have a "look-see" at the deal.

Advantages to a Company Merging into a SPAC

Why would a company merge with a SPAC if it could do a self-filing, reverse merger with a trading or nontrading shell or even an IPO? There are a number of reasons.

First, compare a SPAC with an IPO. Much like any reverse merger, a merger with a SPAC is quicker and less expensive than an IPO. It takes longer than many reverse mergers because it requires filing and obtaining SEC approval of the investor reconfirmation prospectus, but this still takes much less time than an IPO. Also, the underwriter has completed his job of raising money, so the company merging in is not negotiating with the underwriter so much as with SPAC management.

The third advantage over IPOs is less focus on the IPO "window" and Wall Street's appetite for new offerings since the SPAC market is almost by definition active only when IPOs are down. Fourth, very simply the money is already there and the price is set. The company merging into the SPAC does not face the risk of an underwriter not being able to raise money, or trying to change the offering price at the last minute. One might see this in many ways as the most important advantage a SPAC has over an IPO.

The fifth advantage companies see in a SPAC merger, much like the investors, is the management team. The hope is that the post-merger company will retain at least one or two of these prominent players for representation on the board or to assume a key consulting role.

Sixth, in some cases a company simply does not qualify for a traditional IPO, and pursuing a SPAC merger provides an efficient method for getting public and raising large amounts of cash relatively quickly.

Why do some companies think a SPAC merger is better than other types of reverse mergers? First and foremost, unlike most shells, SPACs have cash. Even if a non-SPAC shell does have cash, odds are it won't have as much as a SPAC will. (Most non-SPAC shells with cash have less than $5 million.)

Second, a SPAC is preferable to other shell mergers because of the existence of a trading market for the securities. Although some shells trade, very few have active trading markets. Plus, the identity of investors and their interest in the company merging in is greater because the investors know up front that the SPAC planned to invest in a company in their industry. In other trading shells that had a history, the holders of publicly tradable stock had invested in a completely different company, and how they will react to the merger is rarely clear in advance.

Third, companies favor SPACs over reverse mergers with other trading shells because the SPACs are totally clean. This is also true of Form 10-SB shells, and so this benefit applies to other types of transactions. Trading shells that are not SPACs, however, have a history and a background that must be reviewed and scrubbed prior to a deal.

Fourth, sometimes owners or promoters of trading non-SPAC shells are unsophisticated, unpredictable, and greedy. They think their shells are worth paying a premium for and frequently insist on rather aggressive deal conditions. The operators of SPACs are typically professional, experienced, senior-level management in the particular industry in question. Underwriters who have completed many deals and are true professional investors are advising them. This generally makes the deal process smoother and more predictable. Again, the Form 10-SB shell promoters also generally fit the professional mold, as many are experienced investors or investment bankers, so this advantage may not apply as compared with other nontrading shells.

Why would a company prefer a SPAC merger to a self-filing? In general, the same analysis applies as to the benefits of a self-filing, but as mentioned in the chapters covering self-filings, a SPAC might be preferable for a number of reasons. First, a company doing a self-filing is not likely to raise the large amount of cash that's sitting in the SPAC. Second, a SPAC likely will be completed more quickly than a self-filing. Third, a SPAC brings along a professional team of lawyers, auditors, investment bankers, and industry-tested management, whereas a self-filing is very much the do-it-yourself creation of a public company.

Disadvantages of SPACs

Investors see several disadvantages to investing in a SPAC. First is simply the opportunity cost of making the investment. If after two years investors decide not to be part of the ultimate merger, depending on the deal's structure, they might receive up to 95 percent of their money back. Nevertheless, during those two years they could have invested that money elsewhere and actually made a profit, rather than lose 5 percent.

Even putting the money in a money market account would yield more like 3 to 4 percent profit over two years as against a 5 to 7 percent loss in the SPAC. And investing more aggressively in the equities markets, as most hedge funds do, could yield even greater returns.

The second disadvantage to investors, while also an advantage with respect to return on investment, is the time limit. Some investors become concerned that a SPAC will rush into a deal toward the end of its time limit without as careful a vetting process as if the deal came along six months after going public. Most SPACs require at least a letter of intent or some clear outline of a deal within eighteen months of going public; then they have another six months to complete the deal. Finding a deal within eighteen months is the greatest challenge a SPAC faces. This time limit, borrowed from Rule 419, was the main reason many former shell promoters from the 1980s decided not to pursue forming Rule 419 shells. Although it may seem beneficial that some underwriters are deferring their fees until a merger is completed, so that underwriters have an incentive to find and close a deal, arguably that also creates an incentive to close a mediocre deal when time is running out so that the deferred fees can be earned.

Similarly, some investors become concerned that a deal simply will not come along, in which case their money, minus expenses and commissions, gets returned. Again, this represents a small loss which is not in their control and a lost opportunity to have invested the funds elsewhere.

Third, some investors believe the underwriters may not share their interest in ensuring that a private operating company can be put into the SPAC. Personally, I disagree with this concern, and knowing the underwriters well, I believe they understand that their ability to keep doing SPACs rests squarely on their talent for finding successful deals; however, some investors perceive otherwise. This has led to the recent trend where underwriters have been forced to take several points on their commission and delay receiving them until a deal comes along and gets closed.

Fourth, some investors worry about the large interest in the SPAC given to management, typically as much as 20 percent of the company. They would prefer more of this interest be given to management of the company merging in as an incentive to encourage their performance. The counter-position to this argument is that an investor is investing in this SPAC management team, and it is critical to give them a meaningful stake to maximize their motivation. The operating company should have more than enough equity interest after the deal to provide incentive.

Disadvantages to a Company Merging into a SPAC

Companies thinking about a SPAC merger also have concerns.

If a company can achieve an IPO with an established investment bank that routinely raises the money it promises to raise, there may be very few advantages to a SPAC other than a somewhat speedier process. In fact, the aftermarket support that generally follows an IPO is typically stronger than that following a SPAC. As indicated in earlier chapters, sometimes this IPO post-deal support is manufactured and does not last. But the same may be said for some post-deal SPAC trading markets. If one is pursuing an IPO with a questionable underwriter that may not be able to launch a fully committed deal, however, the advantage of having the money in the SPAC can make a difference. In addition, the SPAC offers a seasoned management team, whereas an IPO does not. Also, as is the case with most every alternative IPO deal structure, SPAC mergers generally are completed much faster than IPOs.

SPACs and reverse mergers with other types of trading or nontrading shells are indeed different in their benefits. Assuming the company needs significant cash immediately and can benefit from the SPAC management's expertise, the SPAC would probably be favored. But compared to a more traditional shell merger, the SPAC requires a time-consuming and expensive process of preparing an investor proxy, and runs the risk of not receiving approval of the deal from investors. Trading and nontrading shells (other than Rule 419 shells, which are all but extinct at this point) generally do not require this cost and delay. Thus, a merger with a non-SPAC shell happens much quicker and with less cost.

Most non-SPAC shells, even those with intent to raise PIPE financing upon completing a reverse merger, simply cannot compete with a SPAC holding $50 million, if that is the amount of money the private company needs and deserves.

The line becomes a bit blurry in the case of a SPAC with $20 million or $30 million. Here, most PIPE players may be interested in raising that amount of money in a non-SPAC shell, and can do so more quickly than with a SPAC, and with much less cost and hassle. SPAC players will say, don't forget that their money is in the bank, whereas the PIPE guys have to go raise it. Also, a SPAC promoter will point to his broad shareholder base and existing ticker symbol as benefits.

But it is certainly a very close debate for a company looking to go public and raise less than $30 million as to whether a SPAC or non-SPAC shell makes the most sense. Factors such as timing and the need for more immediate market support would probably drive the decision-making process.

Another disadvantage SPACs have in the marketplace of shells is the simple fact that they tend to have an industry or geographic focus. Most non-SPAC shells have no such focus and can merge with any business they deem appropriate. Although SPAC promoters feel their management team and industry focus are good for investors, it clearly limits the field of potential companies they can merge with. If a target company does not operate in a suitable industry or geography, short of obtaining shareholder approval to change industries, the SPAC is simply out of luck if they have interest in a merger with the company.

This disadvantage becomes particularly conspicuous as private equity and venture capital firms begin, as they have recently, to recognize the value of reverse mergers. After learning how a SPAC operates, many of these investors soon realize that most of their portfolio companies are not SPAC-worthy, if you will, simply because of the industries in which they operate.

When comparing a Form 10-SB shell with a SPAC, one should consider that each is appropriate for different markets and purposes. As a SPAC-meister recently said to me, "Form 10-SB shells should not be marketed as the anti-SPAC." And he's right. Most view a SPAC as best used by a company that otherwise might qualify for a traditional IPO, whereas Form 10-SB and other shells are more commonly used by companies at slightly earlier stages, hence the "public venture capital" concept and all the interest from private equity-type investors.

Compared to self-filings, SPACs have some disadvantages.

In a self-filing, the company has much more control over the process. In a SPAC, much is out of the hands of the company merging in and depends on the investors and management team of the SPAC. Also, in a self-filing there tends to be less total dilution to company management than in a merger with a SPAC, even if the company pursuing the self-filing also completes a financing. A merger with a SPAC probably is quicker than a self-filing, but not by much. And of course the self-filing company faces that added market support challenge.

There are some other disadvantages to SPACs. Companies hoping to raise money in significant amounts by merging with a SPAC also may be considering an outright sale. In that case, if a SPAC is competing with a financial or even strategic buyer of the company, the SPAC may have a difficult time getting the deal. The buyers can usually move fast, and can essentially guarantee a deal will go through, whereas a SPAC must get its investors' approval, which takes a number of months and is not assured in advance.

Here are three other concerns some companies might raise with regard to SPACs. First is the "overhang" of the warrants that most SPACs offer to investors. Although the exercise of warrants after closing a merger will bring additional money into the company, it also further dilutes the ownership of the management of the former private company, to an extent that may not be desirable.

Another concern is the 20 percent of the company typically given to SPAC management. In some cases, the former private business has no interest in using the services or contacts of the SPAC management team and, therefore, the only thing they did was find the deal. Companies merging in may feel the dilution of their interest for the benefit of the SPAC managers is not worth it.

One last issue companies sometimes raise is the two-year time limit. They may feel rushed by SPAC management who are eager to consummate a transaction. This pressure might be applied at an inopportune time when the private company is examining other alternatives. In business circumstances as important as this, a company needs to take its time to determine the best way to pursue its strategic options.

Are Junior SPACs Next?

Recently, several so-called SPAC-meisters have discussed with me a conundrum. As the recent wave of SPACs has seen success and raised more and more money, the underwriters and dealmakers must shed themselves of smaller deal opportunities, even those they deem exciting and worthy of investment. They say they wish there was a method in place to complete these deals.

I have made several suggestions to these players, and we may see one or more of them pursued in the near future. First, of course, I suggested that they consider forming nontrading Form 10-SB shells to use for smaller deals. While some are indeed moving in this direction, the concern, they say, is that their SPAC investors are used to having a shell that trades, and some are required to be able to mark to market their investment, which means a nontrading shell may not work.

The second suggestion is one I have been making for some time now. I take some credit for developing it as a concept. The idea is to take full advantage of the Rule 419 exemption provided by the SEC. Form a SPAC not with $20 million or $50 million or $100 million, but with the minimum $5 million necessary to claim the exemption.

One way to do this is to raise the money privately, with the underwriter serving as placement agent, before the shell goes public. Then the private shell has the money in the bank as an asset, and claims the exemption by filing a Form SB-2 resale registration for the investors. In this case, no company public offering is involved; therefore, the NASD compensation review is not undertaken, state blue sky review is streamlined, and the process is a bit simpler. In addition, the placement agent can own part of the shell, which is much more difficult to do when it serves as an underwriter of an IPO of a traditional SPAC.

The other approach is to do an IPO of a shell, much like a SPAC does, but only raise $5 million. The advantage is that investors have tradable shares immediately, but the NASD, SEC, and state reviews are more difficult, and the investment bank realistically cannot own stock.

Either way, the key to what I have started calling a "junior SPAC" is to eliminate most of the SPAC and Rule 419-type protections, since the SEC simply does not require them. The placement agent, now also the promoter of the shell, goes to its closest investors to raise the money, those who trust that they will not act improperly and who have invested successfully with them in the past.

I have suggested to several clients the following approach to structure a junior SPAC:

1 The money raised (approximately $5 million), minus deal and operating expenses, is placed in escrow much like a SPAC.

2 The stock is permitted to trade just like a SPAC (it is not clear that the Bulletin Board will permit this, but the Pink Sheets will).

3 There is a self-imposed time limit to complete a deal, but it is longer, possibly two and a half years or even three years.

4 No shareholder reconfirmation or ratification of the deal is sought or required (this would depart from the typical SPAC structure), but see below regarding my suggestion for a transaction advisory committee.

5 There is no industry or geographic focus (unlike SPACs, the junior SPAC could be opportunistic and pursue any deal, which also eliminates the need for issuing large chunks of stock to SPAC management).

6 The size of the merger deal would not have to be related to the amount of money raised (in a SPAC the merger deal must have a value of at least 80 percent of IPO proceeds).

Thus, the two key differences would be the lack of industry focus and the lack of shareholder confirmation of the merger deal. It is true that many investors see a primary benefit of SPACs in their ability to see a merger and opt in or out. Therefore, I have suggested that clients consider a less formal route, through the creation of a "transaction advisory committee" from among its investors. This committee would not have any power to approve a deal, but would be required to be consulted prior to entering into a merger. It is unlikely that the junior SPAC's management would pursue a deal that this committee thinks is not advisable.

The committee could include representatives from the junior SPAC's largest investors, who might even receive additional equity or preferred stock for agreeing to serve in this role. But because it has no legal power, the committee members should not face any liability exposure for performing this function.

I believe the industry focus is generally of less interest to SPAC investors than the right to have a look at the eventual merger deal. The fact that a broad contingent of investors has been investing in every SPAC, almost regardless of industry or geographic focus, seems at least partially to prove that point.

Will investors be interested in this concept? I believe so, especially those who have already made money with larger SPACs.

Wrap-Up on SPACs

Although some professionals in mid-2005 began to wonder if the SPAC market was saturated with pre-IPO deal activity, or whether all the trading SPACs would find successful merger partners, as of the time of this writing, it seems clear that the SPAC market is evolving and proliferating. SPACs are serving a need in the marketplace, and as the deals get larger and the players more sophisticated, it looks to be a fascinating few years ahead in this dynamic area of finance.

CHAPTER 15

Form 10-SB Shells

Many believed through most of the 1990s that setting up a Form 10-SB shell, although seemingly a permissible way around Rule 419, was disfavored by the U.S. Securities and Exchange Commission and other regulators. To briefly recap, Rule 419 was passed in 1992 under the Securities Act of 1933, which governs the public offering market. Rule 419 applied only to those seeking to register for public sale individual shares to be sold by a company, or resold by existing shareholders.

Form 10-SB is filed under the Securities Exchange Act of 1934. Form 10-SB allows a company to voluntarily subject itself to the SEC reporting requirements under the Exchange Act without registering individual shares for sale or resale. In order for a trading market to develop in these companies, shares have to be registered for sale at some point, or become able to be sold under an exemption from registration. This is similar to the self-filing approach discussed in earlier chapters, except here we are talking about creating a shell to be used in a later reverse merger through a Form 10-SB self-filing rather than taking an operating business public through the same filing.

In any event, a blank check can go public by filing a Form 10-SB and thereby avoid the proscriptions of Rule 419. But some tried, as our law firm did on behalf of a client in 1993, to create a Form 10-SB shell. As mentioned earlier, the SEC commented on our Form 10-SB filing by saying that we were prohibited from taking a shell public through Form 10-SB because of Rule 419. Our client, you may recall, chose not to fight, and we withdrew the filing, even though the SEC's analysis was, respectfully, incorrect at the time.

By 1998, a significant number of Form 10-SB shells had been formed, and it has finally become clear that these shells are not only legally permissible, but acceptable to regulators. Indeed, the dozens of Form 10-SB shells we have formed for clients have been met with virtually no comments from the SEC and have truly sailed through, whereas those forming Rule 419 shells have recently met with very stiff resistance in the form of dozens and dozens of difficult comments from the SEC staff. As a result, almost no one is pursuing 419 shells currently.

This chapter examines this dramatic new trend and discusses the mechanics of creating a Form 10-SB shell. Compared with the process of creating a SPAC, creating a Form 10-SB shell, although it involves some dicey legal issues and nuances, is relatively straightforward.

First, the chapter describes the specific steps required to create and take public a Form 10-SB shell. That is followed by a discussion of a few legal issues specific to Form 10-SB shells, and finally, a review of some of the advantages and disadvantages of this method of creating a shell.

Mechanics of Creating a Form 10-SB Shell

A Form 10-SB shell is completed in five major steps. The first step is forming the entity and capitalizing it. Next is preparing and filing the Form 10-SB. Third is understanding the responsibilities of the promoter following the effectiveness of the registration. (During this time, some anticipate raising money and/or putting together a shareholder base in the shell.) Fourth is the completion of the merger itself, and fifth is pursuing a resale registration following the merger to permit trading to begin.

Getting Started: Forming and Capitalizing the Entity

The first step in forming a shell is actually setting up a corporation. Our clients form their shells almost exclusively in Delaware. Why, then, are so many older shells incorporated in Utah, Nevada, or Colorado? In part, this was done because many promoters were located there. There are also certain tax benefits in those states to penny stock companies wishing to issue hundreds of millions of shares. My clients generally are seeking to keep the authorized shares under 100 million.

We prefer Delaware in part because it is considered the most legitimate place to incorporate and is where virtually every major corporation is set up. Of course, we are also very familiar with Delaware corporate law, of which there are many favorable aspects. The initial shock, however, comes when a client receives a franchise tax bill from the state suggesting that their new shell owes over $200,000 in franchise taxes! Have no fear, however, as there is an alternative method of calculating the tax that, in the case of a shell, reduces the tax to only a few hundred dollars.

When the shell is formed, its certificate of incorporation has to say how many shares the company is authorized to issue. Most of our clients have used between 50 million and 100 million shares. This allows for sufficient shares to complete a merger with a number of shares left for the merged company so it can grow and issue shares for a while before having to go back and increase its authorized shares. Most of the certificates of incorporation also include the availability of preferred stock, not just common stock, so that after a merger, management has some flexibility in how it raises money or completes acquisitions.

How is it determined that 100 million is enough? We go through a theoretical reverse merger and work backward. For example, assuming that a company merging in will be worth about $20 million, and that the shell founders will hope to have a stock that trades at around a dollar, and that some shares are left over for shell founders and investors, one might imagine the need for about 25 million shares after a merger. If one has 50 million to 100 million total authorized shares, this leaves a large comfort zone for future post-merger activities.

After incorporating, the entity needs to apply for an Internal Revenue Service employer identification number (EIN), the equivalent of a company's social security number. Armed with its EIN, the company can open bank accounts and deposit initial monies to pay expenses.

Cost of Creating the Shell

We estimate approximately $40,000 to $50,000 is sufficient to complete the process of getting the shell public, and another $20,000 to $25,000 per year, at most, to keep the entity public. This includes attorneys, accountants, auditors (separate from accountants), EDGAR filing services, tax return filings, franchise taxes, and corporate services used to create the entity.

That's right. A nice, clean, nontrading shell costs about $40,000 to $50,000 upfront. Compare this to the $450,000 to nearly $1 million to acquire an OTC Bulletin Board trading shell! Just recently, I heard about a shell that had turned down $1.2 million to sell nearly 100 percent of the stock. Again, as mentioned earlier, some smart promoters can acquire shells for less, but this is not easy. This is part of the reason so many have pursued this technique, realizing that it is possible to create ten to twenty absolutely clean Form 10-SB shells for the cost of acquiring one trading shell that requires scrubbing.

Founder Stock

The next decision is how many shares to issue to founders, who typically are the individuals who have set up the shell. Unlike a SPAC, the founders may include broker-dealer affiliates. Again, we imagine a likely deal structure. Using $20 million as the value of a company merging in, if shell owners are usually permitted to keep around 5 percent to 10 percent of the stock, issuing around 1.5 million to 2 million shares to founders generally makes sense. Some, however, issue fewer shares, especially those forming shells who realize that investment banks and others will step in and request additional shares prior to the merger.

It is generally better to issue more rather than less shares. Why is this? If the number requires adjustment upon a merger, it is easier for the holders to simply relinquish or forfeit some shares to reduce the number than it would be to issue additional shares at the time of the merger, as this may have negative tax consequences. A forward stock split can alleviate the tax concern of issuing more shares, but that split may require shareholder approval and a proxy process.

Officers and Directors

The new, still private, shell next has to choose its board of directors, along with president, secretary, and any other corporate officers. Delaware requires only a president and secretary to be officers, but they can be the same person. That same person also can be the sole director or there can be multiple directors.

Most of the shells we are creating have one or two officers and directors, and they are typically affiliated with the founders or the investment banking firm that is driving the process. These officers and directors technically take on liability exposure for the decisions they make, including what company with which to merge. This exposure, however, manifests more intensely if the shell chooses to take in a large group of shareholders holding significant equity at some point. It is helpful if the officers and directors have no "bad boy" backgrounds, as this probably would have to be disclosed in the Form 10-SB.

Preparing and Filing the Form 10-SB

The next two steps happen simultaneously. The basic Form 10-SB document is prepared, and the audit process begins.

Financial Information and Audit

Yes, even though it has conducted no activity other than incorporating and issuing its initial shares, a new shell must file audited financial statements with its Form 10-SB. In some cases, this process can move so quickly that the audit takes only a few weeks after the date of incorporation. In any event, it needs to be done.

The first step is the preparation of a set of financial statements for the auditors to audit. Financial statements that are audited are not prepared by the auditor; rather, they are merely reviewed, items checked, and changes made. In fact, the auditor cannot assist at all in preparation. When one of my clients sent financials to his auditor, the auditor came back and insisted that footnotes be added. The accountant asked, "What footnotes?" The answer, "We're not allowed to tell you."

So an accountant other than the auditor, or someone very knowledgeable in these matters, prepares the financial statements. A QuickBooks report will not do the trick. The financial statements are then submitted to the auditors, who must take a number of steps regardless of whether the audit is of an inactive shell company or General Motors. They ask us, as legal counsel, to confirm in writing that there is no outstanding litigation or threats thereof. They review bank statements, the corporate minute books, and the like. A good, efficient auditor should be able to complete an audit of a new shell about three to four weeks after receiving everything necessary to get it done.

Once the audit is completed, the financial statements, along with a statement from the auditor, are embedded in the Form 10-SB. The statement typically includes what is known as a "going concern" opinion if there is not much cash in the shell. This expresses the auditor's opinion that there is substantial concern about whether the shell can continue as a going concern without additional financing. The auditors also insist on reviewing and signing off on all the content of the form before it is filed with the SEC, often including a final review of the version that is formatted for EDGAR.

Filing the Form

Form 10-SB itself is divided into sections pursuant to SEC rules. These include a business description, plan of operation, related party transactions, executive compensation, management, share ownership, capitalization, the financial statements, and exhibits which typically include the company's certificate of incorporation and bylaws.

Most of these shells' business descriptions are essentially the same, describing their desire to find a company to merge with and some of the criteria they may use to identify an appropriate company. The ownership and management sections are unique to each set of shells, and include five-year biographies of the officers and directors. Because only a few founders exist, the description of share ownership is fairly simple, as is the required description of the manner in which the company has sold unregistered shares prior to the filing.

When the shareholders, officers, directors, and auditors have approved, the form is sent to be prepared for EDGAR filing. Company representatives must approve the electronic version of the filing. Then, the button is pushed and the form is filed.

Getting the Form 10-SB Effective

Filings of Form 10-SB registration statements under the Exchange Act are deemed automatically effective sixty days after they are filed. During that time, the SEC may comment on a filing, but even if it has not finished making comments within the sixty-day period, the form is effective and the company has succeeded in becoming a full reporting company unless the SEC requests that it withdraw and refile. If not, the comments and amendments continue on a "post-effective" basis after the sixty days.

Our law firm has been fortunate in that the SEC has made few, if any, comments to the many Form 10-SB shells our clients have filed since early 2005. More recently, in most cases it has even declared a rare "no review" of many clients' filings. Even when we have received comments, the SEC has typically made it clear that any amendment we file to respond to the comments will not even be reviewed, and the filing will be effective after sixty days.

Of course, during the time the Form 10-SB is pending, not only are shares not tradable, but also the promoters may not speak with potential merger candidates at all. That said, we understand that a number of our clients forming the shells are investment bank affiliates. Thus, obviously they are talking to companies every day about possible financing transactions and strategic alternatives, which might include going public.

But I generally advise them not to disclose that they are considering forming their own shells or even that they have done so until after the Form 10-SB is effective. As with the registration for a SPAC, the Form 10-SB declares that management has had no discussions with a potential merger candidate about merging with the shell.

Post-Effective Responsibilities Prior to a Merger

After the Form 10-SB is effective, the shell is officially a public shell, or as the SEC now calls them, a shell company. As a full SEC reporting company, it is now subject to all the same filing obligations of any public company, including quarterly and annual reports to be filed on Form 10-QSB and Form 10-KSB, as well as forms to be filed by large stockholders, officers, and directors to declare their ownership. These include an initial filing on Form 3 and Schedules 13D or 13G for management and shareholders with more than 5 percent ownership.

The company also is subject to the SEC's proxy rules and restrictions on insider trading. That said, again no shares are trading, even though the shell is public and reporting. This is the concept of a nontrading shell. In the current market, many investors generally are willing, however, to invest in a reverse merger with a nontrading shell as long as the shell is and was fully reporting, and trading will commence around the time that the investor's shares are registered and able to trade. Most PIPE funds, for instance, have built into their agreements with investors that they may invest in companies that report to the SEC, not specifically companies which have a trading market for their securities.

In a series of letters between the SEC and Nasdaq from 1999 and 2000 (the famous "Worm/Wulff letters" to be discussed in greater detail below), and in subsequent informal guidance, the SEC has expressed the view that all shares issued in a blank check never qualify for an exemption under Rule 144. Therefore, shares in the new public company must ultimately be registered with the SEC in order for them to trade. This is another reason the shell's stock cannot trade, even if holders have waited the requisite period under Rule 144.

Raising Money and/or Shareholders

Some newly minted shells wish to increase their attractiveness to potential merger candidates by putting either money or a large group of shareholders, or both, into the shell. Shells with cash and shells with lots of shareholders are typically more valuable. In order for the OTC Bulletin Board to permit trading, they generally (but unofficially) require at least thirty-five to forty unaffiliated holders of at least one hundred tradable shares each to be present in the company.

Some shells have raised token amounts of money by offering to forty or fifty people the opportunity to buy one hundred or two hundred shares at, say, $0.25 a share. Thus, they write a check for $50 to buy two hundred shares and voilà, there's a new shareholder with enough shares. Others have done full-fledged financings of several million dollars into the shell. In each case it depends on the market that the shell founders seek to pursue.

These financings theoretically could take place prior to the Form 10-SB being effective. But it just creates more information for the SEC to review and comment on, and, more important, it is simply easier to raise money or bring the shareholders in when they are investing in a full-fledged public company.

Some shell founders have not chosen to add shareholders, believing that they can add the requisite number of holders at the time of a financing that is combined with a merger. This avoids whatever dilution (though typically minor) associated with the financing at the time the company is still a shell.

Selling a Shell

Sometimes our clients are approached to flip their Form 10-SB shells. Some of these shells, as of this writing, are selling for $200,000 for a 99 percent interest, typically completed at the same time as a reverse merger effected by the buyer. Although this is a steep discount to the price of trading shells, it provides a reasonable profit for the hassle and expense of setting up the shell, and provides the buyer an immediate clean entity rather than having to wait to create one themselves. Indeed, some of my clients who are in the process of forming shells can't do it fast enough, and have approached me to purchase shells from other clients who have completed the process. Some believe this $200,000 price will climb as demand increases for these shells and recent offers have gone up to $250,000. By way of providing a disclaimer, I could benefit personally from this as I have formed a number of Form 10-SB shells as a principal myself.

Technically the SEC, through its earlier letters, takes the position that a shareholder may not sell his shares of a shell, even privately, to a third party, without first registering them. Thus, several clients have taken to having the shell itself redeem, or repurchase, their shares, for cash if a third party wishes to come in. This redemption does not appear inconsistent with the SEC letters, since no sale to a third party is involved, only a sale back to the company itself. In general, the SEC does not appear to look with favor upon shell owners simply flipping their ownership.

PRACTICE TIP

Do not form shell companies with the purpose of selling them for cash.

Merging with a Form 10-SB Shell

There are some structural advantages to using a Form 10-SB shell when completing a merger. First, the officers and directors of the shell are not concerned about trading issues in the shell, as its stock does not trade. Therefore, worries about when to disclose things, insider trading and the like, are simply not present or are of less concern. Management also worries less about liability for choosing a deal, since shareholders typically either are affiliates of management's company or are very small holders brought in to round out the shareholder base. This exposure is greater where a larger cash financing has taken place in the shell.

From the perspective of the company merging in, the due diligence process with a Form 10-SB shell is much simpler than with a shell that is trading and has an operating history of a prior business. Form 10-SB shells are clean: there has been almost no activity in the shell before the merger. It is essential to check the backgrounds of the shell's promoters, but the documentation of its activity should be very easy and quick to review, similar to a SPAC.

Another major advantage of using a Form 10-SB shell is the speed with which a transaction can occur, similar to a reverse merger with a trading shell. Once the due diligence is completed, a merger document is negotiated, and a disclosure document (the super Form 8-K) to be filed upon the merger under the new SEC rule is prepared, a closing can take place. If there is to be a contemporaneous financing, the disclosure document can be used to provide investors proper information about the deal.

In addition, since Form 10-SB shells are much less expensive to create, and since most of the players creating them are investment bankers planning a much broader total role with the company merging in, there is expected to be less pressure to give very high percentages of equity or cash to the former shell owners.

Some of our clients expect to keep very small percentages of the resulting combined entity after a merger instead of the more typical 5 percent to 10 percent. Why bother, then? First, in some cases the client already typically has a large stake in the private company merging in. Second, they typically expect to earn fees and receive equity for raising the combined company money.

Third, some are simply less interested in the equity they keep in the shell than they are in knowing simply that a shell is available and owned by friends. This also helps moot any arguments that they milked the transaction through their interest in the shell, especially given any potential conflicts of interest. Last, having the shell allows a merger and PIPE (private investment in public equity) to be completed quickly, even though it is not trading and the promoter will not receive much equity.

Of course, not all Form 10-SB owners are going to be this generous. Some expect the full 5 percent to 10 percent in merged equity that is typical in these transactions, and it would seem appropriate for them to receive it. But the marketplace ultimately will work this out.

Post-Merger Registration

Life used to be so simple. Companies merged with shells, after which any shareholders holding restricted, or untradable shares, would register their shares for resale and be able to sell them in a matter of a few months. Sometimes, this registration encompassed almost all the shares outstanding in the merged company. Trading then commenced, and the reverse merger technique was validated.

Life is not as simple today. Recently, some groups of examiners within the SEC have begun to take the position that any attempt at registering a large percentage of a company's shares for resale really is what is known as a "primary" registration, requiring the company to offer the shares at a fixed price, in some cases pursuant to a firm commitment underwriting. In contrast, typically resale registrations permit a shareholder to resell his shares to the public "at the market," or whatever price is prevailing at the time. Also, no underwriter is required.

In addition, in these attempted registrations involving large percentages, the SEC has been seeking to insist that all members of management, as well as all broker-dealer affiliates whose shares are to be included, agree to remove their shares from the registration and wait a full year before attempting another registration for them.

In general, however, it appears, though has yet to be made clear, that keeping a resale registration to less than 50 percent of a company's outstanding shares may satisfy the SEC's concerns about registering a large percentage of stock.

PRACTICE TIP

Do not seek to register more than 50 percent of a post-merger company's stock in a single resale registration, or risk the SEC's ire.

This should be taken into account when structuring the registration rights of investors, shell founders, and management of private companies merging in. In our PIPE deals, we are now using a two-stage registration rights approach. First, PIPE investors are promised that the company will immediately register some percentage less than 50 percent.

After the registration is effective, and a certain amount of time has passed, the investors have a right to demand that the company register additional shares. (These are, surprisingly, called demand registration rights.) The second tranche is not automatic because the SEC will probably argue (I think correctly) that two automatic registrations in a row are the same as doing one giant one. By making the second tranche optional, and its initiation up to the investor (and not all investors will need this because many will be able to make use of Rule 144 sales after one year), it should be possible to sidestep the problems of the two-step automatic registration.

In early 2006, I had a conversation with several high-ranking SEC staff members. I explained that the existence of the Worm/Wulff letters prohibiting any sale of shell shares except through registration, combined with this new attempt to limit whose shares are registered for resale, is the equivalent of putting off for a very long period the opportunity for shell owners to obtain liquidity, supposedly a goal of the SEC. The staffers acknowledged the concern and promised to look into the matter. I believe they will.

In addition, in a resale registration statement on behalf of a company whose shares are not yet trading, as a technical matter it may be required that initial sales of stock before a trading market develops be completed at a predetermined fixed price. Thus, as of this writing, clients are currently examining the best way to approach this as the first sets of registrations on Form 10-SB shell mergers are being filed.

Three approaches are being considered. One is a registration requiring the sale at a fixed price, and a subsequent posteffective amendment to that registration when trading commences, which permits sales of shares "at the market." Then, those that wish to wait for that market can hold off on selling until it develops. The second notion is to provide in the registration that the fixed price is only required until a symbol and listing for trading are in place, then at-the-market sales are permitted. It is not clear how the regulators will react to such a filing, but either way, after the initial sales, at-the-market resales should be possible.

The third idea being considered is to file a registration providing for at-the-market sales, and simply responding to any comments the SEC has about it, with the hope that the SEC may permit the sales to occur at the market presuming a ticker symbol and listing for trading exist.

The other recent development in the SEC review of resale registrations is the desire to make it difficult to register shares owned either by broker-dealers or their affiliates. If the shares have been held by the broker-dealer or its affiliate for less than six months after a PIPE or other private offering, the SEC and National Association of Securities Dealers (NASD) have been arguing that a full underwriter's compensation analysis has to be performed as if the company had undertaken its own public offering.

At the moment, they are mostly limiting their review to shares held by a broker-dealer in its own name, but there is a proposal on the table to expand this. As of this writing, the prospects for final passage of this NASD rule proposal are unclear, but significant opposition has been expressed by the NASD members who are most affected by it.

While waiting for the Form SB-2 resale registration to become effective, the company takes the necessary steps to acquire its listing for trading and ticker symbol. This is done by a market maker who applies to the OTC Bulletin Board by filing Form 211. But first comes the exciting moment when the company gets to reserve its ticker symbol with the NASD and obtain a CUSIP number from the CUSIP (Committee for Uniform Security Identification Procedures) bureau. These are the first basic steps to getting trading going.

The hope is always that the process of obtaining Nasdaq approval for trading does not take any longer than the approval of the Form SB-2 and its effectiveness, so that the *right* to trade thereupon matches the *ability* to trade on the OTC Bulletin Board.

Legal Issues Regarding Form 10-SB Shells

Four major issues crop up when creating Form 10-SB shells, each of which may be dealt with in a variety of ways.

Can Entities Own Shares? Auditors Disagree

An accounting issue, based upon a 2004 IRS ruling relating to so-called variable interest entities, or VIEs, creates some potential complications for Form 10-SB shells. The ruling followed the Enron debacle where off-balance sheet entities were used to off-load underperforming assets to help the company's financials look better. Despite the close affiliation these entities had with the company, their financial results never had to be reported by Enron. The new rule sought to remedy this by stipulating that where there is common control of multiple entities, an audit of one entity may require the audit of the other and the consolidation of their results for financial and IRS reporting purposes. Some accountants have confided to me that it is one of the most difficult to understand rulings they have ever read.

So, for example, following the passage of the VIE ruling, a client of mine had a distribution business doing nearly $100 million in annual sales. He wanted to go public through a traditional initial public offering. The company's financials were in good shape, auditable and clean, and he wanted to go public to grow and acquire similar businesses.

But the auditors discovered that the distribution business sold almost 25 percent of its goods to a group of customers that were owned by my client, the owner of the distribution business, and his family members. The auditor determined, based on this new VIE release, that the retail stores also would have to be audited and their financials combined. My client disclosed that the customers, for a variety of reasons, probably could not be audited. As a result, the IPO was shelved.

How does this relate to Form 10-SB shells? Some auditors believe that if an entity, rather than an individual, owned 100 percent of the stock of the shell as its founder, the VIE rules would apply because of common control. Some believe any control percentage in an entity (probably above 20 percent at least) is sufficient to raise this concern. Other auditors, however, believe that what matters is if the entity owning the stock of the shell makes a legally binding commitment to financially support the shell, only then are the financials combined. Even if the controlling entity shareholder actually does support the shell, without that binding commitment, there is no VIE problem. They have opined as such in allowing a number of shells to be audited even though a 100 percent ownership interest is in the hands of an entity.

The auditors who feel that the key is percentage ownership have simply said that ownership should be in the name of individuals rather than an entity, and the VIE problem goes away. Thus, a number of our clients have done just that, putting stock in people's names rather than investment companies or other entities.

Either way, the answer is far from clear, and most clients have been comfortable to take the advice of the auditors they choose. As lawyers, we do the smart thing and do the same.

PRACTICE TIP

If in doubt, allow only individuals to be in a control position with regard to share ownership in a Form 10-SB shell.

The Worm/Wulff Letters

A series of groundbreaking letters written by the SEC between 1999 and 2000, collectively referred to as the "Worm/Wulff Letters," are important enough to be included as an appendix to this book. Before beginning this discussion, it is important to note that the advice the SEC gave in this series of letters applies to any shareholder of a shell, whether it is a SPAC (specified purpose acquisition company) or even a trading shell, so all should pay heed.

In 1999, the NASD sought advice from the SEC on issues surrounding the tradability of shares of a blank check (the term *shell company* had not yet been created as a concept) if they have not been registered. The response from Richard Wulff, then the head of the SEC's Small Business Policy division, which came in 2000, made a significant impact on those creating and managing shells.

The specific language of Wulff's response provides that affiliates or promoters of blank check companies can never sell their shares either publicly or privately under Rule 144 or Section 4(1) of the Securities Act without those shares being fully registered first. Therefore, Rule 144, which allows the public sale of shares without registration if they have been held for one or two years, does not apply, according to the letter, to affiliates and promoters of shells.

This also means, technically, that even a private sale of shares by an affiliate or promoter directly to a third party would not be permissible even though it is arguable that Securities Act Section 4(1) permits it. (Technically, the language of the statute does not directly relate to a transfer by a holder to a third party, but longstanding practice is to recognize what is known as the "4(1½)" exemption, although the SEC has never officially sanctioned it to my knowledge.)

It appears that, as mentioned above, a redemption of shares by a company which simply repurchases shares from a promoter or affiliate would be permitted. The reason is that this sale would not be pursuant to Section 4(1) but rather would be exempt under Section 4(2) involving transactions with issuers themselves. Section 4(2) is not mentioned in the Wulff letter as being an unavailable exemption.

What was the SEC's reasoning? To summarize: shares acquired by affiliates and promoters of a blank check are always purchased with the intention of distributing them publicly, rather than holding them as an investment. Therefore, this makes the holders underwriters, thus making Rule 144 unavailable. In addition, the underwriter analysis makes a Section 4(1) exemption unavailable.

What's the real reason behind this? The only trading of shares in a shell that the SEC wanted were shares that were issued either (a) pursuant to a proper Rule 419 public offering of a shell, but such trading would only occur following a merger; (b) shares issued and becoming tradable prior to the company being a shell; or (c) shares that are registered following a merger.

What has this wrought? Since the issuance of the original letter, those forming shells knew they had to wait until a merger and subsequent registration for their shares to trade. In most cases, this is not a problem, especially for legitimate players. Since the letter came out, however, the SEC staff has made it clear that they view the impact as broader than even the specifics of the letter itself.

For example, the SEC staff takes the position that a passive, nonaffiliate, nonpromoter who purchases a small percentage of the shares in a shell as an investor is subject to the letter and its restrictions. This is true even though the letter addresses only affiliates and promoters.

Just before completing this book, at the SEC's request, I withdrew what was a request for a no-action letter for one of my clients. In this type of request, one can ask the SEC staff to declare that they would recommend that the Commission take no action against someone for taking a certain course of action. Technically, no one can rely on a no-action letter, as they are specific to the situation and each one actually declares that no one can rely on it except the person to whom it is addressed. Also, the SEC commissioners could always act on their own and counter to their staff. As a practical matter, however, most practitioners do rely on these letters at least as an indication of how the staff will react to certain situations. The fact that the letters are publicly accessible and routinely searched is evidence that even the SEC acknowledges their quasiprecedential value. Because of this, the staff will at times simply refuse to grant any no-action letters on certain topics.

In this request for a client creating a Form 10-SB shell, I asked for the SEC to rule that a nonaffiliate, nonpromoter investor in the shell be permitted to sell under Rule 144 *after a merger is completed*, if they have held for at least a year or two as applicable. I argued that the passage of the new rule requiring substantial disclosure after a merger no longer makes the need for protection of trading after a merger necessary.

I didn't suggest the SEC permit trading of the shell when it is a shell, which I think would have killed the request, nor did I suggest giving affiliates or promoters this ability to sell without registration. If it rules, however, that these nonaffiliate, nonpromoters may not sell, they are codifying their views as going even further than Worm/Wulff. I recently withdrew the letter at the staff's request. It is not clear whether this means a more formal rulemaking in this area is forthcoming, but one can only hope.

In the meantime, the SEC staff still officially says one cannot sell shell shares privately or publicly to a third party under Rule 144 or Section 4(1) without registration. Period. But some questions simply have not been answered and are becoming more problematic, and this may indeed be the right time for the SEC to move to clarify some dicey Worm/Wulff issues.

For example, the following recently happened to a client of mine: An investment banker raised money for a real operating public company and received warrants as part of his compensation. A year later the company collapsed, leaving behind the public shell. A year after the company became a public shell, my client desired to exercise his warrants and purchase the shares. Are these shares subject to Worm/Wulff and does that mean they can never be sold without registration because my client purchased shares of a shell? Or are they exempt because the original warrant was issued while the company was a real company? One can argue that the banker is not acting as an underwriter but counter that a real investment decision was made to invest in the shell. The result is unclear.

Here's another scenario: Former management of an operating public company owns shares that were never registered. Now the company is a shell. Can those shares be sold under 144, or are they subject to Worm/Wulff? It is not clear, although here at least there is not a new investment decision into a shell.

Here's another easy mistake to fall into: Some buy into a shell just prior to a merger without having a clue that they have purchased shares which must ultimately be registered.

> ### PRACTICE TIP
>
> *Upon a merger, all holders of shares in the shell who might be subject to Worm/Wulff must obtain registration rights to ensure they have the ability to sell in the public market.*

Another more recent wrinkle: Worm/Wulff refers to restricting the sale of shares in blank checks. But recall our earlier conundrum about blank checks that are not shell companies and shell companies that are not blank checks. One could have a shell company with nominal assets but a business plan to be a real company. It is stuck with the shell definition when it goes public, but is Worm/Wulff applicable? One would assume the SEC may seek to expand its applicability to these situations, but it is not even remotely clear.

> ### PRACTICE TIP
>
> *Wait and see (and be cautious).*

With the greater proliferation of manufactured clean and legitimate shells, along with the significant investor protections achieved by filing the "super Form 8-K" after a merger, the hope is that the SEC will permit a loosening of the Worm/Wulff reins and at least allow Rule 144 to apply after a merger is completed. This would save companies the complications of what under current rules truly are unnecessary registrations for these shares.

Proper Capitalization

Initially, a small amount of money may be put into a shell to purchase founder shares. Money will also be put into the shell later to pay lawyers and auditors. But a legal doctrine known as "piercing the corporate veil" comes into play. This doctrine stems from the fact that the major benefit of a corporation is that the shareholders are not held liable for the debts and obligations of the corporation merely by virtue of their stock ownership. They might be liable for actions as managers, officers, and directors. But if a company goes defunct, and no personal guaranties are given, the shareholders cannot be sued individually.

There are a few exceptions to this general rule. One is a vestige under New York law (New York Business Corporation Law Section 630) that gives employees the right to sue the ten largest shareholders of a corporation formed in New York for unpaid compensation. This right goes away if the company is a reporting company or incorporated elsewhere, so it does not apply to Form 10-SB shells or their post-merger world. In any event, as discussed, our clients' shells, and most Form 10-SB shells in general, are formed in Delaware.

Another exception is a concept built over many years of court-made or common law, which says, if the corporation is merely an alter ego of the person or persons controlling it, we will not respect the protection provided by shareholdings. The basic three-part test to look through an entity and sue its shareholders is to see if one or more of the following are present:

1 Money is commingled between personal and corporate accounts; or

2 Corporate formalities (in particular the issuance of stock) are not observed; or

3 The company is undercapitalized.

It is important in forming a shell that it not be undercapitalized for this reason. This requires that monies be put into the shell either for purchase of stock or loans to ensure that it looks "real." In general this is not a problem as significant cash needs to be put into the shell to pay expenses.

PRACTICE TIP

Ensure the shell is not undercapitalized.

Challenges in Post-Merger Registration

As mentioned above, recently the SEC has made it difficult for post-merged companies to register a significant portion of their shares in a resale registration. Keep the percentage to be registered as low as possible so as to avoid this issue. Also be careful, if the registration includes broker-dealers or their affiliates, to be sensitive to SEC and NASD concerns. And be cautious around the "fixed price" versus "at the market" resale issue.

Advantages and Disadvantages of Form 10-SB Shells

In this section, we compare and contrast the Form 10-SB shell with other types of shells that can either be formed or purchased.

Advantages of Form 10-SB Shells

There are eight principal advantages to using these types of shells. First, and very important, the SEC seems to tolerate them. SPACs have faced SEC challenges. Rule 419 shells are now very difficult to do. The Footnote 32 shells are under direct attack by the SEC's staff. Yet the Form 10-SB shells have had virtually no review as they go public.

Why is this? I believe the primary reason is the simple fact that the Form 10-SB shell involves no public offering whatsoever, and that it is honest in its status as a shell. All the other types of manufactured shells have some sort of offering, and the Footnote 32 shells are arguably out-and-out frauds. Also, the SEC seems to like that the stock of the Form 10-SB shell will never trade until after a merger and after disclosure about the company that merged in. This is not true with SPACs or Footnote 32 shells.

In the case of the Form 10-SB shell, offerings to raise money or shareholders are private, not public, and typically take place before or after the Form 10-SB is effective. In addition, the affiliates of the shell admit that it is a shell looking to merge and not effect an improper end around Rule 419.

The second major advantage flows from this: Namely, the Form 10-SB is easy and quick to form and take public because the SEC lets them fly through. There are only typically a few shareholders upon going public, so the SEC filing is fairly straightforward. SPACs have complex structures and offering terms, as do most Rule 419 shells. Footnote 32 shells require fanciful descriptions of the supposed business, risk factors, and so on. Trading shells face their scrubbers to look at their background.

Third, Form 10-SB shells are inexpensive. It takes about $40,000 to $50,000 to get one formed and public. Rule 419 shells cost a little more, and SPACs are very expensive (though much more money is raised) and cost several hundred thousand dollars before underwriting commissions. Buying a trading shell, if on the OTC Bulletin Board, can run anywhere from $400,000 to $1 million, plus equity in the merged company.

The fourth advantage is that the structure of the Form 10-SB shell is fairly simple. Several shareholders purchased some shares, and now they seek to have a fully reporting public nontrading shell. The other types of shells typically have much more complex capitalizations and structures.

Fifth, while industry-related management in a SPAC helps sell the deal to investors, the promoters and underwriters ultimately place control of the entity in management's hands, which involves some risk. In a Form 10-SB shell, broker-dealers can own shares, which is very difficult in a SPAC, and they control and manage the shell themselves, making it a relatively simple process ultimately to decide to raise money or approve a merger. Other trading shells also have similar challenges in worrying about board approval of a deal, liability exposure to public shareholders for the merger choice, and so on.

Related to this issue is the fact that promoters of a Form 10-SB shell can avoid unknown shareholders, which can be true in all other types of shells except possibly a Rule 419 shell. Even in a SPAC, if underwriters control the initial purchasers of shares, as the stock trades, unknowns creep in and can theoretically cause problems. This is also true of Footnote 32 shells. Because the Form 10-SB shares do not trade, the founders can totally control the identity of shareholders prior to a merger.

Sixth, like SPACs, these shells are absolutely clean. A trading shell with a prior business requires careful review to ensure that the company merging in does not face unknown liabilities or reputational problems (such as the prior involvement of bad players) from the past business of the shell. Footnote 32 shells are scarred by the SEC rulemaking in June 2005, and in order to work need to have operated (or pretended to operate) a real business, which may have created liabilities. Form 10-SB shells were created for a specific purpose and have no prior business in them.

Seventh, the shell can raise money fairly easily in a private offering if it wishes. I suppose this is true of all shells, but trading shells face the challenge of pricing the offering either with some relationship to the trading price of the shell's stock (which might not be favorable) or being on the defensive to explain why it needs to raise money at a very substantial discount to the public trading price. Because the Form 10-SB is nontrading, it does not face that same valuation issue in raising money.

Last, but certainly not least, is speed. Form 10-SB shells get formed and go public quickly, and can complete mergers quickly. If an auditor is fully cooperative and the shell founders are engaged and responsive, a Form 10-SB can be prepared and filed within about six weeks of forming the corporation. Since, in general, we have been able to avoid delays at the SEC, the filings have become effective sixty days after the original submission. *Thus, going from incorporation to public company status can take as little as three and a half months.* Contrast this with SPACs, which at best take about six to eight months from start to finish, and Rule 419 shells, which lately have been held up by the SEC for many months as well. Footnote 32 shells also take time for their IPO prospectus to get through the SEC, thus as much as eight to twelve months or more from incorporation to public company status.

Mergers happen quickly as well. Of course, there may be some delay in preparing the newly required super Form 8-K to be filed within four days after closing. And getting the financing organized may take time. But these details are present regardless of the type of shell. SPACs and Rule 419 shells are required to delay the closing of their merger so that a disclosure document about the company merging in is filed and fully reviewed and approved by the SEC, which can easily take months. It is true that other trading shells, including Footnote 32 shells, have this same advantage of completing a deal quickly, however.

Disadvantages of Form 10-SB Shells

Those seeking to create Form 10-SB shells face four principal drawbacks. First, like the Rule 419 shell, the stock of the shell may not trade prior to a merger. In the case of the 419 shell, a disclosure document is approved about the merged company, and then a closing and trading can occur. In the case of a Form 10-SB shell, a merger can happen quickly, but a resale registration (not dissimilar to the Rule 419 disclosure document) must be approved by the SEC before trading can begin.

As mentioned earlier in the book, in the end, Rule 419 shells and Form 10-SB shells take about the same time to get to trading. But the big difference is that a merger with a Form 10-SB shell can happen first, including the closing of a PIPE, then a registration and trading. With a 419 shell, the financing must wait until approval of the disclosure and closing of the merger.

As has been reviewed, however, although the marketplace deems lack of trading to be a negative, I believe that trading in a shell is not only irrelevant, but can even be a negative and is an illusory benefit at best. These shells avoid concerns about insider trading, timing of disclosure, short selling, and defections by shareholders of the prior operating business in a trading shell. And having trading in a shell by no means guarantees the creation of an active trading market immediately following the merger.

The second drawback is the existence of the Worm/Wulff restrictions on owners of the shell. Only Footnote 32 shell promoters may avoid these restrictions, although again, I don't believe I would trade the avoidance of these restrictions for the significantly enhanced scrutiny the SEC is placing on these Footnote 32 shells. In a trading shell that had an operating business, shares issued prior to it being a shell can trade, allowing for more trading post-merger, theoretically, and earlier profit for insiders.

In a SPAC, Worm/Wulff restrictions generally are avoided since the shares that trade have been registered, which is what Worm/Wulff requires.

The third drawback is that Form 10-SB shells typically have smaller shareholder bases than trading shells or SPACs. This can be a negative as the company seeks to develop its trading market. But proponents respond that trading will develop over time, to be patient with regard to development of market support, and that the other advantages of Form 10-SB shells outweigh this negative.

The fourth disadvantage of Form 10-SB shells is simply the time it takes to get to a point where real trading can begin. Especially with the SEC's relatively new attitude seeking to limit the number of shares being registered for resale at one time, this becomes even more difficult. This same problem, however, exists with Rule 419 shells and even to some extent with other trading shells. And again, if you are management of the shell merging in, you will not likely be selling large numbers of shares any time soon. The challenge, however, is in subsequent rounds of financing while still waiting for the market to develop. It is, as discussed in Chapter 5, more difficult to convince a PIPE investor to either ignore a thinly trading stock's price or do a separate valuation of a company not yet trading. The response: The importance of this issue depends on the need to raise large amounts of cash in the three to six months following the financing which takes place as part of the reverse merger.

The analysis of this issue is similar to the discussion on market support. In some cases, biting the bullet on purchasing or merging with a trading shell, including the additional cost and risk of liabilities, in exchange for a faster and more active trading market, may make sense. A similar analysis is true when comparing SPACs. Many companies pursuing a Form 10-SB shell, however, take a longer-term view to going public and would rather not deal with the negatives of trading shells. In the end, it depends on a company's timing and priorities.

Endnote on SPACs and Form 10-SB Shells

The marketplace has changed dramatically in just a few years. In the original outline for this book in 2003, there was no mention of SPACs or Form 10-SB shells. It was all about traditional reverse mergers (except for a short chapter on self-filings). Now, there are two full chapters on this exciting set of developments.

The existence of these relatively new vehicles adds a layer of legitimacy and depth to the reverse merger marketplace. Not every company can benefit from a SPAC or Form 10-SB shell, but it is an option that should be considered along with others as a company is seeking to pursue alternatives to becoming public.

CHAPTER 16

The Experts Speak

A Look Ahead

Τhis final chapter includes commentary from experts in the field about current trends in reverse mergers and other alternative techniques to initial public offerings.

Any attempt at pinning down current trends in the area of alternatives to IPOs is like taking a picture of a fast-moving train as it speeds past you. What was true a year or two ago, or even six months ago, is not true today. Some of what appears in this book may not even be applicable by the time the book is published due to changes in the financial marketplace, regulatory amendments, and the like.

Even though it is difficult, the intent of this chapter is to predict the future. What is an important trend now? What trend is up-and-coming? What will be an important trend one year from now? For this, we turn to the experts.

The cast of characters, in alphabetical order, includes: Dan Burstein, managing partner of Millennium Technology Ventures Advisors, LP; Alan Gelband, head of AGC Investment Banking; Tim Keating, president of Keating Investments, LLC; Mitchell Littman, partner at the law firm Littman Krooks LLP; David Nussbaum, chairman of EarlyBirdCapital, Inc.; and Charles Weinstein, managing partner of accounting firm Eisner LLP.

Recent Developments

There are a number of interesting and exciting new developments in this field. First is the very recent and dramatic interest of private investment in public equity (PIPE) investors and investment bankers in reverse mergers and related financings. Second is the growing interest of private equity investors in reverse mergers for their portfolio companies. Third is the rapid replacement of the small-cap IPO by a reverse merger combined with a PIPE, or by a specified purpose acquisition company (SPAC) as the going-public vehicle of choice for micro-cap companies. Fourth, interest in transactions from overseas companies, particularly China, grows daily. Fifth, SPACs abound in this market, causing an explosion in the number of new trading shells with significant cash. And, last but by no means least, the price of public shells continues to rise as their overall quality declines. This is no doubt powered by the increasing popularity of these deals on Wall Street. One effect is an upsurge of interest in self-filings and nontrading manufactured shells.

No summary of recent developments would be complete if it failed to mention the meaningful change in the regulatory environment as a result of the June 2005 SEC rulemaking on reverse mergers in June 2005 and the proliferating ramifications of the Sarbanes-Oxley Act of 2002.

The New Small-Cap IPO

Because of the strong interest from PIPE players in reverse mergers, along with the unavailability of IPOs for most small- and mid-cap companies since 2001, a reverse merger along with a PIPE has in many ways replaced the traditional small-cap IPO. Accountant Charly Weinstein comments on this trend particularly in the biotechnology arena: "In our public companies audit practice, we are seeing a new trend developing. More development stage biotechnology and research and development companies are using the reverse merger process to create a public market and to raise capital of between $5 and $10 million. Reverse mergers are replacing traditional IPOs for smaller biotechnology companies."

Will this continue? Industry veteran Alan Gelband is uncertain: "I believe that the reason reverse mergers are happening now is that it is an excellent way for hedge funds to participate in private equity-type transactions. I believe that the hedge funds and others will continue to fund private companies by merging them with public companies. The distinction between private equity and hedge funds is going to continue to blur. Therefore, the outsized returns enjoyed by private equity will be a target for hedge funds. For the next few years, I think this trend will continue; however, further out I think the SEC will change the laws to make it more economical to do IPOs and I think this will be a better financing alternative for companies than merging with shells and getting hedge fund money."

Agreeing at least in part is investment banker Tim Keating: "If a company can complete a traditional IPO on favorable valuation terms and with acceptable costs and with the certainty that the IPO will actually happen, it should do so under all circumstances." Keating continues, "If valuation, cost, or certainty of completion is a question mark, an issuer should seriously consider a reverse merger as a rational alternative to a traditional IPO."

Keating adds his thoughts on why reverse mergers are replacing small IPOs. "PIPE investors have increasingly looked to the reverse merger market as a source of quality new issue deal flow. The reverse merger coupled with contemporaneous financing has largely supplanted the small-cap IPO as a source of opportunity for those institutional investors seeking to finance newly public growth companies. In 2004—a decent year for IPOs—the average amount of capital raised in an IPO was $174 million. Of the approximately 196 IPOs in 2005, there were only thirteen issuers that raised under $25 million in new capital. Given these market conditions, it is extremely unlikely that the typical VC (venture capitalist) or private equity fund will be able to rely on a traditional IPO as a realistic exit for its micro-cap portfolio investments."

The Opening of China

A very important driver for growth in reverse mergers in the last three to five years has come from overseas. Foreign companies, like domestic ones, see the opportunity to access U.S. capital markets by going public in this country through a reverse merger or similar technique. Although there is a smaller countertrend of some companies going public outside the United States to avoid the Sarbanes-Oxley restrictions (in particular on the London Stock Exchange's AIM or Alternative Investment Market), deals continue to come to the United States from Israel, Hungary, the United Kingdom, Korea, Germany, and other countries.

But no country has had a more dramatic impact than the People's Republic of China. The "China bubble" has continued to grow despite some early predictions of its demise and several well-publicized scams. It appears that over time, American reverse merger players have learned to avoid bad guys even in a communist country.

In early 2005, the Chinese government caused a short-lived scare when it passed a series of decrees requiring all reverse mergers (and other deals where Chinese nationals would control a foreign company) to seek approval from the central government's foreign exchange regulators, the

State Administration of Foreign Exchange, also called "SAFE." This approval was to be based on standards that would be promulgated at some point in the future. A quiet panic hit players in the reverse merger business who were betting heavily on Chinese deals. They wondered about the approvals process and time line, not to mention how they would comply with rules lacking any clarity.

What triggered this new decree? Initially, the government supported ownership of foreign companies by Chinese nationals; however, this led to money not only coming into the country but going out as well, which apparently caused the government concern. One of the challenges of developing a fully open Chinese trade market is their continued protectionism, encouraging foreign investment but not repatriation of profits outside the country.

Following an outcry, however, in October 2005, the Chinese government effectively reversed itself. It now requires registration, rather than approval, of deals, and only at the local SAFE office, which is expected to be much easier than filing with the central government.

Tim Keating, who has been involved with a number of Chinese reverse mergers, says, "With today's historically high stock market valuation and low dividend yields, it is hard to imagine how equity markets will be able to repeat the 10 percent-plus annual returns that they have enjoyed over the last eighty years. In part, this is why we at Keating Investments firmly ascribe to the view that every investor in the world should own a small piece of China in his portfolio."

Chinese deals do promise some large potential upside and there is a seemingly endless supply of interesting growing companies; however, these deals are not easy to consummate. Due diligence can be more challenging, in part because the Chinese culture simply resists revealing information. The language barrier can be difficult, whereas deals with most other foreign countries involve principals who speak and write English. Most U.S. players looking for deals rely on native representatives on the ground in China who are believed to be reliable, but are not fully able to trust their own deal instincts.

In addition, Chinese accounting rules can be difficult to reconcile with U.S. generally accepted accounting principles. Also, Chinese executives wish to do deals, but are very careful, leading to a slower process than one might typically find elsewhere.

The structure is also more complicated. Most deals require establishing two new entities, one in China known as a "wholly foreign-owned enterprise" or WFOE (practitioners pronounce it "woofee," which rhymes with "whoopee"). Then the WFOE gets permission from the Chinese government to acquire the assets of the company, effectively privatizing it. Not that long ago the Chinese government owned all businesses, more recently they owned a piece of all businesses, and now they are prepared to relinquish all ownership to WFOEs in certain situations.

The shareholders of the WFOE (the former owners of the private Chinese enterprise) then sell their shares of the WFOE to a non-U.S. entity, typically formed in the British Virgin Islands (BVI), which is beneficial for Chinese regulatory and tax reasons. After that, the former owners of the private business own 100 percent of the BVI company, which in turn owns 100 percent of the WFOE. Then, finally, the owners of the BVI company (again, the former owners of the private Chinese enterprise) exchange their shares for shares of the U.S. shell.

The process of getting ready to do the deal takes quite a bit of time on the Chinese side. It is not that difficult, just time-consuming. And it is important to note that these structures may not be applicable if the company is based in Taiwan rather than mainland China.

PRACTICE TIP

Make sure that Chinese counsel and auditors are of the highest quality. Some are excellent, but some, unfortunately, are willing to be paid to declare whatever result management wishes for them to declare. Others are simply incompetent.

That said, the Chinese "yuan rush" has yet to fully play out. Modern business in China is only in its infancy, and U.S. management gurus are treated like rock stars when they go to China to lecture and teach Chinese managers about business. In addition, there are many very profitable and growing businesses seeking the benefits of a U.S. public trading stock.

Nevertheless, I recall seeing a billboard in Shanghai that said in Chinese, "You will like our product. You should buy it." When I asked a Chinese friend if I missed something in the translation, she said, unfortunately, things are really that bad in terms of understanding principles of marketing and yes, that is the language. This creates an obvious challenge and an opportunity. U.S. reverse merger players embrace both, with no end in sight to the increase in the number of deals done each year.

What could cause the flow of Chinese deals to stop? Another government misstep comes first to mind. The government could develop and act on a fear of foreign investors. Another possible logjam could occur if an increasing number of deals turn out to be either scams or market failures. And, of course, the broader Wall Street community could lose interest in these deals. Any major political problems either between China and the United States or internally in China also could interfere with this trend.

What could cause the flow of Chinese deals to continue or even increase? If U.S. players continue to play by the book and look at deals conservatively rather than with an Internet-era style frenzy. Or if the government continues to see more money coming into the country than going out. Or if the populace of China avoids rebellion even as it gets richer and richer while still being controlled rather dramatically by the government in their day-to-day lives. Or if the cultural and language barriers continue to come down.

My bet? At least several good years lie ahead, perhaps until the 2008 Olympics in Beijing, when the entire world will be tuned in to the China phenomenon. In the meantime, those doing deals in China will continue to walk a tightrope.

SPACs Are Back

Why have SPACs come back with such a vengeance? Who better to ask than David Nussbaum of EarlyBirdCapital, who says, "SPACs were created to allow talented and experienced dealmakers a vehicle to provide growth capital to attractive operating companies that wish to raise money through an IPO. This vehicle is attractive to investors who get to align themselves with these dealmakers and ultimately vote on the proposed transaction after receipt of a full disclosure document describing the deal. The quality of the management teams that have embraced the SPAC vehicle, as well as the investor safeguards built into the SPAC charter, have been principally responsible for fueling the dramatic growth of SPAC financings."

Alan Gelband of AGC Investment Banking divides the market. Gelband says, "I think the SPAC market falls into two different categories. There are SPACs which have under $50 million and those which have over $50 million. The smaller SPACs will find it easier to merge with a public company and therefore provide both capital and liquidity for the private company's shareholders. In a transaction like this, the SPAC shareholders will probably wind up owning between 20 and 49 percent of the merged entity.

"The other type of transaction involves a larger SPAC of over $50 million. In this case, it is more likely for them to purchase a company and, therefore, far more challenging. They will be competing directly with private equity funds which can move faster and are more flexible. The institutional investors are aware of this challenge and therefore demand that these management teams put some real skin in the game and the underwriters defer fees until a company is acquired. In this case, the management team invests directly in the company and will lose their investment if a deal is not consummated. In a variation of this, the management team agrees to buy virtually all the warrants and, of course, will lose this investment if a merger is not consummated as the warrants will become worthless."

So where does Gelband see all this going? "I think that in the next couple of years there will be new structures for SPACs which will give the investor better economics after a merger is consummated. I think that the interests of the management team, the investors and the brokers will be much more aligned."

From the lawyer's perspective, Mitch Littman comments, "While, of course, SPACs are themselves a unique financing technique, it is important to remember that the primary purpose of a SPAC is to locate an unidentified target company otherwise ready to go public. Thus, investors are willing to pay for front-row seats of a show that has not yet been written. I believe that the demand for SPACs is a reflection of a pent-up demand for IPOs for small- to mid-cap companies and expect the capital markets to show a significant increase in these types of transactions over the course of the next two years."

The story of the new SPAC surge will not be completely written until the dozens of SPACs currently public or in registration complete deals (or fail to do so). One hopes not only that most SPACs will do deals, but that they will do successful deals. If that happens, we can expect a much longer life for this latest round of SPACs. If many end up returning the money to investors or post-merger stocks do not do well, it may impact negatively on the market for these vehicles. My bet? We'll see at least two to four more years of mega-SPACs and the beginnings of interest in junior SPACs.

Shell Market Mayhem = Nontrading Shells and Self-Filings

In the last few years, we have witnessed an extremely dramatic increase in the price of a trading shell, whether to purchase for cash or merge. Demand has far outstripped supply, and this has fueled the upward price trend. The SEC's attack on Footnote 32 shells also reduces the attraction of many existing shells in the marketplace. Sellers of shells have decreased their interest in selling for cash just at the time that PIPE players and investment banks wish to purchase shells for cash then reuse them for their own deals.

Therefore, we have seen the sudden and rapid emergence of those seeking to manufacture Form 10-SB and other types of nontrading shells, such as those formed through a bankruptcy procedure. In addition, more and more companies are looking at, and some are actually doing, self-filings. Tim Keating is not so sanguine about self-filings. He notes, "Self-filing is always an option for private companies to go public without having to pay fees to investment bankers … just as fixing a plumbing problem is always an option for a do-it-yourselfer not wanting to pay a plumber." My response is that those considering self-filing should consult with an investment banker for help with both determining whether or not a self-filing is appropriate and navigating the process.

There is a controlled yet intense rush to create Form 10-SB shells. They sail through the SEC and are totally clean. They avoid all the tumult that a trading shell creates prior to, during, and even after a merger. That said, as of now they have created only a small blip on the radar screen with respect to available shells, and the value of these shells should continue to be strong for years to come.

Of course, as with the new SPAC surge, it is not yet clear that self-filings and Form 10-SB shells will lead to good public companies which develop strong market support. They are simply too new as options. My guess is that, if the marketplace has patience and helps a company build support, these can be very successful techniques in the years ahead.

New, More Positive Regulatory Environment

The June 2005 reverse merger rulemaking, which is now fully effective, exposed the reverse merger technique to the highest level of securities regulation in the form of the full SEC commission. The result: An official declaration by the SEC that reverse mergers are a legitimate technique. Add to that a favorable *Wall Street Journal* article titled "Reverse Mergers Move into Fashion," published on the same day the SEC announced the new rules, and indeed, things are certainly looking up.

At times, this new support from the highest level has yet to fully translate to the folks on the front lines who review SEC filings on a daily basis, some of whom still harbor a bias against reverse mergers. One hopes that will begin to change as deal activity increases along with access to information and data on deal activity.

In the meantime, we are all operating under the new rules, which create more work but also much greater transparency and legitimacy in deals. How should we deal with this new regime? Says accountant Charly Weinstein, "With the complexity of the new SEC filing requirements for reverse mergers, our clients are planning much further ahead when entering into these transactions. They are preparing audited financial statements and other filing documents, most times even before they have settled on which shell company they are going to use." This is good advice.

PRACTICE TIP

> *Those running a private company and thinking about a possible reverse merger or similar transaction should start writing and start hiring. Get auditors to start auditing. Get lawyers to start working on the company story that will eventually be needed for filings. And bring in an investment banker to help orchestrate it all.*

Sarbanes-Oxley also has had an impact, but not a terrible one. The most draconian aspect of SOX, the development of internal financial controls, has been put off until 2007 for most every company expecting to go public through one of these techniques, and the SEC's Advisory Committee on Smaller Public Companies has recommended eliminating the requirement entirely for smaller companies. Audit costs are definitely higher, but still manageable. Legitimate company managers should be comfortable signing the certifications that their financial statements are materially true to the best of their knowledge.

A Broader Point of View

Author, venture capitalist, and philosopher Dan Burstein offers a good summary of where the marketplace stands and may be going. He says, "In our current world, where hedge funds and other large pools of capital are flush with vast amounts of investable cash sitting largely on the sidelines seeking above-market returns (because the standard returns available in the markets are unacceptably low), we will continue to see managers, deal sponsors, and entrepreneurs explore new markets (China, India), new vehicles (SPACs) and new ways to obtain public listings (reverse mergers, PIPEs, London's AIM, and the like).

"Because this is driven largely by hedge fund and mutual fund money, there is a special desire to invest in vehicles that are 'public' and allegedly 'liquid,' even though the reality of many of these new kinds of companies and markets is that they are very thinly traded and are just barely public vehicles in a functional sense. But the holders of securities can list them on their reports as public, and that's what matters.

"There is nothing inherently good or bad, prudent or imprudent, about anything in the foregoing, but there are mini gold rushes and bubbles in all the aforementioned investment sectors, which means some people will inevitably abuse these opportunities or think about them without sufficient attention to the risks, while other people will indeed, discover, perfectly good and functional above-market investment situations. Because these markets and structures are comparatively new and still in the process of emerging, there is simply a different risk/reward equation at work."

And So It Goes

There is much to talk about in this rapidly growing field. We have only just scratched the surface of certain topics within this text; however, at last we have a much needed comprehensive resource on reverse mergers and other public offering alternatives.

Where is this business headed? I believe these alternatives will continue to gain in popularity and legitimacy, as long as there is constant vigilance on the legitimacy part. When boy scouts turn into bullies, no one wins. When greed overtakes logic, no one wins. When companies turn into just deals, no one wins. My advice to those seeking to somehow take unscrupulous advantage of the recent surge in activity in this area: please find somewhere else to steal. The rest of us will seek to move to the high road.

As to the future, when and if small-cap IPOs return, I believe there will be a place for reverse mergers and self-filings for many companies. Armed with these past years of increased acceptance, there is nowhere to go but up.

One key to continued growth in this field, as with most things, is education. This book serves to help the industry grow by arming people with the information to make decisions on as fully informed a basis as possible. Overturning prior biases, misunderstandings, and negative press has not been easy, but we have been doing it, interview by interview, article by article, conference by conference, regulator by regulator and now, hopefully, with this book.

ACKNOWLEDGMENTS

As I WRITE THIS, my book is nearly finished and I cannot believe how many people there are to thank.

First thanks must go to those who helped me with this book. At the top of the list is my contributor Steven Dresner. Steven is directly responsible for bringing me to Bloomberg Press. His contributions, charts, and data were critically important. In my office at Feldman Weinstein & Smith LLP, Stacey Spinelli, Jen Volpe, and my former assistant Sandra Berrios all helped in ways that they well know. I also appreciate valuable input from my partner Joe Smith and our counsels Joe Krassy and Rich Ellenbogen and associates Mike Nertney and Jamie Bogart on some of the more technical aspects of the legal discussion. On the research side, Nathan Bull, Randi Taub, Alex Katz, Ryan Hayward, Hannah Gray, Melanie Figueroa, Sarah Bravin, Charlene Ong, Minna Lo, and Tara Laszlo all pitched in when they were students working in my office. Thanks guys! Over at Bloomberg Press, thanks to Jared Kieling, Janet Coleman, Andrew Feldman (no relation) and their team for doing a tremendous job on every level, from marketing to content.

Next, I would like to thank several people who helped me develop expertise in this subject: my first reverse merger client, Larry Kaplan, and his partner (but not relative) Stan Kaplan, and the first people who gave me the opportunity to lead a conference on the subject, Burt Alimansky and Arlene West, owners of the conference company Capital Roundtable.

I also owe a debt of gratitude to the many mentors and colleagues who have helped me over the years as I developed my practice: my uncle Len Rivkin and son John at Rivkin Radler LLP, coach and day-camp boss George Coleman, networker extraordinaire Bob McMillan, Carl Kaplan, Merrill Kraines, and Gerald Eppner for so much help in my early years at the old Reavis & McGrath (now Fulbright & Jaworski), Howard Griboff for our shared introduction to entrepreneurship in the radio business, Gideon Cashman and Selig Sacks of Pryor Cashman Sherman & Flynn, and David

Mazure of Smith Mazure Director Wilkins Young Yagerman & Tarallo. Thanks also to David Smith, Kenny Lindenbaum, Bob Stein, and my best man and a partner at Paul Weiss, Eric Goodison, for your personal advice.

Let me also thank all my incredible partners, counsel, associates, and staff at Feldman Weinstein & Smith LLP, nearly thirty in all. To my fellow name-partner and close friend Eric Weinstein, thanks for your advice and friendship. In my practice, I especially wish to thank partner Adam Mimeles and associates Mike Nertney and Jamie Bogart (and former associate Jodi Zotkow and former counsel Scott Miller).

Thanks also to Sam Katz of McAndrews & Forbes for his leadership of Youth Renewal Fund, Peter Boneparth of Jones Apparel Group and President of the Board of Lawrence Woodmere Academy, and Alan Bernstein, its headmaster. I am also thankful to the members of the greatest business networking group ever, the Strategic Forum.

I am devoted to my alma mater, the Wharton School at the University of Pennsylvania, and currently have the honor of serving as chairman emeritus of the school's worldwide alumni association board. I am enthused by the dedication and stature of Dean Patrick Harker, and the leadership of Jon Huntsman, Sr. (not to be confused with his namesake son, the Governor of Utah) at the helm of the school's board of overseers. Here's to Wharton as it celebrates its one hundred twenty-fifth anniversary during the year of publication of this book.

On a personal level, my wife, Barbra, and children, Sammi and Andrew, are truly amazing. Barbra, you are an awesome wife and mother and I am so proud of your accomplishments in the community. Sammi and Andrew, thanks for tolerating the too many Saturdays I spent writing the book ... I'm finally back now!

No acknowledgements would be complete without offering thanks to my mother Judy, my father Dr. Ted Feldman, who died in 2001, my sister Carol, my sister Laurie, who died in 1995, and the rest of my wonderful family, including my in-laws Janet and Nat, sister- and brother-in-law Rachele and Mort, nieces Lizzie and Tracey, nephews Scott and Matthew, and aunts, uncles, and cousins. Scott, thanks for your help editing the book!

To all my clients, business friends, and referral sources, I truly owe my success to you, and I thank you very much for all your business, your friendship, your support, and the joy of being able to use my brain every day to assist you and of looking forward to coming into work each morning.

APPENDIX

The Worm/Wulff Letters

In 1999, the NASD's Ken Worm requested that the SEC clarify a number of issues concerning the tradability of shares in blank check companies. The clarification came in early 2000 in a response from the SEC's Richard K. Wulff. The request and response, therefore, are familiarly known as the Worm/Wulff letters. Reprinted below are the letters between Worm and Wulff and the NASD Notice that summarizes these letters.

INQUIRY-1:
NASD
REGULATION
9513 Key West Avenue, Rockville, MD 20850

November 1, 1999

Richard K. Wulff
Assistant Director
Office of Small Business
Division of Corporation Finance
450 5th Street, N.W.
Washington, D.C. 20549

Re: Tradeability of Securities Distributed by Means Other than Public Offerings

Dear Mr. Wulff:

The purpose of this letter is to request the guidance of the Division of Corporation Finance ("Division") as to whether certain specific factual scenarios present potential violations of Section 5 of the Securities Act of 1933 ("Securities Act"). The Market Regulation Department's OTC Compliance Unit ("Unit") reviews Form 211 filings submitted by potential market makers to determine whether they are in compliance with SEC 15c2-11 and NASD Rule 6740 before they are cleared to initiate or resume quotation of a non-Nasdaq security in any quotation medium. During the course of these reviews, the staff has been presented with certain factual scenarios that, based on the nature of the initial security distribution of blank check shell company issuers, either the initial distribution or the redistribution of the shares in the aftermarket may constitute violations of Section 5 of the Securities Act. Set forth below are various scenarios that the Unit has encountered or feels that it may encounter, while reviewing Form 211 filings. The staff requests that the Division provide its opinion on the following scenarios with respect to potential violations of the securities rules:

1. As a gift the issuer transferred a nominal amount of its shares (less than 10% of the total float) to between 20 and 50 individuals under Section 4(2) of the Securities Act. After the gift recipients have held their shares for two years, a broker/dealer submits a Form 211 citing the gifted shares as the only free-trading securities. The application does not disclose whether the recipients are sophisticated investors, although the individual who controls the issuer frequently has gifted shares of other companies to the same individuals on other occasions.

2. The issuer transferred a significant amount of its shares to one individual under Section 4(2) of the Securities Act. Then that individual in turn gifts a nominal amount of the shares to between 20 and 50 individuals. After the gift recipients have held their shares for two years, a broker/dealer submits a Form 211 citing the gifted shares as the only free-trading securities. The application does not disclose whether the recipients are sophisticated investors, although the individual who gifted the shares frequently has gifted shares of other companies to the same individuals on other occasions.

3. The issuer transferred a significant amount of its shares to one individual under Section 4(2) of the Securities Act. That individual holds the shares for two years and then in turn gifts a nominal amount of the shares to between 20 and 50 individuals. After the gift recipients have held their shares a few months, a broker/dealer submits a Form 211 citing the gifted shares as the only free-trading securities. The application does not disclose whether the recipients are sophisticated investors, although the individual who gifted the shares frequently has gifted shares of other companies to the same individuals on other occasions.

4. A smaller number of shareholders (less than ten) hold all of the free-trading shares. A broker/dealer submits a Form 211 indicating that the concentration of ownership in the hands of so few shareholders will not result in an ongoing distribution because it expects the market for the security to develop slowly.

5. A small number of shareholders (less than ten) control nearly all (more than 90%) of the free trading shares in the issuer. The remaining nominal amount of free-trading shares (less than 10%) are widely dispersed among a larger number of shareholders (50 or more individuals). A broker/dealer submits a Form 211 indicating that the concentration of ownership in the hands of so few shareholders will not result in an ongoing distribution because it expects the market for the security to develop slowly and considers the number of total shareholders to be determinative.

6. An issuer controlled by one individual issued shares to another company controlled by the same individual pursuant to SEC Rule 701. The issuer filed a Form 10 with the SEC that became effective by default. The second company then sells all its shares in the issuer through a brokerage firm. A second broker/dealer submits a Form 211 indicating that the shares sold through the first broker/dealer are all free-trading securities.

7. A reporting shell company merged with a private company and the former controlling shareholder of the reporting shell company sold his shares to numerous individuals more than three months after he ceased to be an affiliate of the post-merger company. A market maker submits a Form 211 citing the post-merger shares sold by the former control person as the only free-trading shares.

Thank you for your attention to this matter. We look forward to receiving the Division's guidance on whether any of these scenarios are of regulatory concern to the Division. If you have any questions, please do not hesitate to contact me at (301) 978-2097.

Sincerely,

Ken Worm
Assistant Director
OTC Compliance Unit

Mr. Ken Worm
Assistant Director
OTC Compliance Unit
NASD Regulation, Inc.
9513 Key West Avenue
Rockville, MD 20850

Re: NASD Regulation, Inc.
    Incoming letter dated November 1, 1999

Dear Mr. Worm:

You have raised a question regarding the "free trading" status[1] of securities initially issued by so-called blank check companies in a number of factual scenarios.

A blank check company is a development stage company that has no specific business plan or purpose or has indicated its business plan is to engage in a merger or acquisition with an unidentified company or companies, or other entity or person. In 1990, the U.S. Congress found that offerings by these kinds of issuers were common vehicles for fraud and manipulation in the market for penny stocks which undermines investor confidence and inhibits legitimate capital formation by small, issuers and other companies.[2] The Commission has adopted several rules, as Congress directed, to defer fraud in connection with registered offerings by blank check companies.[3] The Commission has also excluded blank check companies from eligibility for several exemptions from Securities Act registration requirements.[4]

Each of your scenarios suggests the availability of Rule 144 or Section 4(1) of the Securities Act following the lapse of some period of time following the issuance of shares in the blank check company regardless of whether a merger has occurred. In a number of cases, promoters of these issuers appear to be in the business of creating blank check companies, then gifting or selling the securities of the companies without registration, either directly or through intermediaries.

Section 4(1) exempts transactions not involving issuers, underwriters or dealers. The availability of the exemption depends upon the facts and circumstances of each particular situation, which the staff generally is not in a position to determine. Nonetheless, transactions in blank check company securities by their promoters or affiliates, especially where they control or controlled the "float" of the "freely tradable" securities, are not the kind of ordinary trading transactions between individual investors of securities already issued that Section 4(1) was designed to exempt.[5]

Furthermore, as the Commission had indicated, purchasers who are mere conduits for a wider distribution of the securities are "underwriters." When they do sell, these purchasers assume the risk of possible violation of the registration requirements of the Securities Act and consequent civil liabilities. Persons engaged in the business of buying and selling securities who function in this capacity are subject to careful scrutiny.[6]

---

1. Because the Securities Act of 1993 establishes the requirement to register securities for sale, subject to a series of exemptions, the concept of freely tradable securities is not a technically accurate one. In common parlance, the term is used to describe securities subject to the exemption provided by section 4(1) when it is available because no issuer, underwriter or dealer is engaged in the transaction.

2. Securities Enforcement Remedies and Penny Stock Reform Act of 1990, S. 647, Pub. L. 101-429. See H. R. Rep. No. 101-617; 101 Cong., 2d Sess. at 23.

3. Rule 419 under the Securities Act of 1933 and Rule 15g-8 under the Securities Exchange Act of 1934.

4 See. e.g., Rule 504 under Regulation D and Regulation A.

5. SEC v. Cavanagh, 1 F. Supp. 2d 337 (S.D.N.Y 1998).

6. Release No. 33-4552 (Nov. 6, 1962).

It is our view that, both before and after the business combination or transaction with an operating entity or other person, the promoters or affiliates of blank check companies, as well as their transferees, are "underwriters" of the securities issued. Accordingly, we are also of the view that the securities involved can only be resold through registration under the Securities Act.[7] Similarly, Rule 144 would not be available for resale transactions in this situation, regardless of technical compliance with that rule, because these resale transactions appear to be designed to distribute or redistribute securities to the public without compliance with the registration requirements of the Securities Act.[8]

Each of your scenarios illustrates what we believe to be a scheme to evade the registration requirements of the Securities Act. Consequently, it is our view that the resale of the shares in scenarios 1 through 7 would require registration.

In addition, with regard to scenario 6, we are of the view that Rule 701 is not available for issuances to companies or entities, but only to individuals. In view of the business of a blank check company which generally has few or no employees, it seems unlikely that reliance upon this exemption would be appropriate. It is our view that Rule 701 would generally not be available to blank check companies for issuing shares to their consultants or advisors.

Moreover, we have been advised by staff of the Division of Market Regulation that Rules 101 and 102 of Regulation M[9] impose restrictions on issuers, selling shareholders and distribution participants when they effect transactions in securities that are part of a distribution. Generally, a distribution exists when a sufficient magnitude of shares is being sold and special selling efforts are employed to sell these shares. If a distribution exists, the persons involved in the distribution are prohibited from bidding for or purchasing the securities in distribution. The rule covers persons selling securities, their affiliates, and others participating in the distribution. Persons selling in the manner described in your letter should carefully analyze the facts surrounding the sales to determine whether the security being sold is in distribution for purposes of Regulation M. This analysis should specifically consider the actions taken by any persons assisting with the transactions. In particular, selling through a market maker into an illiquid market raises heightened concerns regarding compliance with Regulation M.[10]

Because these positions are based upon representations made in your letter, any different facts or conditions might require a different conclusion.

Sincerely,

Richard K. Wulff, Chief
Office of Small Business

---

7. This view is analogous to the one the Commission has expressed with respect to business combinations under Rule 145 where affiliates of parties to the transaction are viewed to be "underwriters." Further, the nature of these types of resale transactions are closely analogous to shares from an unsold allotment held by professional underwriters. Generally, these securities are only resaleable through registration. Shares purchased by non-affiliates in a registered transaction such as one offered in compliance with Rule 419, however, would not be subject to this restriction.

8. Release No. 33-5223 (Jan. 11, 1972).

In view of the objectives and policies underlying the Act, the rule shall not be available to any individual or entity with respect to any transaction which, although in technical compliance with the provisions of the rule, is part of a plan by such individual or entity to distribute or redistribute securities to the public. In such case, registration is required.

9. 17 CFR 242.101 - 102.

10. See Release No. 34-38067 (Dec. 20, 1996).

NASD Notice to Members 00-49

SEC Interpretive Guidance

SEC Issues Staff Interpretation On The "Free Trading" Status Of Blank Check Company Securities Under Certain Scenarios

The Suggested Routing function is meant to aid the reader of this document. Each NASD member firm should consider the appropriate distribution in the context of its own organizational structure.

- Legal & Compliance
- Senior Management
- Trading & Market Making

- Blank Check Companies
- Freely Tradeable Securities

Executive Summary

A unit of the NASD Regulation, Inc. (NASD Regulation℠) Market Regulation Department recently asked the Securities and Exchange Commission (SEC) for interpretive guidance regarding initial distribution or the redistribution in the aftermarket of the shares issued by "blank check" companies[1] and whether these distributions were in compliance with SEC Rules.

NASD Regulation's request for guidance and the SEC's response are included with this *Notice*.

Questions/Further Information

Questions regarding this *Notice* may be directed to Ken Worm, Assistant Director, Market Regulation Department, NASD Regulation, at (301) 978-2097.

Background

The Market Regulation Department's OTC Compliance Unit (Unit) reviews Form 211 filings submitted by potential Market Makers to determine whether they are in compliance with Rule 15c2-11(a) of the Securities Exchange Act of 1934 (Exchange Act) and NASD Rule 6740 before Market Makers are permitted to initiate or resume quotation of a non-Nasdaq® security in any quotation medium. During the course of these reviews, the Unit's staff has raised concerns regarding certain factual scenarios where either the initial distribution or the redistribution in the aftermarket of the shares issued by blank check companies may violate Section 5 of the Securities Act of 1933 (Securities Act) based on the nature of the initial distribution of the securities of certain issuers. As a result of these concerns, the Market Regulation Department

requested guidance from the Division of Corporation Finance (Division) of the SEC on whether certain factual scenarios may present potential violations of Section 5 of the Securities Act. In response to the NASD Regulation staff request, the Division issued a staff interpretation dated January 21, 2000, on the "free trading" status[2] of securities initially issued by blank check companies in a number of factual scenarios.

As an initial matter, it is important to emphasize that the restrictions on trading of securities of blank check companies, as described in the Division's response letter, are not limited to the scenarios described within this *Notice*. Based on the Division's response letter as well as subsequent conversations with Division staff, in most, if not all, cases, the resale of securities of blank check companies is restricted and such securities can only be resold through registration under the Securities Act. In addition, Rule 144 would not be available to promoters or affiliates of blank check companies or to their transferees either before or after a business combination with an operating company or other person.

Moreover, NASD Regulation staff will require a Market Maker, when seeking NASD Regulation clearance pursuant to NASD Rule 6740 to initiate or resume quotation of a security of a blank check company, to provide an independent opinion from its own counsel detailing why the sale of such securities would not violate the registration requirements of the Securities Act. In addition, the NASD Regulation staff will continue to scrutinize closely such filings and will vigorously pursue disciplinary action and/or refer the staff's findings to the SEC for further action.

NASD Notice to Members 00-49

Specific Factual Scenarios Presented To The SEC

In its November 1, 1999 letter to the Division, NASD Regulation staff requested guidance on whether the following factual scenarios presented potential violations of Section 5 of the Securities Act.

Scenario 1: The issuer transfers a nominal amount of its shares (less than 10 percent of the total float) as a gift to between 20 and 50 individuals under Section 4(2) of the Securities Act. After the gift recipients have held their shares for two years, a broker/dealer submits a Form 211 citing the gifted shares as the only free-trading securities. The application does not disclose whether the recipients are sophisticated investors, although the individual who controls the issuer frequently has gifted shares of other companies to the same individuals on other occasions.

Scenario 2: The issuer transfers a significant amount of its shares to one individual under Section 4(2) of the Securities Act. That individual subsequently gifts a nominal amount of the shares to between 20 and 50 individuals. After the gift recipients have held their shares for two years, a broker/dealer submits a Form 211 citing the gifted shares as the only free-trading securities. The application does not disclose whether the recipients are sophisticated investors, although the individual who gifted the shares frequently has gifted shares of other companies to the same individuals on other occasions.

Scenario 3: The issuer transfers a significant amount of its shares to one individual under Section 4(2) of the Securities Act. That individual holds the shares for two years and then subsequently gifts a nominal amount of the shares to between 20 and 50 individuals. After the gift recipients have held their shares a few months, a broker/dealer submits a Form 211 citing the gifted shares as the only free-trading securities. The application does not disclose whether the recipients are sophisticated investors, although the individual who gifted the shares frequently has gifted shares of other companies to the same individuals on other occasions.

Scenario 4: A small number of shareholders (less than 10) hold all of the free-trading shares of an issuer. A broker/dealer submits a Form 211 indicating that the concentration of ownership in the hands of so few shareholders will not result in an ongoing distribution because it expects the market for the security to develop slowly.

Scenario 5: A small number of shareholders (less than 10) control nearly all (more than 90 percent) of the free-trading shares in the issuer. The remaining nominal amount of free-trading shares (less than 10 percent) are widely dispersed among a larger number of shareholders (50 or more individuals). A broker/dealer submits a Form 211 indicating that the concentration of ownership in the hands of so few shareholders will not result in an ongoing distribution because it expects the market for the security to develop slowly and considers the number of total shareholders to be determinative.

Scenario 6: An issuer controlled by one individual issues shares to another company controlled by the same individual pursuant to Rule 701 of the Securities Act. The issuer files a Form 10 with the SEC that became effective by default. The second company then sells all its shares in the issuer through a brokerage firm. A second broker/dealer submits a Form 211 indicating that the shares sold through the first broker/dealer are all free-trading securities.

Scenario 7: A reporting shell company merges with a private company and the former controlling shareholder of the reporting shell company sells his shares to numerous individuals more than three months after he ceases to be an affiliate of the post-merger company. A Market Maker submits a Form 211 citing the post-merger shares sold by the former control person as the only free-trading shares.

Division Response

In its response letter, the Division indicated that each of the scenarios initially suggests the availability of Rule 144 or Section 4(1) of the Securities Act following the lapse of some period of time after the issuance of shares in the blank check company, regardless of whether a merger has occurred. The Division noted that in several of the scenarios, promoters of the issuers also appear to be in the business of creating blank check companies, then gifting or selling the securities of the companies without registration, either directly or through intermediaries.

Section 4(1) exempts transactions not involving issuers, underwriters,

NASD Notice to Members 00-49

or dealers. The availability of this exemption depends upon the facts and circumstances of each particular situation. The Division indicated that transactions in blank check company securities by their promoters or affiliates, especially where they control or controlled the "float" of the "freely tradable" securities, are not the kind of ordinary trading transactions between individual investors of securities already issued that Section 4(1)was designed to exempt.[3] Moreover, the Division noted that purchasers who are mere conduits for a wider distribution of securities may be deemed "underwriters." When such purchasers sell their securities, they assume the risk of possible violation of the registration requirements of the Securities Act and consequent civil liabilities. Persons engaged in the business of buying and selling securities who function in this capacity are subject to careful scrutiny.[4]

The Division noted in its response that both before and after the business combination or transaction with an operating entity or other person, the promoters or affiliates of blank check companies, as well as their transferees, would be considered "underwriters" of the securities issued. As a result, the securities involved can only be resold through registration under the Securities Act.[5] Similarly, Rule 144 would not be available for resale transactions in this situation, regardless of technical compliance with that rule, because these resale transactions appear to be designed to distribute or redistribute securities to the public without compliance with the registration requirements of the Securities Act.[6]

Accordingly, the Division concluded that each of the scenarios illustrates what it believes to be a scheme to evade the registration requirements of the Securities Act. Consequently, the resale of the shares in scenarios 1 through 7 would require registration. In addition, with regard to scenario 6, the Division noted that Rule 701 is not available for issuances to companies or entities, but only to individuals. In view of the business of a blank check company which generally has few or no employees, it seems unlikely that reliance upon this exemption would be appropriate; therefore, Rule 701 generally would not be available to blank check companies when issuing shares to their consultant or advisors.

Moreover, the Division was advised by staff of the SEC's Division of Market Regulation that Rules 101 and 102 of Regulation M[7] impose restrictions on issuers, selling shareholders, and distribution participants when they effect transactions in securities that are part of a distribution. Generally, a distribution exists when a sufficient magnitude of shares is being sold and special selling efforts are employed to sell these shares. If a distribution exists, the persons involved in the distribution are prohibited from bidding for or purchasing the securities in distribution. The rule covers the persons selling securities, their affiliates, and others participating in the distribution. Persons selling in the manner described in the scenarios above should carefully analyze the facts surrounding the sales to determine whether the security being sold is in a distribution for purposes of Regulation M. This analysis specifically should consider the actions taken by any persons assisting with the transactions. In particular, selling through a Market Maker into an illiquid market raises heightened concerns regarding compliance with Regulation M.[8]

Compliance Guidance

Based on the Division's response letter as well as subsequent conversations with Division staff, in most, if not all, cases, the resale of securities of blank check companies is restricted and such securities can only be resold through registration under the Securities Act. In addition, Rule 144 would not be available to promoters or affiliates of blank check companies or to their transferees either before or after a business combination with an operating company or other person.

Moreover, NASD Regulation staff will require a Market Maker, when seeking NASD Regulation clearance pursuant to NASD Rule 6740 to initiate or resume quotation of a security of a blank check company, to provide an independent opinion from its counsel detailing why the sale of such securities would not violate the registration requirements of the Securities Act. Member firms are reminded that, in complying with these requirements, a Market Maker cannot reasonably rely on a legal opinion provided by the issuer or the issuer's counsel, or by counsel acting for any individual or entity involved in the transaction.[9] To ensure reliability of the opinion, the Market Maker must obtain an independent opinion from its own counsel.[10] The NASD Regulation staff will continue to closely scrutinize such filings and will vigorously pursue disciplinary action and/or refer the staff's findings to the SEC for further action.

NASD Notice to Members 00-49

Endnotes

[1] A blank check company is a development stage company that has no specific business plan or purpose or has indicated its business plan is to engage in a merger or acquisition with an unidentified company or companies, or other entity or person.

[2] The concept of "freely tradable" securities is used to describe securities that are exempt from the registration requirements pursuant to Section 4(1) of the Securities Act because no issuer, underwriter, or dealer is engaged in the transaction.

[3] See SEC v. Cavanagh, 1 F. Supp. 2d 337 (S.D.N.Y. 1998).

[4] See SEC Release No. 33-4552 (Nov. 6, 1962).

[5] This view is analogous to one the SEC has expressed with respect to business combinations under Rule 145 where affiliates of parties to the transaction are viewed to be "underwriters." Further, the nature of these types of resale transactions are closely analogous to shares from an unsold allotment held by professional underwriters. Generally, these securities are only resaleable through registration. Shares purchased by non-affiliates in a registered transaction such as one offered in compliance with Rule 419, however, would not be subject to this restriction.

[6] SEC Release No. 33-5223 (Jan. 11, 1972).

> In view of the objectives and policies underlying the Act, the rule shall not be available to any individual or entity with respect to any transaction which, although in technical compliance with the provisions of the rule, is part of a plan by such individual or entity to distribute or redistribute securities to the public. In such case, registration is required.

[7] 17 CFR 242.101 - 102.

[8] See SEC Release No. 34-38067 (Dec. 20, 1996).

[9] See James L. Owlsey, 54 S.E.C. Docket 739, SEC Release No. 34-32941 (June 18, 1993) (citing SEC v. Datronics Engineers, Inc., 490 F. 2d 250, 253-254) (4th Cir. 1973).

[10] SEC v. Harwyn Indus. Corp., 326 F. Supp. 943, 954-55 (S.D.N.Y. 1971). The Market Maker's duty to seek independent counsel stems from its obligation to make a "searching inquiry" and to conduct a meaningful investigation of the surrounding circumstances in order to ensure that it is not engaged in the distribution of an unregistered security on behalf of an issuer, any person in a control relationship with an issuer, or an underwriter. See Stead v. SEC, 444 F. 2d 713 (10th Cir. 1971) cert. denied , 404 U.S. 1059 (1972); see also SEC Release No. 33-4445, Distribution by Broker-Dealers of Unregistered Securities (Feb. 2, 1971).

GLOSSARY

4(2) analysis. The method by which one determines whether a private offering is exempt from registration with the SEC because the issuer is involved with a nonpublic offering.

accredited investor. As defined in Rule 501 under Regulation D, refers to the type of investor that is not required to receive detailed offering materials in a Regulation D offering. Generally means an individual with $200,000 in recent and expected annual income (or $300,000 when combined with one's spouse) or $1 million in net worth, a broker-dealer, bank or institution, any entity not formed for the purpose of the investment in question with at least $5 million in assets, or an entity all of whose equity owners are accredited.

Advisory Committee on Smaller Public Companies. Group established by the SEC in 2005 to review all aspects of SEC regulation of public companies with less than a $700 million market capitalization. The final report from the committee was issued in April 2006.

affiliate. A person or entity which controls another, is controlled by another, or is under common control with another. In a corporation, affiliate status is presumed if one is an officer or director or control shareholder (generally holding at least 20 percent of the outstanding capital stock).

aftermarket. Trading activity of a stock immediately following the event by which an operating business's stock becomes publicly tradable. More commonly referred to in connection with an IPO, but also applies following a reverse merger.

aftermarket support. The extent to which brokerage firms and market makers and their customers participate in the aftermarket following a reverse merger or self-filing.

alternative investment market (AIM). A stock exchange based in London, England which lists stocks of companies that may not qualify for the London Stock Exchange or similar broader exchanges.

alternative public offering (APO). Somewhat misleading term used to refer to the variety of methods of going public other than an IPO. The term generally describes reverse mergers, self-filings, Rule 504 offerings, and Regulation A offerings; however, a number of these methods do not include public offerings, which is why the term is somewhat misleading.

American Stock Exchange. A major U.S. exchange where a public company's shares can trade. Listing and maintenance requirements are more stringent than on the Over-the-Counter Bulletin Board, but it is generally considered easier to list on the American Stock Exchange than on the Nasdaq or the New York Stock Exchange.

asset acquisition. One method used to complete the combination of two entities. Rather than a direct merger or share exchange, one entity, in the case of a reverse merger typically the public shell, acquires the assets of an operating business.

audit. Detailed review of a company's financial statements and performance, where thorough checks of inventory, expenses, revenues, and the like are performed by an independent certified public accounting firm. SEC rules under the Sarbanes-Oxley Act of 2002 require an audit of a public company to be performed by an accounting firm that is registered with the Public Company Accounting Oversight Board.

audited financials. The state of a company's financial statements after being approved by an auditor.

auditor. The accounting firm performing a financial audit.

backdoor registration. A method by which a company's shares can become publicly tradable through a merger directly with a public shell, after which the private operating company survives the merger and succeeds to the public status of the shell.

bankrupt shell. A public shell that has been created either through issuance of shares following a bankruptcy (these shares are publicly tradable under a provision of the Bankruptcy Code) or a public operating business that was sold or liquidated through a bankruptcy, leaving behind a public shell with virtually no liabilities.

beneficial owner. Either the record owner of securities or someone deemed to be the owner of securities under applicable SEC rules. Examples of beneficial ownership include the presumption that one owns shares which underlie currently exercisable options or warrants, or shares owned by one's spouse.

blank check. As defined in SEC Rule 419, a development stage company with no business plan or whose business plan is to merge with or acquire an operating business. Also referred to as a *blank check company.*

blank check company. See **blank check.**

blank check preferred stock. In a corporation's certificate of incorporation, it may authorize the issuance of preferred stock. If that authorization includes granting the board of directors the power to determine the rights, powers, and preferences of the preferred stock without further shareholder approval, it is known as blank check preferred stock.

blind pool. Term used by some in the industry to refer to a blank check which is raising or which has raised money.

blue sky laws. Securities laws and regulations in each of the fifty states, regulating the offering of securities in that state. According to www.investopedia.com, the term is said to have originated in the early 1900s when a Supreme Court justice declared his desire to protect investors from speculative ventures that had "as much value as a patch of blue sky."

board. See **board of directors**.

board of directors. Governing body of a U.S. corporation. Shareholders generally elect members of the board of directors, which is granted broad powers to elect officers such as the president and secretary and oversee a corporation's business. Also referred to simply as a *board*.

broker-dealer. A firm engaged in the business of effecting securities and other transactions for the accounts of others. They are required to be registered with the SEC and the NASD.

bulletin board shell. A blank check or shell company whose securities trade on the Over-the-Counter Bulletin Board.

bylaws. Set of rules governing many aspects of a corporation's business, including the process of electing officers and directors, calling and conducting meetings, and defining protocols related to shareholders and stock certificates.

cash-and-carry shell. A shell company whose owners wish to sell most or all of the shell's ownership for cash, rather than participate as equity holders in a merger with an operating business.

cashless exercise. The right to exercise an option or warrant without paying the cash exercise price, by returning other options or warrants for their value, which is determined by subtracting the exercise price from the stock's trading price. As an example, if one holds one hundred options exercisable at $1 each, and the stock's trading price is $2, one could return 50 options as the exercise price for the other 50.

certificate of incorporation. The filing with a U.S. state's government (typically the Department of State) to create a corporation. Some states use the term *articles of incorporation*, and often the term *charter* refers to this document. Typically includes the number and type of shares of stock which are authorized, the corporation's name, and limitation of liability of corporate directors. Also referred to as a *corporate charter*.

change of control. A transaction pursuant to which a company's shareholdings, board of directors, and/or officers undergo a majority change. This can occur as a result of the sale of a company, the accumulation of stock by an unfriendly acquirer, or a shake-up resulting from a shareholder vote expressing dissatisfaction with a board or management's performance.

clean shell. A shell company which has no liabilities or other negative attributes as perceived by an operating business seeking to merge with it.

contemporaneous financing. A common technique in reverse mergers where an operating business combining with a shell company raises money at the same time as the completion of the merger, typically through a PIPE or other private placement.

controlling shareholders. Those who have the ability, through their ownership of shares of stock of a corporation, to approve matters required to be approved by shareholders, or to elect the board of directors.

convertible debt. Indebtedness of a corporation, the holder of which has the right to exchange or convert monies owed into stock at a negotiated price.

convertible preferred stock. Preferred stock of a corporation, the holder of which has the right to exchange or convert shares into shares of the corporation's common stock at a negotiated conversion price.

corporate charter. See **certificate of incorporation**.

corporate director. A member of a corporation's board of directors.

corporate officer. An individual elected by the board of directors to be an officer of a corporation. Most states require every corporation to have a president and secretary, but additional officers may be appointed and may include treasurer, vice president, chief executive officer, and chief financial officer. Individuals with titles resembling those of corporate officers are not corporate officers unless elected by the board of directors. Officers have certain fiduciary duties to the board and the corporation's shareholders.

current report. A filing with the SEC, most commonly on Form 8-K, describing an event or transaction that has taken place between the company's filings of periodic reports.

CUSIP number. An identification code issued by the CUSIP bureau identifying a class of stock. Publicly trading securities are required to have a CUSIP number.

delist. To remove a company's securities from a particular market or exchange so that they cannot trade on that market or exchange. Sometimes, a company voluntarily delists, in other cases delisting is involuntary for failure to meet a market or exchange's listing standards.

demand registration rights. The right for a holder of a company's securities to require the company, typically at the company's expense, to file and seek effectiveness of a resale registration statement including those securities.

Depository Trust Company (DTC). The custodian of records reflecting electronic representation of ownership of publicly tradable securities. DTC also serves as record owner on a company's records of all shares held electronically where a physical stock certificate has not been issued.

deregister. Commonly used term to refer to the process by which a reporting company voluntarily seeks to terminate its status as a reporting company, typically through filing of SEC Form 15, which is generally available only if a company has fewer than 300 shareholders of record. The SEC also has the power to effect an involuntary deregistration for failure to follow their regulations.

dilution. The reduction in either percentage ownership or value of one's ownership interest resulting from additional issuances of securities of a company.

dirty shell. A shell company in which it appears shady players have been involved and undertaken questionable transactions or tactics that have the effect of reducing the shell's desirability to a merger partner.

due diligence. The process of reviewing a company's operating history, assets, liabilities, risks, uncertainties, and management in anticipation of entering into a transaction with that company.

EDGAR. The SEC's Electronic Data Gathering, Analysis, and Retrieval system of filing virtually all SEC filings. EDGAR has been fully effective since 1996.

equity. Ownership of a business, whether through shares of stock of a corporation, membership interests in a limited liability company, partnership interests in a partnership, or securities granting the right to acquire any such interests.

escrow. The process by which a third party, at the request of parties to a transaction, holds money or other property as the agent of the parties, with such money or property being released pursuant to the instructions of the parties.

exemptions from registration. The opportunity for securities of a corporation to be sold publicly without being registered with the SEC. The most common exemption is Rule 144.

exit strategy. Term used by venture capitalists and private equity investors referring to the method by which they might liquidate an investment in a company.

fairness opinion. Advice from an independent third party that a particular transaction is fair from a financial point of view. Typically, this advice provides a board of directors with greater comfort as to the value of a transaction, and is particularly helpful when members of the board or shareholders have a conflict of interest in the transaction.

firm commitment underwriting. Public offering of securities in which the underwriter agrees to purchase all securities offered by the company. It then resells the securities to its customers after having purchased the shares at a discount from the company. Distinguished from best efforts underwriting, whereby the underwriter simply promises to use its best efforts to resell the shares.

float. Shares of a publicly held company that are tradable by the public. Most definitions of float exclude shares held by officers, directors, and other affiliates. Also referred to as *public float*.

follow-on offering. Sale of a company's securities to the public after the company is already public by way of an event such as either an IPO or reverse merger.

Footnote 32. Note in the SEC's June 2005 reverse merger rulemaking which acknowledges a questionable tactic whereby individuals take supposedly operating companies public with the intention of shutting down or spinning off the business upon a reverse merger. This allows the promoter to avoid Rule 419 restrictions. The SEC declares these entities shell companies.

Footnote 32 shell. Shells created when individuals take supposedly operating companies public with the intention of shutting down or spinning off the company upon a reverse merger. This allows the promoter to avoid Rule 419 restrictions. The SEC declared these entities as shell companies in its June 2005 rulemaking.

Form 10-K. Annual report filed with the SEC by a company that does not qualify to report under Regulation S-B. Includes detailed company information and three years of audited financials.

Form 10-KSB. Annual report filed with the SEC by a company that qualifies to report under Regulation S-B. Includes detailed company information and two years of audited financials.

Form 10-SB. Registration statement under the Securities Exchange Act of 1934 which registers a class of securities with the SEC but does not register any individual shares for public sale. After effectiveness of the filing, the company is an SEC reporting company.

Form 10-SB registration. The process of filing and seeking effectiveness of Form 10-SB. Filing is automatically effective sixty days after filing. If SEC comments are outstanding after sixty days, they are dealt with through a post-effective amendment.

Form 10-SB shell. Shell company created by filing Form 10-SB on behalf of previously private shell. Creates a clean but nontrading shell.

Form 15. Filing with the SEC undertaken to deregister.

Form 211. Filing with the NASD undertaken by a market maker to commence trading of a company's securities on the Pink Sheets or Over-the-Counter Bulletin Board.

Form 8-A. Simple SEC filing under the Securities Exchange Act of 1934 after which a company is an SEC reporting company, in lieu of using the more complex Form 10-SB. Can only be used by the end of the first fiscal year after a company completes a registration under the Securities Act of 1933, or under certain other limited circumstances.

Form 8-K. Current report required to be filed by reporting companies between periodic reports when certain material events occur, including a reverse merger. The timing of filing was made shorter and the scope of items covered was made more comprehensive following implementation of the Sarbanes-Oxley Act of 2002.

Form D. Required filing made with the SEC under Regulation D describing a private placement whose issuer is claiming an exemption from registration pursuant to Regulation D.

Form S-1. Primary form of registration of securities under the Securities Act of 1933 for companies that do not qualify to report under Regulation S-B.

Form S-4. Form of registration of securities under the Securities Act of 1933 when securities are issued pursuant to combination transactions and upon other events.

Form S-8. Simplified form of registration of securities under the Securities Act of 1933, utilized if securities are issued pursuant to a stock option or other employee benefit plan, or issued to consultants or other advisers. Shell companies may not utilize Form S-8.

Form SB-2. Primary form of registration of securities under the Securities Act of 1933 for companies that qualify to report under Regulation S-B.

Form SB-2 resale registration. Registration of previously issued securities on behalf of owners wishing to be permitted to publicly resell the securities. Used by companies that qualify to report under Regulation S-B.

forward stock split. A process by which each share of a company's stock of is multiplied and increased on a pro rata basis among all shareholders. For example, a company with 100 shares outstanding that completes a two-for-one forward stock split would have 200 shares outstanding following the forward stock split.

founder stock. Shares of a company issued to its original management and investors who started the business.

franchise tax. Annual levy payable to a state in which a corporation is incorporated or doing business.

free-trading shares. Shares of stock in a corporation that have been registered with the SEC for sale or resale or which are able to be traded pursuant to an exemption from registration.

fully reporting company. See reporting company.

general solicitation. Seeking interest from the public at large for an offering either through advertising or some type of mass communication. For a private placement to qualify for the exemption from registration under Regulation D, no general solicitation may take place.

good standing. Status of a corporation in a particular state as both existing (or qualified to do business as applicable) and up to date on paying franchise taxes and completing certain filings which the state may require. A corporation may not effect certain transactions without being in good standing.

go private. Seeking to stop being a reporting company through filing of Form 15, if available, or seeking effectiveness of a filing with the SEC called Schedule 13E-3, describing a plan for qualifying to file Form 15.

grandfathered shells. Shell companies and blank checks which were formed and taken public prior to the passage of Rule 419 were permitted to continue to exist without the restrictions of Rule 419.

hedge. To protect an investment by using certain financial, legal, or trading techniques which generally limit both the gain and potential loss of the investment.

information statement. Filing with the SEC in lieu of a proxy statement where shareholder approval is to be obtained on a matter but proxies are not being requested or solicited, because the requisite number of shareholders either has already approved the matter or is expected to approve the matter at a meeting.

initial public offering (IPO). The process of going public through an offering of securities by a corporation to the public and filing and seeking effectiveness of a registration statement under the Securities Act of 1933.

insider filings. Reports that are required to be filed with the SEC by officers, directors, and at least 5 percent shareholders of reporting companies. Such filings include information about securities holdings or changes in holdings.

insider trading. Technically includes all purchases and sales of shares of a company's stock by officers, directors, and affiliates, but more commonly is used to refer to illegal trading by these insiders or others based on possession of material nonpublic information.

intrastate exemption. Allows shares of a corporation located and incorporated in one state to offer securities within that state in a manner which is exempt from SEC registration. Such an offering may require state registration.

Investment Company Act of 1940. Federal statute passed to regulate mutual funds and other entities established to invest in securities. Most hedge funds operate pursuant to an exemption from regulation under this Act.

investor relations (IR). The process by which a company seeks to garner positive attention from broker-dealers and others in a position to influence investment in the company's public stock. Also includes day-to-day dealings with existing shareholders of a company.

IPO window. The period of time in which IPOs are popular with investors and available to private companies seeking to become public through an IPO. The IPO window is described as open during periods of popularity, and otherwise closed.

junior SPAC. Proposed type of SPAC raising a minimal amount of money to qualify for a Rule 419 exemption, and avoiding shareholder reconfirmation of investment, short time limit, and mandatory industry focus.

liquidity. The ability to easily sell or purchase a public company's securities. Also an often-cited benefit of being a public company.

listed stock. A company's stock which is tradable on a major market or exchange such as the New York Stock Exchange, American Stock Exchange, or Nasdaq.

manufactured shell. A shell company created from scratch for the purpose of being a shell company.

market capitalization. The perceived value of a public company calculated by multiplying a company's per-share trading price by the number of total shares of stock outstanding. Also referred to as *market cap*.

market maker. A broker-dealer that agrees to make a market in a Pink Sheet or Over-the-Counter Bulletin Board stock. Stocks may not trade on these markets without a market maker. A market maker is required to complete transactions from its own account if it is not able to find another party to complete a transaction.

market support. The extent to which brokerage firms, market makers, and their customers participate in the market for a company's stock following an IPO, reverse merger, or self-filing.

merger. A process by which two U.S. corporations combine, with one corporation continuing as the surviving entity and the other disappearing as the nonsurviving entity. Shares of stock of the nonsurviving entity typically are exchanged for shares of the surviving entity or a parent company of the surviving entity.

merger proxy. A complex filing with the SEC in which one party to a merger is a reporting company.

messy shell. A shell company with records that are difficult to obtain and transactions that are not easy to verify. As distinguished from a dirty shell, no unsavory activity is suspected.

Nasdaq. The National Association of Securities Dealers Automated Quotation System includes two trading markets, one known as the Nasdaq National Market and a lower-level market known as the Nasdaq SmallCap Market. Nasdaq also owns and operates the Over-the-Counter Bulletin Board, or OTCBB.

National Association of Securities Dealers (NASD). All broker-dealers must be members of the NASD, which regulates and oversees the operations of broker-dealers.

new listing application. Application made to a market or exchange seeking for the first time for a company's securities to be listed on that market or exchange. The application is typically subject to the market or exchange's new listing standards.

New York Stock Exchange. Considered the most prestigious U.S. stock exchange, with the most stringent listing and maintenance standards.

no-action letter. A publicly available letter from the staff of the SEC indicating that the staff will recommend no enforcement action against the addressee if it follows a certain course of action. Each letter declares it cannot be relied on by others, but most practitioners consider them as having quasiprecedential value.

nonaccredited investor. A purchaser of shares that does not meet the definition of accredited investor.

nonreporting company. A company that either is not subject to the SEC's reporting requirements under the Securities Exchange Act of 1934 or which is subject to the requirements but is not current in its required filings.

nontrading shell. A shell company whose shares do not trade or cannot trade until after a reverse merger.

offering. The process by which a company seeks buyers for its securities, or by which a holder of securities seeks buyers of those securities.

option. The right to purchase securities (typically common stock) of a company for a fixed period of time, generally for a predetermined price.

overhang. The existence of derivative securities such as preferred stock, warrants, or options which may be converted into or exercised for shares of common stock, thereby increasing the number of shares outstanding upon such conversion or exercise.

Over-the-Counter Bulletin Board (OTCBB). A trading market most commonly used following a reverse merger, as its listing and maintenance requirements are minimal, other than being a reporting company. Most OTCBB stocks are not heavily traded.

penny stock. In the Penny Stock Reform Act of 1990, it was defined as "any stock which is not selling on a major exchange and has a purchase price of less than $5 per share." Most post–reverse merger stocks are initially penny stocks when they begin trading.

penny stock market. Typically refers to the trading activity in lower-priced stocks on the Over-the-Counter Bulletin Board or Pink Sheets.

Penny Stock Reform Act of 1990 (PSRA). Following abusive practices in the penny stock market, Congress mandated more disclosure to purchasers of penny stocks and more information be gathered by broker-dealers from customers who are purchasing penny stocks. The PSRA also directed the SEC to pass a rule which ultimately became Rule 419.

piercing the corporate veil. The ability in a corporation to successfully sue shareholders for debts of the corporation if the corporation is effectively an alter ego of the shareholder.

Pink Sheets. A centralized quotation service that collects and publishes market maker quotes for Over-the-Counter securities. Unlike the OTCBB, issuers do not have to be fully reporting companies with the SEC for their shares to be quoted on the Pink Sheets.

pink sheet shell. A shell company whose shares trade on the Pink Sheets.

post-effective amendment. An SEC filing effecting changes or updates in a registration statement after it becomes effective. Rule 419 requires a post-effective amendment to disclose information about the company proposed to be merged into a shell.

post-money valuation. The value of a company immediately after it completes a financing. Generally calculated by adding the amount of financing to the pre-money valuation.

preferred stock. A class of securities in a corporation generally higher in the capitalization structure than common stock, often with special rights or privileges.

pre-money valuation. The value of a company immediately before it completes a financing.

primary registration. A registration statement filed on behalf of a company seeking for it to register its shares for a public offering.

private company. A company that has not conducted a public offering nor become a reporting company.

private equity. A somewhat amorphous term referring generally to a source of financing that involves a private placement.

private investment in public equity (PIPE). A private placement of equity or equity-linked securities effected for a public company, typically with immediate required registration of the equity sold to the investor.

private offering. Offering of securities by a company or a holder of securities that does not involve a public offering. Also referred to as a *private placement.*

private placement. See **private offering.**

private placement memorandum (PPM). A detailed offering document that describes a company's business strategy, financial performance, risk factors and the like, which is utilized in a private offering.

promoter. Entity or person that controls a shell and is actively seeking a private operating company with which to merge. A promoter can also be any investment bank or broker otherwise promoting a deal.

prospectus. Document used for public offering by issuer or shareholders including information required by SEC rules, in form and content approved by the SEC and contained in a larger filing known as a registration statement.

proxy statement. Mailing to shareholders of reporting company in form and content approved by the SEC in accordance with proxy rules. Required when a shareholder meeting is planned and management or another party is soliciting proxies from shareholders. The proxy, or individual designated by the shareholder, appears at the meeting on the shareholder's behalf and votes the shareholder's shares in a predesignated manner.

public company. A company that either has conducted and completed a public offering or has otherwise become a reporting company. May include either a company that has completed a public offering but is not a reporting company or a company whose shares do not trade.

Public Company Accounting Oversight Board (PCAOB). Established by the Sarbanes-Oxley Act of 2002, the body that oversees accounting and auditing of reporting companies. An auditor must be registered with the PCAOB to perform an audit of a reporting company. PCAOB establishes rules for auditors, audits all accounting firms which audit more than one hundred reporting companies, and randomly audits all others.

public float. See **float.**

public offering. The process by which a company seeks to offer and sell its securities to the public, as opposed to a limited distribution of securities as in a private placement. Also refers to the process by which a shareholder may seek to offer shares of a company other than in a private placement. Public offerings typically require registration with the SEC.

public relations (PR). The process by which a company seeks to obtain broad awareness and knowledge of its product or service offerings or of other news concerning the company, often with the assistance of a public relations firm or similar expert and through the issuance of announcements or press releases.

public shell company. See **shell company**.

public venture capital. Often used to refer to a private placement accompanying a reverse merger. Relates to the fact that the investment risk is often similar to a venture capital investment, except that the investment is into a public company.

pump and dump. Illegal practice by unsavory investors or broker-dealers in which misleading or false information is provided to the marketplace, causing a stock's price to rise, upon which questionable players sell their stock. After this, true information becomes available and the stock price generally returns to its prior lower level.

qualified institutional buyer (QIB). An entity, acting for its own account or the accounts of other qualified institutional buyers, that in the aggregate owns and invests on a discretionary basis at least $100 million in securities of issuers that are not affiliated with the entity.

reconfirmation prospectus. Under Rule 419, prior to completing a reverse merger, the shell must prepare and have approved by the SEC a prospectus containing detailed information concerning the private company merging into the shell. This prospectus is delivered to purchasers in the shell's IPO, 80 percent of whom must reconfirm their investment after reviewing the prospectus before the merger can be completed. Those who do not reconfirm receive their investment back, less expenses.

registered broker-dealer. See **broker-dealer**.

registered stock. Shares of a company's capital stock that have been registered with the SEC either for sale by the company to the public or for resale by a shareholder to the public.

registration. The process of obtaining approval from the SEC for a public offering of securities of a company or shareholder by following the SEC's rules for required disclosures in connection with registering individual shares either for sale by a company to the public or for resale by a shareholder to the public.

registration statement. A filing required by the SEC in form and content approved by the SEC in order to effect the registration of shares.

Regulation A. This SEC regulation permits offerings of up to $5 million to an unlimited number of investors, whether or not accredited. An offering circular is prepared and approved by the SEC, but the form is more streamlined than a full registration statement and does not require audited financial statements.

Regulation D (Reg D). Passed in 1982, this SEC regulation offers a safe harbor ensuring that an offering is a private placement and exempt from registration. The most common exemption used is contained in Rule 506, which permits an unlimited amount of money to be raised to all accredited investors and up to thirty-five unaccredited investors. No specific information delivery is required to accredited investors, but nonaccredited investors must receive all information that would be in a public offering prospectus, unless the information is not material.

Regulation S (Reg S). This SEC regulation provides for an exemption from registration for securities offerings by U.S. companies if they are completely or partially from foreigners or by a foreign company, if raising money completely overseas where some directed selling efforts take place in the United States. No specific information delivery or accredited investor status applies.

Regulation S-B. This SEC regulation outlines disclosure requirements for smaller companies in the small business filing system, generally permitting less information in its offerings and periodic reports. A company fits the S-B system if it has revenues of less than $25 million, is a U.S. or Canadian issuer, is not an investment company or asset-backed issuer, and its parent (if a subsidiary) is also a small business issuer. Also, if the company has a public float (held by nonaffiliates) of $25 million or more, it would not fit into the S-B filing system. The regulation may be amended or even overhauled by SEC Advisory Committee on Smaller Public Companies.

Regulation S-K. This SEC regulation, which predates Regulation S-B, outlines disclosure requirements for companies that do not fit into the Regulation S-B system.

Regulation S-T. This SEC regulation provides requirements for SEC filings made electronically through the EDGAR system.

reporting company. A company which is obligated to file periodic and current reports with the SEC as a result of a recent public offering or voluntary registration under the Securities Exchange Act of 1934.

representations. Statements of fact concerning a company, generally provided in an agreement to reassure third parties and allow them to rely on the statement. For example, "The Company has 10 million shares of common stock outstanding."

resale registration. Effecting a registration of shares held by individual shareholders to permit their resale in the public market. Technically the registration is made on behalf of the selling shareholders, but typically the company prepares and handles the filing.

restricted stock. Shares of capital stock of a company which are not registered or which are not able to be sold in the public market through an exemption from registration.

reverse merger. A method by which a private operating company arranges for its stock to be publicly traded following a merger or similar transaction with a publicly held shell company, pursuant to which the equity owners of the private company typically take control of the former shell company.

reverse stock split. A pro rata reduction in the number of shares of capital stock of a company that are outstanding. Typically requires approval of a majority of shareholders. Often used to increase per-share price, or to make more authorized shares available in order to complete a reverse merger.

reverse takeover (RTO). Another term sometimes used for reverse merger.

reverse triangular merger. A reverse merger in which the public shell company creates a wholly owned subsidiary, and which subsidiary merges with and into the private company seeking to merge. As a result, the private company becomes a wholly owned subsidiary of the public shell company. Typically used to avoid shareholder approval at the level of the shell company and to allow the operating business to maintain its corporate existence.

round lot shareholders. Equity owners of a public company that hold at least 100 shares.

Rule 10b-5. This SEC rule, under the Securities Act of 1933, forbids intentionally and materially misleading a third party in connection with the purchase or sale of a security.

Rule 144. This SEC rule, under the Securities Act of 1933, provides a popular exemption from registration, allowing otherwise restricted securities to be sold in the public market if they have been held for a sufficient period of time, typically at least one year and in some cases two years.

Rule 144A. This SEC rule permits qualified institutional buyers, or QIBs, to trade restricted securities between and among themselves and allows for broader exemptions from registration for those offering securities to QIBs.

Rule 419. This SEC rule, passed in 1992, requires significant safeguards in connection with an IPO or other registration under the Securities Act of 1933 of shares of a blank check. These safeguards include requiring almost all funds raised and shares issued to be placed in escrow pending a merger, an eighteen-month time limit to complete a merger, investor reconfirmation of their investment prior to a merger, and other requirements. An IPO is exempt from this rule if it raises more than $5 million, as a result of which all SPACs are exempt from Rule 419.

Rule 419 shell. A shell company or blank check created through an IPO conducted under Rule 419.

Rule 504. This SEC rule, part of Regulation D, permits up to $1 million to be raised by a private company from an unlimited number of accredited and nonaccredited investors, with no information delivery requirements and the ability of the shares to trade unrestricted following such offering. Most states do not permit Rule 504 offerings.

SAFE (China's State Administration of Foreign Exchange). Chinese regulatory agency that oversees foreign exchange and briefly sought to limit or restrict reverse mergers involving Chinese companies.

Sarbanes-Oxley Act of 2002 (SOX). The largest and broadest change in U.S. securities laws since 1934, SOX shortened reporting times for most companies' periodic reports and insider reports, mandated establishment and maintenance of internal financial controls, added corporate governance requirements, in particular with respect to oversight of a company's audit, eliminated all extension of credit to executives, and required top executives to certify as to the material correctness of their financial statements.

Schedule 13D. SEC filing required to be made by any holder of at least 5 percent of a reporting company's stock if it is part of management or if the holder may seek to effect or influence management.

Schedule 13G. SEC filing required to be made by any holder of at least 5 percent of a reporting company's stock if it is not part of management and if the holder does not seek to effect or influence management, or meets other criteria.

Schedule 14F. SEC filing required to be made and mailed to shareholders if, pursuant to a transaction involving at least 5 percent of a reporting company's stock, there is an arrangement or understanding to effect a change in a majority of the board.

scrubbing a shell. Typically refers to the process of completing a thorough due diligence review of a shell and solving problems that arise during that process.

SEC Advisory Committee on Smaller Public Companies. Established in 2005, the committee is charged with reviewing all aspects of SEC regulation of companies with revenues of less than $700 million. Its report was completed in April 2006.

SEC comments. Most registration statements are reviewed by the SEC, which provides comments to the issuer recommending changes or additional disclosure in the registration statement.

SEC Division of Corporation Finance. The division of the SEC charged with overseeing reporting companies and offerings of securities.

SEC examiner. An individual, typically within the SEC Division of Corporation Finance, who takes primary responsibility for reviewing and commenting on an SEC filing.

SEC filing. Any document formally submitted to the SEC under its rules.

SEC Office of Small Business Policy. Part of the SEC Division of Corporation Finance, which develops and assists in implementation of the SEC's policies that relate to smaller businesses.

SEC Reverse Merger Rulemaking in 2005. In June 2005, the SEC passed a new set of rules directly effecting reverse mergers, which became fully effective in November 2005. In addition to requiring substantial disclosure about the fully merged company within four business days after completing a reverse merger with a shell company, the rule requires every single reporting company to declare whether it meets a newly created definition of *shell company*. The rule also eliminated the use of Form S-8 by shell companies.

secondary offering. A public offering by a company's shareholders.

Section 404 of the Sarbanes-Oxley Act of 2002. The section of SOX mandating the establishment and maintenance of internal financial controls in certain reporting companies.

Securities Act of 1933. The first law regulating the securities markets passed during the Great Depression and regulating the offering of securities.

Securities and Exchange Commission (SEC). See **U.S. Securities and Exchange Commission (SEC)**.

Securities Exchange Act of 1934. The follow-up to the Securities Act of 1933 established the SEC and set up the integrated disclosure system, along with regulation of broker-dealers, tender offers, and proxy solicitation.

self-filing. The process by which a private company may seek a public trading market for its securities without an IPO or a reverse merger, by completing its own filings with the SEC either to resell securities held by shareholders or to voluntarily become a reporting company.

share exchange. One method of completing a reverse merger by simply exchanging shares of the public shell company for shares of the private company seeking to merge.

shareholder approval. The process by which consent of shareholders is required under applicable state corporate law in the state where a corporation is incorporated.

shareholder base. The number of holders of shares of stock of a corporation.

shareholder rights certificate. A certificate sometimes used to represent the right to receive shares of stock of a company following a reverse stock split, increase in authorized shares, or other recapitalization.

shareholders of record. Holders of capital stock of a company holding physical stock certificates issued by the company's transfer agent. Does not include holders of capital stock who possess only electronic representation of shares through the Depository Trust Corporation.

shares authorized. The number of shares of a class of stock a corporation is permitted to issue pursuant to the corporation's certificate of incorporation.

shares issued. The number of shares of a class of stock a corporation has issued to holders, including shares which may have been redeemed or repurchased by or forfeited to the corporation and not cancelled and are no longer outstanding.

shares outstanding. The number of shares of a class of stock a corporation has issued to holders, excluding shares that may have been redeemed or repurchased by or forfeited to the corporation.

shell broker. An individual or entity who assists parties seeking to purchase or merge with a shell company by identifying and negotiating transactions with shell managers.

shell company. A company with no or nominal assets (other than cash) and no or nominal operations. Also referred to as a *public shell company*.

shell merger. A reverse merger or similar transaction effected with a shell company.

shell promoter. See **promoter**.

short selling. The selling of a security that the seller does not own, or any sale that is completed by the delivery of a security borrowed by the seller. Short sellers assume that they will be able to buy the stock at a lower amount than the price at which they sold short.

short swing profit rule. Under Section 16 of the Securities Exchange Act of 1934, this SEC rule states that an officer, director, or 10 percent shareholder of a reporting company may not purchase and then sell, or sell and then purchase, any shares of the company's stock within a six-month period and retain profits from the transaction.

specified purpose acquisition company (SPAC). A blank check that completes an IPO pursuant to an exemption from Rule 419 for companies raising more than $5 million. SPACs generally have an industry focus with a related management team, and adopt several of the Rule 419 restrictions to assist in attracting investors.

stock. A form of equity ownership in a corporation.

stock option. The right to purchase stock for a specified period of time and typically for a specified price.

stock split. A pro rata increase or decrease in the number of shares outstanding, typically requiring shareholder approval.

street name. Common term for holding shares electronically through the Depository Trust Corporation rather than through a physical stock certificate.

subsidiary. An entity that is owned more than 50 percent by another entity.

super Form 8-K. Term used to describe the current report required to be filed following a reverse merger with a shell company and including the same information that would be included in a Form 10-SB for the merged company. Also called a *super 8-K*.

super 8-K. See **super Form 8-K**.

thin trading. Common criticism of post–reverse-merged companies or trading shells, which is that only limited stock trading exists.

trading shell. A shell company whose common stock may be publicly bought and sold on an established market or exchange.

transfer agent. Transfer agents keep a company's stock records, issue stock certificates when appropriate, help conduct a company's annual meeting by providing inspection services and current lists of shareholders, and help with stock splits, stock dividends, and similar changes.

unaccredited investor. See **nonaccredited investor**.

unclean shell. Broad term meant to encompass either a dirty shell or a messy shell.

underwriter. Broker-dealer that serves to complete an IPO of a company by purchasing shares from the company at a discount and then reselling them to the broker-dealer's customers.

unregistered broker. Individual or entity performing functions normally required of a registered broker-dealer but which is not registered with the SEC or NASD.

unregistered stock. See **restricted stock**.

U.S. Securities and Exchange Commission (SEC). The administrative agency established by the Securities Exchange Act of 1934, which implements securities laws and establishes and enforces rules and regulations under those laws.

valuation. Process of determining the worth of a company or worth of a share of stock.

variable interest entities (VIEs). Entities that, under IRS regulations, must consolidate their financial statements as a result of a close relationship between the entities.

venture capital. Financing source for early-stage and emerging, typically private companies.

voluntarily reporting company. Company which is not required to provide reports like a reporting company but chooses to do so anyway.

warrant. A security that entitles the holder to purchase another security (typically common stock) at a specified price during a specified time period.

warranties. A promise that something is in a certain state or condition. For example, "All our inventory is in saleable condition," or, "We have complied with all applicable laws concerning our pension plan." They are typically provided along with representations in reverse merger agreements.

wholly foreign-owned enterprise (WFOE). Entity permitted by Chinese regulations to be owned by foreign entities or nationals.

wholly owned subsidiary. A subsidiary all of whose equity ownership is held by one entity.

Worm/Wulff Letters. Series of letters between the SEC and Nasdaq providing that affiliates or promoters of blank check companies can never sell their shares either publicly or privately under Rule 144 or Section 4(1) of the Securities Act without those shares being fully registered first.

Wulff/Worm Letters. See **Worm/Wulff Letters**.

INDEX

ABOUT BLOOMBERG

Bloomberg L.P., founded in 1981, is a global information services, news, and media company. Headquartered in New York, the company has sales and news operations worldwide.

Bloomberg, serving customers on six continents, holds a unique position within the financial services industry by providing an unparalleled range of features in a single package known as the BLOOMBERG PROFESSIONAL® service. By addressing the demand for investment performance and efficiency through an exceptional combination of information, analytic, electronic trading, and Straight Through Processing tools, Bloomberg has built a worldwide customer base of corporations, issuers, financial intermediaries, and institutional investors.

BLOOMBERG NEWS®, founded in 1990, provides stories and columns on business, general news, politics, and sports to leading newspapers and magazines throughout the world. BLOOMBERG TELEVISION®, a 24-hour business and financial news network, is produced and distributed globally in seven languages. BLOOMBERG RADIO℠ is an international radio network anchored by flagship station BLOOMBERG® 1130 (WBBR-AM) in New York.

In addition to the BLOOMBERG PRESS® line of books, Bloomberg publishes *BLOOMBERG MARKETS®* magazine. To learn more about Bloomberg, call a sales representative at:

London:	+44-20-7330-7500
New York:	+1-212-318-2000
Tokyo:	+81-3-3201-8900

FOR IN-DEPTH MARKET INFORMATION and news, visit the Bloomberg website at **www.bloomberg.com**, which draws from the news and power of the BLOOMBERG PROFESSIONAL® service and Bloomberg's host of media products to provide high-quality news and information in multiple languages on stocks, bonds, currencies, and commodities.

ABOUT the AUTHORS

David N. Feldman is considered one of the country's leading experts on reverse mergers, self-filings, and other alternatives to initial public offerings. He is a frequent public speaker, seminar leader, and counsel on issues related to the implementation of these transactions. In his over twenty years of law practice, he has advised hundreds of companies on how to go public, whether by reverse merger or other means.

Mr. Feldman is the founder and managing partner of twenty-three-attorney Manhattan-based Feldman Weinstein & Smith LLP. His practice focuses on corporate and securities matters and representation of public and private companies, investment banks, venture capital firms, and high-net-worth individuals in financing transactions of all types and in general representation.

He received a BS in economics from the Wharton School of Business at the University of Pennsylvania in 1982 and his JD in 1985 from the University of Pennsylvania Law School. An avid supporter of Wharton and the University of Pennsylvania, Mr. Feldman currently serves as chairman emeritus of Wharton's worldwide alumni association board and as a member of Penn's worldwide alumni board. He is also chairman and founder of the New York Business School Clubs, an association of New York-area business school alumni groups.

Mr. Feldman serves as a member of the Business Advisory Board of Sterling National Bank. He is also a member of the Board of Directors of Youth Renewal Fund and the Board of Directors of WhatGoesAround .org. He also serves on the Board of Trustees of Lawrence Woodmere Academy and on the Board of Advisors of Channel Capital Management LLC. He is also president and sole director of six public shell companies. Mr. Feldman has previously been a member of, or associated with, the law firms of Feldman & Ellenoff (which he cofounded); Pryor Cashman Sherman & Flynn; Reavis & McGrath (now Fulbright & Jaworski); and Rivkin Radler LLP.

Steven Dresner is the founder of DealFlow Media, a publishing and events company with offices in New York and California. DealFlow Media publishes *The PIPEs Report*, the first publication dedicated to providing news, information, and analysis of private investments in public equity; *The Secured Debt Report*, which covers asset-backed finance for middle market companies; and *The Reverse Merger Report*, a quarterly focused on the business of shell mergers, SPACs, and alternative IPO techniques. DealFlow Media also produces popular investment conferences including one of Wall Street's largest annual events, The PIPEs Conference, which is the leading forum to discuss primary market deal structures specific to small- and mid-cap companies.

Mr. Dresner currently serves as a general partner of Strategic Alliance Fund LP (www.safunds.com), a specialty asset management vehicle dedicated to making direct investments in both public and private companies through transactions including reverse mergers and private placements. Formerly, Mr. Dresner was an investment banker at Ladenburg Thalmann & Co., and was the founder of VCOM Corporation, a technology development firm focused on the design of Internet-based telecommunications software. Mr. Dresner has a BS in psychology from the George Washington University and both an MBA in finance and a graduate degree in computer communications and networks from Pace University. Mr. Dresner is also coauthor and editor of two books on private placement financing techniques including *PIPEs: A Guide to Private Investments in Public Equity—Revised and Updated Edition* (Bloomberg Press, 2005).

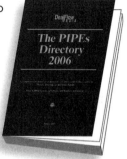

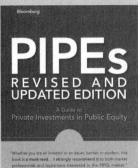